A Socially Critical View
of the
Self-Managing School

A Socially Critical View
of the
Self-Managing School

Edited by

John Smyth

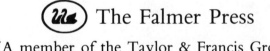 The Falmer Press

(A member of the Taylor & Francis Group)
London · Washington, D.C.

UK   The Falmer Press, 4 John St, London, WC1N 2ET
USA   The Falmer Press, Taylor & Francis Inc., 1900 Frost Road, Suite 101, Bristol, PA 19007

First published 1993

A catalogue record for this book is available from the British Library

Library of Congress Cataloguing in Publication Data are available on request

ISBN 0 75070 212 5 (Cased)
ISBN 0 75070 213 3 (Paper)

Jacket design by Caroline Archer
Typeset in 10.5/12pt Bembo by
Graphicraft Typesetters Ltd, Hong Kong

Printed in Great Britain by Burgess Science Press, Basingstoke on paper which has a specified pH value on final paper manufacture of not less than 7.5 and is therefore 'acid free'.

Contents

Introduction
John Smyth   1

1 Democratic Participation or Efficient Site Management:
   The Social and Political Location of the Self-Managing
   School
   Lawrence Angus   11

2 The New Right and the Self-Managing School
   Jack Demaine   35

3 Paradigm Shifts and Site-based Management in the
   United States: Toward a Paradigm of Social
   Empowerment
   Gary L. Anderson and Alexandra Dixon   49

4 Culture, Cost and Control: Self-Management and
   Entrepreneurial Schooling in England and Wales
   Stephen J. Ball   63

5 Reinventing Square Wheels: Planning for Schools to
   Ignore Realities
   Marie Brennan   83

6 The Evaluative State and Self-Management in Education:
   Cause for Reflection?
   David Hartley   99

7 The Politics of Devolution, Self-Management and
   Post-Fordism in Schools
   Susan L. Robertson   117

8 Pushing Crisis and Stress down the Line:
   The Self-Managing School
   Peter Watkins   137

Contents

9 Managerialism, Market Liberalism and the Move to
   Self-Managing Schools in New Zealand
   John A. Codd   153

10 Teaching Cultures and School-based Management:
   Towards a Collaborative Reconstruction
   Andrew C. Sparkes and Martin Bloomer   171

11 'And Your Corporate Manager Will Set You Free . . .':
   Devolution in South Australian Education
   Brendan Ryan   191

12 Managerialism and Market Forces in Vocational Education:
   'Balkanizing' Education in the 'Banana Republic'
   Peter Kell   213

13 Self-Managing Schools, Choice and Equity
   Geoffrey Walford   229

Notes on Contributors   245

Index   247

Introduction

John Smyth

> I feel like we have been taken to the cleaners. When you go to the
> dry cleaners you get a note that says: 'All care but no responsibil-
> ity'. With this devolution and self-management stuff, 'it's all re-
> sponsibility and no power'. (Teacher, New South Wales Teachers'
> Federation Council, 12 September 1992)

Statements like this nicely capture what lies behind some remarkably similar
themes and patterns that are becoming evident in the educational systems
of various Western countries. Around the world educational bureaucracies
are biting the dust at an alarming rate, or so it seems. It looks as if there
has been a wholesale dismantling of centralized educational bureaucracies
and their replacement by devolved forms of school-based management.
We are being confronted with a bewildering array of terms like 'school-
based management', 'devolution', 'site-based decision-making' and 'school-
centred forms of education' — all of which are occurring in contexts in
which the impression is being given of increased participation and democracy. But appearances can be deceiving, as the contributors to this
book show.

At the level of simple logic there is a problem with this move towards
self-managing schools. We need to ask ourselves the question: why would
the powerful educational mandarins want to blow their collective brains
out in this way by seeming to give away power? That is, unless things are
not what they seem, and they are up to something. If there is one thing
I have learned in over thirty years of studying schools, it is that educational
systems are about acquiring *more* power, *not giving it away*. So, what are
they up to?

Unmasking appearances is basically what this book is about. The
contributors systematically tackle this issue by seeking answers to four
questions:

1   What is this phenomenon of the self-managing school?
2   Why is it happening now?

3 What is it that really lies behind this notion?
4 In general terms, what is wrong with devolution and self-management?

Each of the writers 'calls in the evidence', in a manner of speaking, as it relates to processes of school devolution, relating to their country, state or educational system. And the evidence is not very edifying! If anything, it shows a deliberate process of subterfuge, distortion, concealment and wilful neglect as the state seeks to retreat in a rather undignified fashion from its historical responsibility for providing quality public education.

The contributors to this volume tackle what has become an important policy issue in education — namely, the 'self-managing school'. They do this in four ways: first, they argue that the rhetoric of devolution is occurring in contexts in which there have been substantial thrusts towards recentralization of education; second, they argue that the logic of this contradiction is explainable only when we begin to look closely at the wider structural adjustments occurring in Western capitalism generally (that is, the 'crisis of the state'); third, they show how particular forms of school self-management, far from being emancipatory or liberating for teachers, are in fact another 'iron cage' that serves to entrap them within the New Right ideology of radical interventionism (Quicke, 1988); and, finally, they explore what the dimensions of a more socially, culturally and politically informed approach to school decision-making might look like.

It is clear that the flurry of interest currently being shown towards school-based approaches to management creates something of a problem in terms of an explanation. In all Western capitalist economies (UK, USA, Australia, New Zealand and, I suspect, Canada too) we are currently experiencing the chilling effects of what might best be described as the New Right dogma of 'free marketeering' (McWilliam, 1987) which has taken strong hold in schools in all of these countries. We can see this most clearly in the rhetoric of autonomy and devolution, but in a context in which there has been a vicious attack on person rights and the social, political and economic infrastructure that has traditionally supported them. We are hearing much, for example, about privatization, free choice, and the opening of public education systems to the supposed winds of deregulation and competition, but in contexts in which the overwhelming principles are those of corporate managerialism, increased centralism, and the instrumentalist and technicist approaches that accompany the pursuit of the twin gods of efficiency and effectiveness (Demaine, 1988). The image of schools and their local communities being given greater control — through local managerial responsibility, lowered expectations of state intervention, and the creation of the mythology that these manoeuvres will somehow produce the levels of stability, predictability and control necessary to deliver on the conservative requirement for quality education and new jobs in a context of middle-class mobility — is something that has been carefully orchestrated and nurtured. The paradox is that at precisely the same time we are experiencing a hardening of the educational arteries through moves to make schooling more 'rigorous', 'disciplined' and 'scholarly' (all of which are only *really* possible in circumstances where final decision-making is vested in the hands of an elite decision-making group), we are also being courted by moves that appear to make schools more 'self-determining' and 'self-renewing', with teachers who are more 'autonomous', 'empowered', 'collaborative' and 'reflective'. How do we explain this paradox, and what does it mean?

It is true that educational systems are shrinking and that some of their functions are being pushed out from the centre. But this is happening in ways in which the central residue is becoming even more powerful. Restructurings are occurring in ways in which small elite policy-making groups are intensifying their capacities to set guidelines and frameworks, while divesting themselves of the responsibilities for implementation. Yet, at the same time, educational policy-makers are handing over implementation of centrally decided directions to local groups, along with strict requirements as to accountability and reporting. Marie Brennan in Chapter 5 looks closely at two rival approaches to school level change and shows how in Victoria a democratic, egalitarian and genuinely participative approach was undermined by an approach that treated schools as if they were 'islands', perpetrating managerial foci masquerading as local decision-making. Susan Robertson's case study of Western Australia (Chapter 7) also shows how recent reforms there, far from using devolution to promote genuine participation, amounted to nothing short of a top-down way of severing educational means from ends, of focusing on measurement of outputs, and of dramatically reorganizing and tightening accountability structures over schools. In contexts like these, school self-management has come to mean no more than an opportunity for schools to manage dwindling fiscal resources, within tightened centralist policies over curriculum, evaluation and standards.

The entire exercise appears, therefore, to be primarily concerned with dismantling centralized education systems (which have traditionally supported the work of teachers, students and parents), and replacing them with a free market ideology of 'competition' and 'choice'. It is about making a clear separation between those who conceptualize policy (elite policy-makers and interest groups) and those who execute or implement policy (operatives — i.e., teachers). It is about promising certain things through the use of a particular rhetoric:

more democratic community involvement;

more parental choice;

schools that will be better managed;

schools that will be more effective.

But the reality in New Zealand, according to John Codd (in Chapter 9), where this 'brave new educational world' is well underway, is that:

> schools are pitted against one another for resources and students;
>
> teachers are rewarded according to what they produce;
>
> students are assessed against nationally determined yardsticks.

The self-managing school, therefore, is not fundamentally about 'choice', 'grassroots democracy' or 'parent participation'. It is absolutely the reverse. Gary Anderson in Chapter 3 calls it 'an Alice in Wonderland world where language is turned on its head'. The process is about tightening central controls through national curricula and frameworks; national and state-wide testing; national standards and competences; teacher appraisal and curriculum audit — while in the same breath talking about empowering schools and their local communities. But there is no shift at all of central power. It is all something of a cruel hoax. What we have instead of genuine school-based forms of participation are increasing forms of managerialism, hierarchy, individual competitiveness and task orientation.

The contradiction is a fairly stark one — between an orchestrated rhetoric about democracy (and the need for more community participation in decision-making) and the reality of an economic imperative that demands stronger mechanisms of central control (policy determination, accountability, auditing, reporting and measurement). This contradiction is explainable in terms of the ideology of the New Right. What they are about is producing an amalgam of neo-conservatism (i.e., emphasizing discipline, deference, hierarchy and the authority of so-called traditional values) and neo-liberalism (which emphasizes individual freedom within an unfettered market economy). We can see this most clearly in the reassertion of authority through the regulation of curriculum, standards and traditional teaching methods, while at the same time emphasizing individualism and exposure to market forces and making schools more efficient and responsive to their clients.

What has occurred, the authors in this volume argue, is that there has been a rhetoric of devolution in a context of centralism. Their claim is that this form of *limited discretionary devolution* is fundamentally flawed because it amounts to a 'conservative trajectory' in which participation is 'according to approved formats within an overall government policy and framework' (Quicke, 1988, p. 18). The overarching problem, according to Lawrence Angus (see Chapter 1), is that such forms of tokenism fail to challenge entrenched power relationships and serve only to shape and channel participation in relatively safe directions, while leaving untouched wider educational understandings, practices and arrangements. In particular, Angus highlights the political naivety behind notions of school self-management as espoused by writers like Caldwell and Spinks (1988, 1992), while making the claim that far from being a basis for genuine democratic reform, self-management is being used as a conservative managerial device. The crucial question, he says, is whether citizens are being treated as educational 'consumers' or as educational 'participants' — there is a world of difference!

What, then, are we to make of this? As Jack Demaine argues, there has been a quite dramatic shift in control over teachers' work: away from a form of 'producer capture' — which was supposedly characterized by laxity, an ascendancy of the 'soft subjects', teacher control over the curriculum, declining standards and the like — towards a form of 'consumer capture' that places much greater emphasis on rigour, accountability, common standards, stringent appraisal, assessment and evaluation. In short, the shift has been to a form of privatization of education based on a culture of competitive and possessive individualism (Sachs and Smith, 1988). This has become typified by the situation in England where self-management has come to mean 'cooperativeness', and where teamwork and cooperation have been coopted as part of the new work relations. Involvement of teachers in the policy-making process and the surveillance of their colleagues comes to be just another 'part of the formal organization of schoolwork . . . described as the "corporate development" of the school' (Lawn, 1988, p. 164). The shift in emphasis from *direct* to more *participative* forms of control has been an extremely deft slip of the hand. What has occurred is that in moving from one form of supposed professionalism characterized by classroom-based isolation, we have come to embrace another supposed form of professionalism that involves collective school-wide responsibility 'based on narrowly defined though complex tasks within a context of shared management functions, clearly defined and appraised' (Lawn, 1988, p. 166).

These ideas, while they are dressed up to look democratic, are basically being pushed around by the New Right largely as a way of enabling central educational authorities to increase rather than decrease their control over schools. Jack Demaine in Chapter 2 shows how in Britain notions of school self-management have become an important dogma of the New Right in its moves to divest the state of its responsibility for publicly provided education. The intent is for schools to become individual self-managing 'private' institutions through the creation of a 'free market' in which education is no different from any other commodity. Achieving this, he says, is only possible through increased central control in order to attain a situation of eventual liberation. Brendan Ryan in Chapter 11 argues that self-management is about 'deregulating the economy through reregulating education' (or, as Demaine put it, 'privatization by stealth'). Likewise, Peter Kell in Chapter 12 shows how the 'downside-up' experiment of devolution in technical and further education in New South Wales (a total school system second only to that of the USSR in size before its demise) collapsed under the weight of its own ineptitude and managerialism. Far from delivering the promised autonomy and flexibility, Kell says that the self-managing reforms in New South Wales actually reinforced a despotic managerialist culture, perpetuated old monolithic rigidities, and caused that system to embark on a process of using colleges as mechanisms for redirecting workplace resources into the hands of multinational corporations. Control of education, in these circumstances, is shifted away from educationists as 'producers' and towards 'consumers' (politicians, the business community and parents). There can be little doubt that making schools compete with one another for customers in the manner implied, and of having individual teachers negotiate salary and working conditions, is aimed at turning every school into a self-managing business or mini-corporation.

Why is this happening now? There are several interlocking explanations to this question. The answer basically lies in the declining profits in the corporate sector, driven by the perception of the owners of capital that they are not getting their fair entitlement to a slice of the economic cake. Let us be clear about it: these problems have absolutely nothing to do with the nature of our education system and a lot to do with the massive shifts in international capital out of developed countries in order to take advantage of cheaper off-shore labour in South East Asia. The reality is that sliding profits in the corporate sector in advanced capitalist countries can only be restored if there are massive cutbacks in public sector spending. We saw this clearly under Thatcher with the so-called 'rolling back' of the welfare state. What we are witnessing around the world is a dramatic shrinking of educational budgets, together with the shrill cries to 'do more with less'. That is unequivocally the case, and it has to do with the need for the state to allow the private sector to have more of its nose in the economic trough! The way of managing this shrinkage is to intensify central power, cutting back resources for public services, while giving the appearance of devolving power further down the line. Make no mistake about it — this is not about giving up power; it is about intensifying it.

David Hartley makes this point well (see Chapter 6) through an analysis of how the Scottish educational system has set itself on a course of introducing self-managing schools that are to serve utilitarian ends — which are not, by and large, those of pupils, teachers or schools. In Hartley's view, 'the evaluative state' is handling the crisis of motivation in which it finds itself by directing (while not appearing to do so) notions of choice, ownership and self-management. Hartley sketches a fairly sombre picture in which schools will ultimately be controlled by the educational equivalent of a stock market, replete with its own *Times Educational Index*, the faceless men who monitor the rise and fall of stocks, who direct the financial audit, but who are bereft of even the merest understanding of the need to audit the moral worth of schools and what they stand for.

Peter Watkins in Chapter 8 calls this a 'pushing of crisis and stress down the line'. There is, he says, 'an attempt to displace the stress of economic crisis down to smaller units.' In the case of education that means down to the level of individual schools. All of this happens behind a smokescreen of apparent 'freedom' and 'choice'. Stephen Ball (see Chapter 4) calls it 'the self-management of decline'. He says it is all about deflecting blame off the state in a context in which the vested interests of the private sector are demanding a shrinking of the public sector. By responding in this way, the state can still 'maintain steering at a distance' while leaving the option open of blaming parents when things don't work out, by arguing that they 'made bad or ill-informed choices, or misused their autonomy.'

Individualizing the problem by linking it to notions like the self-managing school allows the state to get off the hook for providing sufficient resources for a public good. Arguments become local squabbles over priorities and ill-informed decision-making, rather than collective pressure to ensure that the state discharges its constitutional obligations. Ball describes this as a way of 'deflecting the focus off the cuts, and focusing on how to cope with the cuts.' It is also, he says, a way of ensuring that 'things are not so much done *to schools*, but rather *by schools*.' According to Mark Considine (1990, p. 177), the whole process is a framework for 'circling the wagons and rationing supplies'. It is a way of bringing about greater discipline and control, by limiting goals and reducing waste through tying work to narrowly prescribed outputs.

What occurs, of course, is a cultural shift away from education to management and other forms of entrepreneurialism. We lose sight of what it is that is being managed, and what we have is the replacement of a professional model of education with what is a largely discredited industrial management model. Why we in education would want to emulate this kind of derelict model that failed so demonstrably as evidenced in the corporate excesses of the 1980s is a complete mystery. Andrew Sparkes and Martin Bloomer's Chapter 10 is a good illustration of this. They use a case study of a particular teacher to show the dramatic nature of the shift in control that is occurring over teachers' work — from a situation Roger Dale (1989) described as 'licenced autonomy' to one of 'regulated autonomy', under the 'symbolic canopy' (Popkewitz and Lind, 1989) of local management of schools. As these commentators note, processes like self-management pose important questions for teachers about the de-professionalization of teaching that is underway, but, more importantly, how teachers through recognizing the specialist nature of their work can challenge the new orthodoxies and demonstrate to the public the qualitative effects of these changes.

The real game is about defusing conflict by providing the additional layers necessary to diffuse criticism about cutbacks. Hans Weiler (1989) says that real decentralization implies a loss of power at the centre, but what is happening in education is that central power is being retained and intensified at the centre, without the centre appearing to lose legitimacy (i.e., appearing to be committed to decentralization, and sensitive and responsive to local needs). According to Weiler, we currently have a situation where the rhetoric is that of decentralization (self-managing schools), but the behaviour is decidedly that of centralization (central setting of goals, targets, the devising of instruments of surveillance and the fixing of resourcing). Participation under these conditions is superficial and restricted to whatever the central authority chooses to allow.

Making schools responsive and accountable to their communities is seen as the mechanism for ensuring that standards are maintained and that targets are met by continuous testing and measurement. The outward appearances are given of power being devolved, while it is still retained. But, as Geoffrey Walford shows (see Chapter 13), school self-management in England and Wales has been used to reorient schools away from a common education for all towards increased competition, in the process creating a hierarchy of unequally funded schools which perpetuate class, gender and ethnic divisions. It is a mechanism of promoting the survival of the fittest through notions of choice. The only problem is that those who are already advantaged by wealth, class or ethnicity will use this to substantiate and extend their already disproportionate advantage in an already differentiated educational system.

In sum, then, among the many drawbacks of this shift to self-management identified by contributors to this volume are the following.

It is a way of the state arrogantly shirking its social responsibility for providing an equitable quality education for all.

It promotes greater inequality as those who have the financial and cultural capital are able to flee by buying a better education, and the rest remain trapped in some kind of educational ghetto.

Treating schools as if they were like convenience stores, managing their own affairs, deflects attention away from the educational issues by making people in schools into managers and entrepreneurs.

Turning principals into mini Chief Executive Officers may have limited rhetorical appeal, but it takes them a long way from being the kind of educational leaders our schools desperately need.

Giving schools budgetary control may not produce staffing profiles of the best trained, qualified and experienced teachers, as principals and their councils cut corners in order to balance dwindling budgets.

Schools need to be properly resourced in order to do their crucial work; school-based management is about cutting resources to schools and getting school communities to own and manage the decline.

Postscript

Since this book was completed, many of the predictions about what was envisaged as likely to happen under a conservative government in Victoria have come to pass (see, for example, those by Watkins in Chapter 8). It is interesting that perpetrators of policies like those behind that of the *Self-Managing School* are so arrogantly self-assured of the 'rightness' of what they are doing and the efficacy of their own narrow minded ideas that they are prepared to go to the extreme of closing off public debate by steamrolling them in without proper public discussion. Could it be that those who deem to 'know best' in respect of these matters understand that were their ideas allowed to be put under the light of careful debate and scrutiny, they would in all likelihood be exposed for the fraud that they are? What other explanations are there for governments who stoop to pushing through controversial measures like this in the dark of night? Far from actions like this being a sign of courage and leadership, they are a shameful and shallow reminder of what is coming to pass as 'democracy' in Western capitalist countries.

References

CALDWELL, B. and SPINKS, J. (1988) *The Self-Managing School*, Lewes, Falmer Press.
CALDWELL, B. and SPINKS, J. (1992) *Leading the Self-Managing School*, Lewes, Falmer Press.
CONSIDINE, M. (1990) 'Managerialism Strikes Out', *Australian Journal of Public Administration*, 49, 2, pp. 166–78.
DALE, R. (1989) *The State and Educational Policy*, Milton Keynes, Open University Press.
DEMAINE, J. (1988) 'Teachers' Work, Curriculum and the New Right', *British Journal of Sociology of Education*, 9, 3, pp. 247–64.
LAWN, M. (1988) 'Skill in Schoolwork: Work Relations in the Primary School', in J. OZGA (Ed.), *Schoolwork: Approaches to the Labour Process of Teaching*, Milton Keynes, Open University Press.
MCWILLIAM, E. (1987) 'The Challenge of the New Right: Its Liberty v Equality to Hell with Fraternity', *Discourse: The Australian Journal of Educational Studies*, 8, 1, pp. 61–76.
POPKEWITZ, T. and LIND, K. (1989) 'Teacher Incentives as Reforms: Teachers' Work and the Changing Control Mechanism in Education', *Teachers College Record*, 90, 4, pp. 575–94.
QUICKE, J. (1988) 'The New Right and Education', *British Journal of Educational Studies*, 36, 1, pp. 5–20.
SACHS, J. and SMITH, R. (1988) 'Constructing Teacher Culture', *British Journal of Sociology of Education*, 9, 4, pp. 423–36.
WEILER, H. (1989) 'Why Reforms Fail: The Politics of Education in France and the Federal Republic of Germany', *Journal of Curriculum Studies*, 21, 4, pp. 291–305.

1 Democratic Participation or Efficient Site Management: The Social and Political Location of the Self-Managing School

Lawrence Angus

Current discourses on the self-management of schools incorporate particular understandings of notions such as democracy, participation, choice, community and society. The problem is that the meaning in context of these notions is quite variable and is influenced by the importance, and perception, of other powerful organizing concepts including those of efficiency, accountability, responsibility and authority. In a period in which educational debates have become characterized by neo-conservative and New Right thinking, and by the marginalization of socially democratic themes which had become partially institutionalized in the work and thinking of many education workers during the 1970s and 1980s (Angus, 1992; Apple, 1991), we have seen the incorporation of all the terms mentioned into a rather simplistic slogan system of market efficiency and quality control of schools.

Such incorporation is not challenged by many of the currently popular texts which purport to offer assistance to participants in local school management. Indeed, one of the most popular of these manuals, *The Self-Managing School*, by Brian Caldwell and Jim Spinks (1988), celebrates the utility and effectiveness of its proposed model of school management which, the authors claim, can be adapted for virtually any occasion or any type of political context. Far from challenging New Right themes, *The Self-Managing School*, perhaps unintentionally, provides a spurious legitimacy to the New Right educational project.

In this chapter, before addressing particular limitations in the approach to school management offered by authors like Caldwell and Spinks, I shall sketch briefly the broad policy context against which models of school-based administration should be understood. This context is extremely complex, not least because of the appropriation into neo-conservative rhetoric of notions like participation that previously have been associated with the increased democratization of education rather than its privatization and incorporation into New Right social and economic policy. It is important to recognize, therefore, that particular forms of school level participation may well serve as conservative managerial devices rather than as genuine democratic reforms (Angus, 1989; Davies, 1990). Versions of participation offered to members of the school community within current policy frameworks, I shall argue, tend to take educational management in educationally, socially and administratively conservative directions.

Advocates of school-based management have long argued that, in education systems which have been characterized by highly centralized bureaucracies, schools should be granted a significant level of autonomy in making decisions about such matters as curriculum, finances and resources, staffing and school policy. A measure of authority should be appropriately devolved from central administration to the school level. The bureaucracy, according to the argument, would then become more responsive to the needs of schools and their communities, and would facilitate the realization of school-determined priorities rather than impose centrally mandated ones. Moreover, in order to develop general commitment to priorities which are decided at the school level, local decisions should be made collaboratively by principal, teachers, parents and, in some cases, students.

This much seems unexceptionable. The problem is that, although there is widespread endorsement in current education debates of terms like 'participation', 'devolution' and 'responsive bureaucracy', the apparent simplicity of these notions is deceptive. Their meanings must be understood in context — in relation to the broader educational policy agenda, which is itself sensible only in relation to broad social and economic policy directions. Perhaps a good starting point is to consider the ostensible relationship between schools and reformed, responsive educational bureaucracy in versions of school-based management.

Responsive Bureaucracy and Participative Democracy

Bureaucracy can be reformed in a number of ways (Rizvi and Angus, 1990). Different approaches in the discourse of educational governance to such reform in the past decade or so provide a key for understanding important differences in approaches to local school management. For instance, in Australia in the early 1980s the state of Victoria witnessed perhaps the most serious attempt anywhere to introduce democratic principles into educational governance. The *Ministerial Papers* published in 1983 and 1984 (see collected version, Victoria, Minister of Education, 1986) provide an outline of what a devolved educational structure in Victoria under a then newly elected Labor government was to look like. Participation was presented as an essential corollary to the devolution of authority from the central office to regions and schools. At the school level the importance of school councils, which were representative of local communities and would have a major say in school decisions, was emphasized.

The most important point about the restructure was that the notion of devolution of authority, so prominent throughout the *Ministerial Papers*, implied that the patterns of educational governance were to alter. Instead of offering obedience to a central authority, those involved in education at the school level — administrators, teachers, parents and students — were invited to participate in the decision-making process in such a way that shared and informed consent to school level decisions would ensure both commitment to such decisions and collective responsibility for their implementation.

Participative, school level goverance was to be facilitated by a 're-sponsive bureaucracy'. Just how the bureaucracy was to be reformed to make it more responsive, however, was not fully spelled out (Rizvi and Angus, 1990). This lack of detail was not necessarily a weakness in the policy. Indeed, it could be argued that it was a potential strength in that, while a clear policy principle of participation was enunciated, its success or otherwise would depend upon the way in which responsiveness was demanded and asserted by participants at various points within the educational process. The government did have a responsibility, however, to facilitate responsiveness not only in rhetoric but with adequate resources. Importantly, the policy linked the notion of participation with notions of equity and redress of disadvantage, as well as responsiveness to the needs of local communities. The rhetoric of democratic governance and community participation in the Victorian policy gave hope to advocates of democratic education, including parents, that a genuine shift of power was likely to occur which would significantly change the system in democratic ways.

In the event, as I have argued in more detail elsewhere (Angus and Rizvi, 1989; Rizvi and Angus, 1990), despite significant gains at the level of particular school communities where participation was strongly asserted from below, and within now-marginalized sections of the education bureaucracy, participative democratic practices have not, in the main, been institutionalized within the Victorian administrative system. This does not mean that we should be pessimistic about the ultimate possibilities of more democratic and participative modes of educational governance. The advocates of reform took on an extremely difficult task in attempting to shift the system — a massive, centralized state bureaucracy — in democratic ways, and may well have underestimated the extent to which managerial expectations and institutionalized power relationships are entrenched in hierarchical management structures (Angus and Rizvi, 1989). Despite the pervasive rhetoric, the extent to which principles of participation and equity actually were shared throughout the system (as opposed to being asserted in particular sites) is also questionable. Moreover, the reassertion of corporate managerial practices and the winding back of reforms in Victoria from the mid-1980s can be seen partly as a response in times of increasing financial restriction to a perceived need for economy and efficiency. It was also a response to an ultimate failure at the system level, despite the system-changing intentions of the policy, seriously to challenge the entrenched acceptance of bureaucratic managerial relationships as being appropriate for educational administration.

Decentralization as Efficient Site Management

The noble but flawed Victorian attempt to reform educational bureaucracy and promote school level participation in the early 1980s can be contrasted with recent reforms in the neighbouring state of New South Wales. There, a major report on education (Scott, 1989) set out to recommend ways of improving the operations of the state's education bureaucracy. The starting assumption seemed to be that the performance of the Education Department could be improved by a more tightly defined structure of roles and responsibilities, a better coordinated, hierarchical accountability system and a clearer definition of goals. In the ensuing report, *Schools Renewal: A Strategy to Revitalise Schools within the New South Wales State Education System* (Scott, 1989), little attention is devoted to the examination of educational goals because these are seen as being independent of the real issues of organizational efficiency and effectiveness. In this sense, the reforms are not directed at changing the system so much as tightening up the system.

The general approach and underlying assumptions of *Schools Renewal* capture much of the essence of recent reforms in the United Kingdom and New Zealand as well as New South Wales. These emphasize the importance of local school management, but, in this version, the notion of school level participation in educational decision-making is accommodated comfortably within the principles of corporate management (Angus, 1989; Bessant, 1988). An important new element in all of these cases is a strong rhetoric of the need to reduce unwieldy and self-serving bureaucracy (the so-called 'educational establishment') and release schools from bureaucratic restrictions. In other words, rather than *reforming* bureaucracy in ways that would render it more responsive, the emphasis is on, as far as possible, *eliminating* bureaucracy. Dramatically symbolic of such a shift was the selling of the historic Bridge Street 'headquarters' of the New South Wales Education Department. To many it seemed then that the Department literally had no 'centre'.

Despite such rhetoric and symbolism, it would be incorrect to describe trends of educational governance exclusively in terms of a shift towards decentralization. Rather, the general pattern of educational organization which seems to be emerging is much more complicated. For instance, the guiding principles which informed notions of decentralization in the state of Victoria in the early 1980s were participation and collaboration in a spirit of democratization and community involvement in local schools. In the neighbouring state of New South Wales, in the 1990s, the emphasis seems to be upon notions of effective and efficient institutionally-based educational management which is argued to result from the reduction of bureaucratic control and interference at the school level. In the New South Wales case, where policies and language that largely echo the British Education Reform Act are employed, the reduction of central control is linked with the deregulation of school zones. This has enabled schools to be placed in relation to each other as competitors in an educational market. Within such a relationship, individual schools will have to compete with other schools for pupils (or market share) in such a way that, according to the advocates of this style of institutional management, the more efficiently managed and entrepreneurial schools are likely to be successful. At the time of writing the people of the state of Victoria are facing an election that almost certainly will be won by the conservative coalition of Liberal and National parties. Part of their electoral appeal is their promise to 'fix' the education 'problem' by putting schools on a market footing. The Shadow Treasurer indicated an extension of New Right themes of accountability and an educational market as he spelled out the thinking behind the Coalition's education policy in a recent speech:

> Resources and authority will be devolved to the school council to run the school, as is already the case in the non-government sector. We will give the school council power to hire and fire the principal, and the principal and the school council the power to hire and fire teachers. They will operate within a core curriculum that will demand excellence but we will impose accountability on them in a host of ways, and I shall now instance two of those ways.

> Firstly, we will ensure that funding follows the student. If a school ceases to attract students, if its enrolments start to decline because it is not delivering what the community wants, that will be reflected in lower funding. . . . Secondly, we will impose accountability, particularly at year 12, through a higher proportion of external assessments so that there is a standardisation of measurements across schools, and the community will be able to see which schools are delivering educational excellence and which are not.

It seems that there is a simultaneous shift in the direction of decentralization for some kinds of decisions and centralization for others. In particular, central governments are assuming, or in some cases returning to, a powerful role in setting broad educational goals, mandating curricula and establishing common methods of accountability so that school level decisions are made within a broad framework of centrally determined priorities and, most importantly, within the constraints of a devolved budget. The imposition of centralized curriculum and evaluation also provides a means of gauging the 'performance' of particular schools. The emphasis on testing, therefore, has less to do with providing educational feedback, or even determining standards, than with providing a basis on which schools can be compared by education consumers and administrators.

A Climate of Conservative Educational Reform

Perhaps the most important point about the context of educational policy and planning is that it is linked directly with national social and economic goals. This linkage has profound implications for the ways in which the purposes of education are regarded. It is significant that in countries like Australia, the United Kingdom and New Zealand the voice of public educators has been largely marginalized in the educational policy arena (Angus, 1992). This is largely because, in Thatcherite terminology, education is believed to suffer from 'provider capture' — self-interested educators and education officials are claimed to have been running the system to suit themselves rather than the needs of children or the nation. This is one of a number of assumptions that seem to be shared by the main political groups. The voices of politicians and their advisers, business and industry representatives, conservative academics and social commentators seem to have displaced those of various education workers, including administrators, teachers and their unions, teacher educators and members of parent organizations. Schools and the education system are seen as key strategic sites in which pupils can be trained to contribute, individually and collectively, to the nation's economic and industrial development and competitiveness. Within this general approach, the essential role for education is seen as one of contributing to the efficient development of a nation's human resources, or human capital, as a major part of the effort to achieve the nation's social and economic priorities.

The dismissal of educational arguments in discussion of education policy seems in part to have resulted from a false perception that schooling has failed to serve the needs of the economy. The obvious problem with this perception is that schools are being blamed for contributing to social and economic uncertainty that is, in fact, a product of the failure of capital, social and cultural change, and shifting economic relativities. In the face of such uncertainty, we tend to fall back too easily upon a general faith in managerialism that has been socially constructed in industrial societies through the institutionalization of practices of bureaucracy and scientific management. These practices, now represented in educational administration in terms of competences and corporate management, need to be recognized as more than neutral managerial devices and as significant contributors to patterns of social relationships. The institutionalization of these as standard and proper ways of managing has led to the taken-for-granted acceptance of the necessity of efficiency and effectiveness, conceived of in a particular managerial fashion.

The pervasiveness of such socially constructed 'common sense' may well explain the widespread acceptance of the belief that education's ills may be remedied by the dismantling of bureaucracy and the imposition of the discipline of the market (Pusey, 1991). It is in relation to this belief that the full implications of local school management become apparent. An educational market, according to proponents, would facilitate increased parental choice among educational institutions, and the resulting competition and consumer pressure, it is argued, would lead directly to higher educational standards and an education that was more relevant to the needs of the closely integrated labour market. Such an approach, the argument continues, will ensure greater efficiency in education because the twin themes of competition and relevance to the labour market will lead to reduced wastage of human capital and a consequent increase in educational quality and productivity.

Within this approach the notion of 'choice' is emphasized and associated with the dezoning of schools so that parents can take their pick from the full market range. The effect of this emphasis in the United Kingdom, as Whitehead and Aggleton (1986) point out, is that the conservative potential of parent and community participation is now in the ascendancy and the notion of democracy seems to have been reduced to a simplistic concept of parental 'choice'. Parents are encouraged 'under the guise of involvement and partnership . . . to become agents in the implementation of central government policies' (Whitehead and Aggleton, 1986, p. 444). The emphasis is on accountability and control rather than personal empowerment. For instance, the right of self-managing schools to opt out of local education authorities (LEAs) is consistent with removal of the 'educational establishment' from interference in educational management. Schools are to operate within market conditions, education is regarded as a commodity and schools are valued to the extent to which they can attract customers.

Within the versions of local school management that are on offer in New South Wales, the United Kingdom, New Zealand, and now Victoria, and in conservative education policy generally, it would appear that what is actually devolved to schools is responsibility for a range of management tasks and control of their budgets. Local decisions about the best and most appropriate form of educational delivery and policy, or about the nature and purpose of schooling, are secondary to, and need to be subordinated to, budget considerations. In other words, while the rhetoric celebrates autonomy and control at the school level, the financial limits within which schools must work are obscured (Ball, 1990). Within a climate of expenditure cuts in education and the public sector generally, local management begins to sound like a euphemism for devolving to schools the blame for cutbacks.

Under New Right versions of local management, each school receives a devolved budget the size of which depends on pupil numbers. This comes very close to a full voucher system for public schools in that each pupil whom the school can attract through the gates becomes a 'walking voucher'. School management needs to be entrepreneurial in attracting both pupils and additional funds. The essential idea, consistent with a market view of the world, is that schools must maximize their local control over their budgets to gain the best competitive advantage over other schools. According to the research of Ball (1990) and his colleagues in the United Kingdom, this has resulted in a situation in which school level decision-making has been dominated by financial considerations. Even more alarming in terms of collaboration within educational organizations, Ball (1990) has warned of a division emerging in schools between managers (concerned increasingly with marketing, image building and financial planning) and teachers (concerned with educational matters). Principals, who must 'prove' themselves as efficient and entrepreneurial managers, may well feel themselves pressed to become more task-oriented and to push a personal agenda in order to make their 'mark' on the school. There is a strong danger that this press many have the effect of eroding team building and collegiality among principal and staff and of limiting rather than enhancing democratic, school level decision-making.

As Apple (1989) has convincingly argued, conservative successes have shifted the ideological ground on which educational debate occurs through their assertion of the logic of the market. The distant, one-directional relationship created by the market and the commodity form, however, is hostile to reciprocal community relationships. The emphasis on competition and parental 'choice', rather than, for instance, democratic participation, equity and redress of disadvantage, also reflects a choice that has been made between very different ways of viewing the role of education in a democratic society. The values inherent in such a choice are by no means universally shared. There certainly has been no groundswell of support for the new educational agenda of school level managerialism, accountability and quality control among educators or parent organizations, whose views on schooling cannot be dismissed simply as naive and self-interested.

One might expect, therefore, that educational workers, including teachers, administrators, parents and students, would be helped in the project of establishing democratic educational communities by having access to accounts of the dynamics of the educational policy arena. These might provide sound analyses of current policy directions and solid arguments for democratic, participative and inclusive approaches to school level educational administration. It is hoped that this volume will contribute to such a project. Unfortunately, however, at least from the perspective of advocates of educational democracy and equity, most publications that are targeted to inform participants in school level management and decision-making tend to reduce the complexity of contested educational debates and policies to simplistic how-to-do-it manuals for school administrators. A reasonably typical example of the genre is Caldwell and Spinks's (1988) best-selling volume on *The Self-Managing School*.

The Self-Managing School

The precise nature of school-based management must be worked out by a range of participants in any particular site. Such working out, however, will be influenced by, among many other things, prevailing discourses of education and educational management, policy and legislative frameworks, and government and community pressures. The push from all these areas, as argued above, is currently for greater school level responsibility for management tasks and budgets. For school participants who may have traditionally regarded the work of schools as helping children to learn, the prospect of involvement in school management may be somewhat daunting. School administrators, teachers and members of school communities seeking guidance on ways in which the local management of schools can be achieved are likely to turn to texts such as *The Self-Managing School* (1988), written by an Australian academic, Brian Caldwell, and Jim Spinks, the principal of a Tasmanian school which had been identified as 'highly effective'.

The approach of Caldwell and Spinks seems to have achieved immense respectability in the United Kingdom, Australia and elsewhere. No doubt, the combination of a well regarded academic and a successful school principal as authors adds significantly to the book's credibility in providing sound and tested advice to the school practitioner. The book (and others like it) can be seen to be empowering in certain respects as it gives practitioners a way of coping with new and confusing demands of school level management. It suggests processes for the orderly arrangement of school business and marks out roles within which various participants may feel relatively comfortable yet purposeful. Most importantly, it links these processes with key areas of curriculum and instruction through the notion of programs which are the focus of decision-making, resource allocation and evaluation.

I want to make it clear that I do not wish to dismiss totally the Caldwell and Spinks approach. I do want to argue, however, that the general model of school level administration outlined in books like *The Self-Managing School* is fundamentally flawed in a number of ways. In particular, I wish to analyze the broad approach suggested by Caldwell and Spinks in terms of its functionalist orientation and its separation of policy and implementation, its advocacy of a particular style of hierarchical leadership, and its assumption of very limited and controlled forms of participation. Most fundamentally, however, despite the book apparently being written at the height of Thatcherism and for the British market, the authors display a total lack of awareness of the profound shift to the right in the educational policy context within which school self-management is to be exercised.

Power and Politics in Education

In essence, Caldwell and Spinks's approach seems devoid of any theoretical or political analysis of educational policy — indeed, it seems to eschew politics. Notions of social, economic or cultural influence on education are not mentioned at all. The connections between school level administration and central control are mentioned, but only in the most instrumental fashion. For instance, Caldwell and Spinks accept without reservation the notion that 'decentralisation is administrative rather than political, with decisions at the local level being made within a framework of local, state or national policies and guidelines' (p. vii). Participants are to operate with limited discretion granted from above and according to approved formats within overall government control. Despite the rhetoric of anti-bureaucracy, this has the effect of reinforcing among educational participants bureaucratic modes of thinking while partially disguising the structures of control within which participation occurs.

Perhaps the most dramatic instance of the failure of the authors to analyze the problematic political foundations of education policy occurs early in the book. Caldwell and Spinks discuss the 1987 Election Manifesto of the British Conservative Party in terms of its educational policy directions which would pave the way for four specific reforms: a national curriculum, local control of school budgets, parental choice of school, and the provision of mechanisms for schools to opt out of the control of local education authorities. Arguably, these were the most controversial education policies ever proposed by a political party entering an election campaign. Yet Caldwell and Spinks blithely conclude of them that 'the values of equity, efficiency, liberty and choice are addressed in the intents to decentralise control of budgets, increase access, foster diversity and allow state schools to be independent of LEA control' (p. 10).

This disarming apparent advocacy, or at best uncritical acceptance, of Thatcherite policies is the most puzzling aspect of the book. It seems obvious that such controversial policies demand analysis, and that notions like equity, liberty and choice, as employed in the Thatcherite New Right project, are highly problematic and require interpretation. Yet there is no discussion, for instance, of the political construction of equity. The bland acceptance of the New Right agenda is all the more curious because

Caldwell and Spinks, during the time in which the book must have been written, had come fresh from an extensive consultancy with the Ministry of Education in Victoria where a very different agenda from that of the New Right had been to some extent asserted (although, by then, some retreat from progressive educational positions was underway there also). Moreover, I am convinced by my personal association with the authors over a number years that both Caldwell and Spinks are personally committed to principles of social justice in education. Therefore, I do not wish to imply that the apparent unquestioning acceptance of the Conservative policy direction and apparent endorsement of particular policies reflect in any way upon their personal values (or policy preferences). Rather, their failure to address problematic issues in the policy agenda, and in Conservative policy in the United Kingdom in particular, betrays the chamelion-like character of their program for self-managing schools. Given its presumed ease of application either within Victoria or in post-Thatcher Britain, it would appear that the authors see their approach as being almost infinitely adaptable to any political circumstance.

Indeed, in what seems a blatant attempt to convince readers of the applicability of their model of management in any conceivable situation, the authors make the extraordinary claim that, although they 'have a preference and a commitment to collaboration', the model can be applied in various ways to cover just about all possibilities — from the principal alone autocratically deciding policy without reference to anyone, to the principal, staff and community working through a formal structure of school council or school board (pp. 58–9). Perhaps even more alarming, the authors display an uncritical acceptance of funding cuts to schools and reassure readers that a virtue of their model of program budgeting is that it 'will enable funding cuts to be translated as programme eliminations or modifications and in this way will detrimentally affect only a small number of programmes in schools rather than affecting all with "across the board" cuts' (p. 181). The policies and politics that have resulted in the funding cuts to education are not discussed at all. Such considerations, it is clearly implied, are beyond the ken of school level participants who are expected to accept the cuts, operate within the reduced budget, and get on and do the job by focusing on their own little domain of the school. As Apple (1991, p. 28) quite rightly warns us, however, 'To the extent that we do not place educational problems within their larger social context, we are playing into the hands of the conservative alliance that seeks to blame us [educators] for nearly all social ills at the same time that it both denies us the resources necessary to take education seriously and continuously creates the abysmal social conditions that make our jobs more difficult to accomplish.' Such is precisely the social context against which school self-management is being constructed, and which Caldwell and Spinks ignore.

The book's concern is with apparently neutral, appropriate consultative and budgetary processes rather than the substance of, or the values inherent within, policy. No consideration seems to have been given to the point that the model's emphasis on program budgets and financial management sits very easily with crude cost-accounting and market approaches to educational provision. There seems to be a clear expectation that participants in school level management need only follow the recommended processes and that these will generally result in consensus and 'good' decisions that can be supported by all parties. The type of participation provided within such processes seems relatively innocuous as the emphasis on process overshadows what participants are participating in and why. Issues of significance are likely to become submerged in the specified procedures and construction of the many timetables, plans, evaluation reports and other documents that the model requires.

The context in which education governance is discussed by Caldwell and Spinks is confined and pragmatic. Apart from responding in an instrumental manner to government policy, schools remain detached from politics and economics, and from historical changes in the social context. Reforms are seen merely as something to be applied in schools to make them fit more closely with the requirements of government and the expectations of an anxious public. The world of *The Self-Managing School* is an unreal world that is remote from social relations of inequality, cultural hegemony, sexism, racism or any of the social and educational disadvantages and conflicts that surround and pervade schooling (Apple, 1982; Angus, 1986).

Even internal disputes within the school are to be resolved by an emphasis on the correct processes rather than through confronting and arguing through the issues about which conflict may have arisen:

> The political nature of the process is evident throughout this account; that is, disagreement may occur at any point in the process on the ends which are being sought or on the means by which those ends are to be achieved. A successful policy will result if this political process is effectively managed and the three criteria of desirability ('Will this alternative resolve the issue, achieving the benefits intended with minimal harm in the area under consideration or in other areas?'), workability ('Can this alternative be implemented with the available resources of personnel, time, facilities and money?') and acceptability ('Will this alternative be accepted by those who will be affected by the policy or who will be required to implement the policy?') are satisfied. (p. 95)

While the existence of conflict is at least recognized, it is merely between individuals and never social structural (Tinker, 1986). It is to be resolved through proper processes, through a proper managerial concern with pragmatic matters of desirability, workability and acceptability. Indeed, according to Caldwell and Spinks, the model should prevent conflict arising in the first place because problems 'often arise because of a failure to clearly and/or appropriately specify responsibility for particular activities and programs' (p. 187). This is classical, functionalist, managerial stuff. Good management entails the clear specification of roles and appropriate strategies of decision-making which 'satisfice' (Simon, 1947).

Functionalist Perspective

With its essential emphasis on program budgeting, *The Self-Managing School* makes the school the unit of analysis for the evaluation of outputs within a managerial orientation towards cost-efficiency. Local management is to be valued for its capacity to enhance both efficiency and the involvement of participants. From this limited perspective, the main thrust of the book as identified at the very start by the Series Editor, David Reynolds, would seem entirely appropriate: 'This book concerns one of today's key educational issues; how schools can be encouraged to develop their own management skills' (p. vi). Reynolds makes it clear that book is 'above all a *practical* guide to the process of school management that gives a large quantity of worksheets, check lists and documents that can be used by any staff group in their own school' (p. vi, emphasis in original). The authors similarly make it clear that their mission is in 'identifying and disseminating information which could help head teachers manage their finances in more efficient and effective ways' (p. viii).

The tone of the book, then, is clearly one which implies the direct and unproblematic application to the work of school participants of universal and appropriate skills and methods of managing budgets. Indeed, to Caldwell and Spinks, this is what being a self-managing school is all about: 'We define a self-managing school as one for which there has been sufficient and consistent devolution to the school level of authority to make decisions related to the allocation of resources' (p. 5). The authors quote with approval the view of the chairman of the Solihull education committee (apparently one of the 'trailblazers' in local management of schools) who is reported to have said that 'if you applied the same sort of procedures to running a school as he used in running a small business there could be some improvement in performance, and that if you are spending your own money you take more care than if you are spending someone else's' (p. 11). Good school management, then, is much like good management in business. This connection is rammed home in a long section in which the 'lessons' of Peters and Waterman's (1982) study of supposed best management practice, *In Search of Excellence*, are uncritically translated into specific guidelines for school administration and leadership. A number of commentators writing within the school effectiveness movement, another body of literature with which Caldwell and Spinks seem to be enamoured, make similar connections. According to one of these authors:

One of the most successful compilations of recent theory and practice in the business world is the best-selling book *In Search of Excellence* (Peters and Waterman, 1982). Many of the basic principles identified by the authors in their study of forty-three successful companies will look familiar to readers of the school effectiveness literature. What is found in successful companies is also often found in successful schools. (Dunlap, 1985, p. 1)

Caldwell and Spinks certainly agree.

The efficiency-oriented conception of local school management is further reinforced by the extensive display in the book of diagrams, worksheets, checklists and sample documents that lead the reader through an apparently neutral, apolitical and largely unproblematic process for doing school-based management. The recommended process has all the hallmarks of traditional approaches which have linked 'managed democracy' (Angus and Rizvi, 1989) with efficiency of production — emphasizing, for instance, typical managerial objectives such as program development and delivery, cost effectiveness, staff involvement and accountability (Coleman, 1987; Conway, 1984; Seddon *et al.*, 1990). Participation in the process is therefore regarded as being of instrumental value as it is assumed that it will advance the apparently neutral and supposedly agreed purposes of the school. It seems that, in keeping with a broadly functionalist perspective, Caldwell and Spinks assume the harmony and functionality of schools and education within the social system. The significance of this point becomes even more apparent when considered in relation to the neutral perspective that Caldwell and Spinks adopt to issues of power and politics.

Caldwell and Spinks's functionalist approach is also apparent in their clear separation between policy and implementation, and in their precise allocation of specific roles to particular individuals and groups. This represents classical bureaucratic rationality (Rizvi, 1986). Caldwell and Spinks go so far as to argue that one of the special contributions to the literature on educational management made by their elaboration of the so-called 'collaborative school management cycle', which underpins their approach to school-based management, is its 'clear and unambiguous specification of those phases which are the concern of the group responsible for policy-making in schools ("policy group") and of other phases which are the concern of the group responsible for implementing policy ("programme teams")' (p. 22). Of the six phases of the collaborative school management cycle, the 'policy group' (which, it should be remembered, may consist of a single person) is responsible for policy-making, goal-setting and need identification, and approval of budgets, while the 'programme teams' are responsible for implementing, and preparing plans and budgets that must be approved by the 'policy group'. Responsibility for evaluation is shared between the policy and implementation groups, but the division of tasks here is quite specific:

While programme budgets are prepared by programme teams, they must be approved by the policy group; they must reflect the policies and priorities established earlier by that group. Following implementation by programme teams, the evaluating phase is again a shared responsibility, with programme teams gathering information for programme evaluation and the policy group gathering further information as appropriate to make judgements on the effectiveness of policies and programmes. (p. 23)

By working carefully and systematically through the phases of the collaborative school management cycle, Caldwell and Spinks assure their readers, school participants should find that policy theorists have generally exaggerated the complexities of the policy process. The fact is, they say, that 'building a base of policies for a school is not as complex a task as is often suggested. Most policies can be quickly written by documenting the current approach in the format recommended for a policy' (p. 41). In such ways activity is encouraged but is channelled into relatively safe directions as participants, in a functionalist and utilitarian manner, are directed to work through approved tasks and formats which do not challenge taken-for-granted assumptions.

Managerial Leadership

In keeping with its functionalist assumptions and the literature on school effectiveness, the tone of *The Self-Managing School* betrays an expectation that particular leadership tasks can be ascribed to a hierarchical position and that these will be instrumental in the realization of organizational goals. Most of the managing of the 'self-managing' school is to be done by the principal who is expected to take seriously the task of leadership. Caldwell and Spinks further develop their prescription for effective leadership in a new book, *Leading the Self-Managing School* (Caldwell and Spinks, 1992), which, according to a colleague of Caldwell's at the University of Melbourne, 'tells principals how to tell schools how to do it [be self-managing]' (Beare, 1992, p. 4). The broad thrust of their view of leadership is made perfectly clear, however, in *The Self-Managing School*.

They strongly emphasize the importance of 'appropriate' leadership. Again, what is considered appropriate seems to have been heavily influenced by United States management literature such as *In Search of Excellence* (Peters and Waterman, 1982) and the school effectiveness literature (e.g., Purkey and Smith, 1985). In particular, Caldwell and Spinks give special attention to the so-called 'higher-order attributes of leadership, namely the capacity to articulate and win commitment to a vision for the school and ensure that vision is institutionalised in the structures, processes and procedures which shape everyday activities' (p. 21). Once the 'vision' of the principal has been asserted or imposed, the next step is 'to build the enduring school culture which is critically important if excellence in schooling is to be attained' (p. 54). While the authors do not spell out what 'excellence in schooling' means precisely, they are unequivocal about the need for the headteacher to foster 'vision' and school culture.

Shrewd leaders are expected to manipulate people and situations so that the leader's 'vision' is willingly shared by followers. The active leadership of the leader is required in order to incorporate the desires and needs of followers into a corporate agenda that is set by the leader. The approach draws heavily on the work of Sergiovanni (1984) and Starratt (undated), who in turn incorporate much of the perspectives of such scholars as Weick (1976), Burns (1978), Viall (1984), Bennis and Nanus (1985) and Deal and Kennedy (1982). It seems that Caldwell and Spinks uncritically endorse current management thinking in which it is believed that leaders of vision are able to bring about a negotiated order which accords with their own definitions and purposes and ensures that any change is directed into reasonable, predictable channels by their own overriding moral force. Other organizational participants, such as teachers, parents and students, if mentioned at all, are generally viewed as essentially passive recipients of the leader's vision. By asserting and defending particular values, Caldwell and Spinks argue, leaders so strongly articulate and endorse their own vision that it becomes also the vision of followers and so bonds leader and followers together in a shared covenant which then informs the non-negotiable core beliefs and values of the organization. This core, according to the argument, amounts to an organizational culture which effective leaders can manufacture and manipulate.

The process is argued to work as follows: the leader (principal) articulates a vision for the school which becomes shared by other school members; the vision then 'illuminates' the ordinary activities of school members and invests them with 'dramatic significance'; at this point the leader 'implants the vision in structures and processes of the organisation, so that people experience the vision in the various patterned activities of the organisation'; this leads to the happy situation in which day-to-day decisions are made 'in the light of the vision', which by then has become 'the heart of the culture of the organisation'; one can recognize that the leader's vision has been institutionalized in this way when 'all members of the organisation celebrate the vision in rituals, ceremonies and art forms' (pp. 174–5).

This conception of leadership as a moral and cultural enterprise is consistent with the broadly functionalist perspective within which Caldwell and Spinks's approach to self-management is located. Through their undue emphasis on the role of the principal in schools, they seem to suggest that it is possible to reduce complex educational questions to administrative issues that can be solved merely by the application of correct techniques, skills and knowledge. 'Several years are required', Caldwell and Spinks suggest, 'for people in schools to acquire the knowledge and skills of self-management' (p. 1). However, the main skill required of most participants, the authors imply in their account of leadership, is for them to adopt the leader's vision and slot into the leader's definition of school culture.

Like so much else in *The Self-Managing School*, the particular notion of school culture being applied here is curiously unproblematic. There is virtually no sense, for instance, of an anthropological concern with culture as a shifting and contested concept which is continuously being constructed and reconstructed and which must be subjectively understood. There is also no strong democratic concern with the nature of cultural politics in which organizational members, as active and knowing agents, have the capacity to influence organizational culture while also adapting to some extent to strongly institutionalized cultural expectations, both in schools and in society more broadly. Instead, there is only a managerial concern with the manipulation of, and intervention in, culture by leaders to shape it in ways that enhance school effectiveness. Not only is there a lack of appreciation of the importance and complexity of cultural politics, but also there is a taken-for-granted assumption that the appropriate cultural expectations of those associated with a school will be embodied in the particular values and vision of the leader. The elitist implication of this view is that not only are leaders more visionary than anyone else, but also they are more trustworthy. The general approach seems totally consistent with the tradition of managerial reforms which have attempted to secure the consent of subordinates and build it into otherwise unchanged forms of management control (Braverman, 1974; Clegg and Higgins, 1987; Wood, 1985).

Citizens as Education Consumers or Educational Participants

The attitude of the authors of *The Self-Managing School* to the nature of participation and of participants compounds many of the problems of the book addressed above. Caldwell and Spinks seem to assume the existence of a shared and consistent pattern of meanings, beliefs and basic assumptions among the various participants in the school, whose shared world is represented as being disconnected from issues of power and control, and tensions between competing values and positions. This view of participation, as I have attempted to explain, assumes harmony rather than difference and so minimizes any analysis of an individual's or group's capacity to challenge institutionalized expectations. The role of the individual or group is represented as one of participating according to appropriate rules, policies and processes.

The important point is whether the form and nature of the involvement in schooling that is offered to various participants in models like that proposed by Caldwell and Spinks challenge previously accepted thinking about education under the prevailing bureaucratic rationality (Angus and Rizvi, 1989). The way people participate has been influenced by ent enched structures and their associated pattern of power relationships. Despite a rhetoric of reform, these are likely to be sustained in often subtle ways that involve the culturally and historically constituted dispositions of particular groups. Among the strongest of these are institutionalized expectations about the nature of education and educational administration, and the familiar roles of education participants. Because of widely shared historical understandings of these matters, participants in educational governance tend to shape themselves to fit the pattern of established, 'neutrally' defined role positions. There is a fairly common set of expectations, for instance, of people who occupy the roles of pupil, teacher, parent, principal and so on. Caldwell and Spinks do not challenge the traditional, conservative construction of these role positions. Instead, participants in education are expected to fit the roles and management processes defined by the authors.

Substantial educational reform requires that school participants penetrate the level of immediacy of everyday actions and consider the practices of schooling in relation to the social, cultural, political and economic context of education. Established and taken-for-granted goals and values, however, are unlikely to be confronted within Caldwell and Spinks's carefully constructed and functionalist approach to school self-management because they advocate leaders whose role it is to manage the process, the various participants and the various interests that impinge on schools — but to do so in a way that is detached from politics and ideology, and even (and this point is significant although I have not developed it here) from educational thought.

Current emphases contribute to a particular vision of schooling and society which exists in competition with alternative visions. In the managerial, market-oriented perspective, society is envisaged as a collection of possessive individuals who, as human capital, seek from education the best return for their investment of time, effort and money. The dominance of values associated with this approach has meant the marginalization or incorporation of other values associated especially with equity, justice and community. However, Caldwell and Spinks fail to take up the point that competing understandings of the fundamental purposes of schooling reflect different educational visions, different notions of the good society and, importantly, different conceptions of the appropriate relationship between schools and their communities.

Caldwell and Spinks have very little to say about the participation of parents in school management. Yet there seems to be broad agreement across the ideological spectrum about the necessity of parent participation in the process of establishing quality schooling. The profound disagreements are over the appropriate nature and form of such participation. From a social democratic perspective, the notion of citizens being members of their school community implies an expectation that they will have an active commitment to the institution of the school in which there will be an active exercise of collective community control, community discussion and an attempt to incorporate community expectations and values. The notion of collectivity in such a relationship needs to be strong. If, however, the notion of acquisition of marketable credentials reflects the type of values that a school projects, then one might anticipate that the relationship of the citizen to the school is much more likely to be one of an individualistic consumer rather than a co-participant with a commitment to the joint creation of an institution to be organized around a sense of the common good. The interest of the consumer parent or the consumer community will be specifically in the maximization of immediate satisfaction from what the school is able to offer students in terms of their own economic advancement in a competitive marketplace. Parents may be welcomed as school governors or school councillors if they can contribute valuable financial management skills, but their main role in education is to make the right choice of school.

Within such a market relationship, which now prevails or is being pressed vigorously in countries like the United Kingdom, Australia, New Zealand and the United States, schools will be required to maximize their market appeal and reputation, and seek to attract clients from across a broad geographic range, rather than serve specific local needs in concert with the community. As Ball (1990) and Gintis (1991) point out, the competitive market orientation is likely to exacerbate social inequality by de facto fostering racial, ethnic and social class differences, and favouring higher income families. Yet local school management is presented within this context by authors like Caldwell and Spinks merely as the best means of ensuring 'effective schools'. In fact, at one point in their book Caldwell and Spinks claim that their approach 'may well be the best, if not only, means by which much of the rhetoric of decentralisation and school effectiveness can be brought to fruition' (p. 56).

As I have emphasized, there is a curiously unproblematic conception of schooling here in which education is reduced to school management problems that are represented as being amenable to direct solutions within the school. Within the broad educational arena, such a view pervades the rhetoric of accountability, corporate management, school effectiveness, centralized curriculum, national testing and the like. The narrow focus on schools as neutral institutions that are to deliver quality outputs, which is characteristic of current rhetoric in educational policy, diverts attention from the problematic nature of education in its social context and from the social and cultural issues which education must address. It should be clear that what is most effective in a managerial sense is not necessarily what is most effective educationally, and is extremely unlikely to be effective in promoting democratic participation in education.

Conclusion: Schools and Communities

Market rationality has become a dominant feature in educational debates. Its emphasis on efficient management, which becomes increasingly complex as greater budgetary powers are devolved to self-managing schools, may well increase rather than decrease the distance between communities and schools. Community representatives in the form of school councillors or governors increasingly must spend meeting time working on (or giving approval to) school budgets rather than considering educational issues. The pressure is strong for education systems to be integrated into the mechanisms of the commercial market, yet schools have long been regarded as significant social institutions. By treating education as a commercial product and schools as competitors in a marketplace, we are altering the nature of participation in what for many people is the most significant social institution after the family (Bastian *et al.*, 1986).

Although the discourse of the right has been predominant in recent years in a number of countries and has been reflected to a large extent in government policy formation, the eventual outcome of the current reform (or reconstruction) process in education is uncertain. It will depend on, among other things, the state of the economy, the strength of popular movements, and struggles within and between political parties and dominant groups. However, given the shift to the right and the reduction of education to the service of the market, the economy and national interests, the priority given to schooling as a public good in the past will need to be reasserted. From the emerging New Right perspective, the citizen as individual is sovereign, with freedom *from* interference of others in the pursuit of individual interests. The community in this perspective is simply the locale in which the market operates, and decentralized school management pits schools against each other to win customers. Within an alternative view, one which emphasizes social democracy, citizens may be seen as active social and political beings (Held, 1989) whose individual existence merges into membership of a collectivity which brings with it rights and responsibilities of participation — including participation in local school governance — in the general interests of members.

The press for genuinely collaborative forms of educational governance should not be allowed to slip from the educational agenda. We should learn from the equivocal success of the Victorian example discussed above, especially its ultimate failure to resist the emergence of New Right themes. An educational project which questions whether the best education for children is to be provided in the individualist and competitive approach favoured by the right needs to be asserted. Such a project would embrace genuine school level participation, and would be developed collectively with the partnership of school and community. The genuine democratic participation in school governance that might result from such a project would probably deliver efficient site management. It would probably result in better decisions and greater commitment to those decisions, and would also stimulate greater democratic awareness of, and commitment to, democratic participation in a broader sense. All of these are significant, but, in my view, democratic participation would be most important because it can raise for scrutiny a host of issues that are left dormant under bureaucratic rationality. These include contested issues of justice, relevance, cultural discrimination in schools and the connections between education and society. In collectively challenging the taken-for-granted in education, a number of important questions may be raised by school participants in relation to these issues. These would include questions that have long troubled those with a socially critical perspective on schooling, such as: What counts as education? What counts as knowledge? Whose interests are served or restricted by the selection, production and distribution of such knowledge? What aspects of society and economy are legitimated by forms of knowledge? What kind of society do we want? How might schools contribute to the formation of such a society?

Such critical questioning does not come easily to us because we have long been socialized into acceptance of institutionalized expectations about schooling. Current conservative reforms narrow, but do not essentially challenge, such expectations. This is precisely why experience in participative democracy in schools and school communities is important: participation is itself educative as participants learn to contribute to dialogue over issues that are problematic. The democratic possibilities of school level participation, therefore, can best be realized through the engagement of teachers, administrators and their school communities in critical reflection on the purpose and meaning of education. In these circumstances various educational positions would be scrutinized in an attempt, without any guarantees, to work towards sound and socially responsible education for all students.

References

ANGUS, L. (1986) *Schooling for Social Order: Equality, Democracy and Social Mobility in Education*, Geelong, Deakin University Press.

ANGUS, L. (1989) 'Democratic Participation and Administrative Control in Education', *International Journal of Educational Management*, 3, 2, pp. 20–6.

ANGUS, L. (1992) ' "Quality" Schooling, Conservative Educational Reform and Educational Change in Australia', *Journal of Education Policy*, 7, 4, pp. 379–97.

ANGUS, L. and RIZVI, F. (1989) 'Power and the Politics of Participation', *Journal of Educational Administration and Foundations*, 4, 1, pp. 6–23.

APPLE, M. (1982) *Education and Power*, New York, Routledge.

APPLE, M. (1989) 'How Equality Has Been Redefined in the Conservative Restoration', in W. SECADA (Ed.), *Equity in Education*, Lewes, Falmer Press.

APPLE, M. (1991) 'The Social Context of Democratic Authority: A Sympathetic Response to Quantz, Cambron-McCabe and Dantley', *The Urban Review*, 23, 1, pp. 21–9.

BALL, S. (1990) 'Education Inequality and School Reform: Values in Crisis!', Inaugural lecture in the Centre for Educational Studies, King's College London, University of London.

BASTIAN, A., FRUCHTER, N., GITTEL, M., GREER, G. and HASKINS, K. (1986) *Choosing Equality: The Case for Democratic Schooling*, Philadelphia, Pa., Temple University Press.

BEARE, H. (1992) 'Is There Life after Brian?', *Principal Matters*, 3, 4, p. 4.

BENNIS, W. and NANUS, B. (1985) *Leaders: The Strategies for Taking Charge*, New York, Harper and Row.

BESSANT, R. (1988) 'The Role of Corporate Management in the Reassertion of Government Control over the Curriculum of Victorian Schools', Mimeo, Centre for Comparative and International Studies in Education, La Trobe University, Bundoora.

BRAVERMAN, H. (1974) *Labor and Monopoly Capital*, New York, Monthly Review Press.

BURNS, J. (1978) *Leadership*, New York, Harper and Row.

CALDWELL, B. and SPINKS, J. (1988) *The Self-Managing School*, Lewes, Falmer Press.

CALDWELL, B. and SPINKS, J. (1992) *Leading the Self-Managing School*, Lewes, Falmer Press.

CLEGG, S. and HIGGINS, W. (1987) 'Against the Current: Organizational Sociology and Socialism', *Organizational Studies*, 8, 3, pp. 201–22.

COLEMAN, P. (1987) 'Implementing School Based Decision Making', *The Canadian Administrator*, 4, 4, pp. 1–6.

CONWAY, J. (1984) 'The Myth, Mystery and Mastery of Participative Decision Making in Education', *Educational Administration Quarterly*, 20, pp. 11–40.

DAVIES, L. (1990) *Equity and Efficiency? School Management in an International Context*, Lewes, Falmer Press.

DEAL, T. and KENNEDY, A. (1982) *Corporate Cultures: The Rites and Rituals of Corporate Life*, Reading, Mass., Addison-Wesley.

DUNLAP, D. (1985) 'New Ideas for School Improvement', *OSSC Report*, 23, 3.

GINTIS, H. (1991) 'Review of John E. Chubb, and Terry M. Moe, *Politics, Markets and America's Schools*', *British Journal of Sociology of Education*, 12, 3, pp. 381–4.

HELD, D. (1989) *Political Theory and the Modern State*, London, Polity Press.

PETERS, T. and WATERMAN, R. (1982) *In Search of Excellence: Lessons from America's Best-run Companies*, New York, Harper and Row.

PURKEY, S. and SMITH, M. (1985) 'School Reform: The District Policy Implications of the Effective Schools Literature', *The Elementary School Journal*, 85, pp. 353–89.

PUSEY, M. (1991) *Economic Rationalism in Canberra: A Nation Building State Changes Its Mind*, Cambridge, Cambridge University Press.

RIZVI, F. (1986) *Administrative Leadership and the Democratic Community as a Social Ideal*, Geelong, Deakin University Press.

RIZVI, F. and ANGUS, L. (1990) 'Reforming Bureaucracy: An Experiment in Responsive Educational Governance', in J. CHAPMAN, and J. DUNSTAN (Eds), *Bureaucracy and Democracy: Tensions in Public Schooling*, Lewes, Falmer Press.

Scott, B. (1989) *Schools Renewal: A Strategy to Revitalise Schools within the New South Wales Education System*, Management Review, NSW Education Portfolio, Milsons Point, NSW.

Seddon, T., Angus, L. and Poole, M. (1990) 'Pressures on the Move to School-Based Decision-Making and Management', in J. Chapman (Ed.), *School-Based Decision-Making and Management*, Lewes, Falmer Press.

Sergiovanni, T. (1984) 'Leadership and Excellence in Schooling', *Educational Leadership*, 41, 5 (February), pp. 4–13.

Simon, H. (1947) *Administrative Behaviour*, New York, Macmillan.

Starratt, R. (undated) *Excellence in Education and Quality of Leadership*, Occasional Paper No. 1 of the Southern Tasmania Council for Educational Administration.

Tinker, T. (1986) 'Metaphor or Reification: Are Liberal Humanists Really Libertarian Anarchists?' *Journal of Management Studies*, 23, 4, pp. 363–83.

Vaill, P. (1984) 'The Purposing of High Performing Systems', in T. Sergiovanni and J. Corbally (Eds), *Leadership and Organizational Culture*, Urbana, Ill., University of Illinois Press.

Victoria, Minister of Education (1986) *Ministerial Papers 1–6*, Ministry of Education, Melbourne.

Weick, K. (1976) 'Educational Organizations as Loosely Coupled Systems', *Administrative Science Quarterly*, 21, 1, pp. 1–19.

Whitehead, J. and Aggleton, P. (1986) 'Participation and Popular Control on School Governing Bodies: The Case of the Taylor Report and Its Aftermath', *British Journal of Sociology of Education*, 7, 4, pp. 433–49.

Whitty, G. (1989) 'The New Right and the National Curriculum: State Control or Market Forces?', *Journal of Education Policy*, 4, 4, pp. 329–41.

Wood, S. (1985) 'Work Organization', in R. Deem and G. Salaman (Eds), *Work, Culture and Society*, Milton Keynes, Open University Press.

2 The New Right and the Self-Managing School

Jack Demaine

In many countries today there is growing political pressure for education reform (see Demaine, 1990). Much of the argument for change involves the issue of developing self-managing schools. Of course, most schools already exercise a degree of self-management in the sense that teachers, working with their headteacher, take responsibility for the day-to-day running of their school and for much of the detail of school policy. They usually work in consultation with parents, governors, local authority advisers and other interested parties.

In Britain the 1977 Taylor Report, which had been commissioned by the then Labour government, recommended major reforms to the structure of school management. In particular, Taylor recommended a formal structure for the election of parents, teachers and community representatives to the governing bodies of schools. During the 1980s many of Taylor's recommendations were implemented by the Conservatives, although not in precisely the form set out in the report. A major difference between the Taylor recommendations and the subsequent development of moves towards school self-management concerns the issue of financial management. The Taylor Report had not recommended devolution of financial control to the individual school, although it did recommend that the local authorities involve governors more in the drawing up of expenditure plans along the lines of the 1945 'model articles' for school management (see Taylor Report, Ch. 7). In contrast with Taylor's rather modest recommendations with respect to school finance, very radical proposals for financial self-management have come from the so-called New Right.

The New Right argues that schools should become private, independent self-governing charitable trusts with control over their own budgets and their own pupil enrolment policy. Their income would be derived from education vouchers and from cash paid by parents as 'top-up' fees. At the same time the New Right regards the removal of teachers' national pay scales, the rewriting of individual teacher contracts and the break up of teachers' capacity for trade union activity as necessary to the provision of an improved educational service. The governing bodies of school should be 'free to hire and fire' teachers, while parents would be 'free to choose' the school at which their education credit voucher plus cash would be spent. This chapter examines the arguments of the New Right on the need for schools to become more or less private, self-managing units.

The chapter also examines the 'progress' that has been made along the path of privatization in Britain during the Conservative administrations of the 1980s and 1990s. There have been several attempts to demonstrate the links between right-wing lobby groups and the Conservative Party and Conservative governments (see, for example, Ball, 1990; Knight, 1990), but this is not the objective of the chapter. Rather, here, it is a matter of examining New Right policy thinking and comparing it with the development of education policy in Tory Britain. It is certainly possible to draw comparisons between New Right thinking on the one hand and Tory policy on the other, but it is also possible to find differences.

While the New Right has been politically active and very forceful in arguing for education reform, it should be noted that writers who claim no right-wing credentials such as Caldwell and Spinks, in their book *The Self-Managing School* (1988), and Hill, Oakley Smith and Spinks, in *Local Management of Schools* (1990), are enthusiastic about the development of the kinds of administrative arrangements that right-wing policy would bring about. They are not the only non-right thinkers who want to see change. While not accepting right-wing arguments on education reform, A.H. Halsey, a British Labour Party supporter widely acknowledged as one of the chief architects of the British comprehensive system, has also argued for school self-management and the abolition of local authority control (Halsey, 1981).

Finally, in contrast to the New Right lobby groups and other individuals who are concerned to see further developments in school self-management, there are yet others (including the British Labour Party) who regard the proper management of schools as a task involving 'partnership and participation' of parents, teachers, local politicians and community representatives (see, for example, Gee and Maden, 1988). For those favouring such policy, the financial responsibility for schooling, and particularly teachers' pay, would remain in the hands the local authorities working in cooperation with central government, as the Taylor Report had envisaged. This chapter explores the differing arguments on education reform, with particular reference to the question of responsibilities of the self-managing school.

New Right Argument on the Reform of Education

The term 'New Right' (see Bosanquet, 1983) refers not to any specific group but to a movement represented by a collection of lobby groups concerned, among other things, to bring about the 'liberation' of public services from 'excessive state control' through their 'privatization'. The political philosophy of the New Right is that of 'liberalism', defined in F.A. Hayek's sense of limiting the powers of government in the interests of the liberty of the individual and a 'free society'. Hayek (1960) argues that contemporary liberalism is sometimes misleadingly presented as a doctrine of minimal government, where the latter limits itself to the maintenance of law and order. In fact, liberals are not necessarily opposed to government concerning themselves with social welfare or economic affairs; the important issue is the character and extent of their involvement (Hindess, 1987).

As far as education is concerned, the objective of the New Right is the transformation of whole systems of national, state or local authority controlled schooling, so that most schools would become individual self-managing 'private' institutions. Schools would have the legal status of non-profit-making charitable trusts, much like the existing English public (i.e., private) schools. As one leading proponent of right-wing policy explains, the plan is 'to create, as near as practicable, a "free market" in education. To use a popular term, it is in some sense to "privatise" the State education system' (Sexton, 1987, p. 10).

The New Right argues that education should be regarded as a 'commodity' and teachers as its 'producers'. Hitherto, education has provided an inadequate service because it has suffered from the effects of 'producer capture'. According to the right-wing Adam Smith Institute Omega Report, *Education Policy* (1984), producer capture involves education serving the interests of teachers and administrators rather than the interests of the customers. The hallmarks of producer capture of education are said to include 'employment laxity, giantism and resistance to change' (Omega Report, 1984, p. 3). The New Right sees producer capture as a central characteristic of 'welfare state socialism' typified by the British comprehensive school system.

The New Right remedy for the problems of producer capture is an education voucher system. This, together with forms of school self-management in which 'parental interest' are strongly represented, would, it is said, provide mechanisms for 'liberating' schools and would lead to an improved education service. The terms 'education credits' (Sexton, 1987) and 'pupil entitlements' (Hillgate Group, 1987) are favoured by some sections of the right because the term 'education vouchers' is said to have lost political credibility (see Seldon, 1986). Although the terminology is new, discussion of the principle of vouchers is not. The Institute of Economic Affairs (IEA) booklet, *Education: A Framework for Choice* (Beales, 1967), discussed proposals for voucher schemes and suggested that the notion of vouchers was canvassed by Cardinal Bourne, Archbishop of Westminster, as long ago as 1926. Arthur Seldon (1986) even suggests that the idea can be traced back to Tom Paine's *The Rights of Man* (1792). There was renewed discussion of education vouchers during the early 1980s, in the IEA *Journal of Economic Affairs* (see especially Barns, 1981; Peacock, 1983; Seldon, 1982; West, 1982), culminating in the publication of Seldon's *The Riddle of the Voucher* (1986).

There are minor differences between the various right-wing proposals for vouchers, but, schematically, the suggestion is that every parent or legal guardian of a child of school age would be issued annually with a voucher on its behalf. The value of the voucher, credit or entitlement would be that of the average per capita cost of schooling within a specific locality, taking into consideration differences in costs for children of different ages. Schemes recommended by the New Right suggest that parents should be allowed to 'top up' the value of the voucher with cash. However, the New Right envisages that some schools would remain available where the education credit voucher would be sufficient to pay the fees without any parental top-up money. This would be necessary to retain the principle of 'free' compulsory education (Sexton, 1987).

The New Right concedes that the introduction of vouchers and privatization cannot be achieved quickly because both 'politically and financially it would not be possible or desirable to make a *sudden* change' (Sexton, 1987, p. 30). Instead, there should be a 'phased introduction of educational credits, with every step a gentle step' (p. 46). Sexton's pamphlet, *Our Schools: A Radical Policy* (1987), presents very detailed plans for a process of gradual reform, delineating three distinct stages. What Sexton calls 'gradualism' is proposed in the hope that in making slow progress towards privatization there will be less likelihood of 'offending the educationalists and the bureaucrats' who are said to have 'enormous vested interest' in the status quo (Sexton, 1987, p. 4). Since 'the public' needs to be introduced gently to the idea of paying for education in a 'free market', a step towards this long-term objective is the implementation of a scheme of direct grants from central government to the newly opted out self-managing schools. Once the cost of education is more fully understood and accepted by the public (something that has not really happened in Britain), the next stage would be to allow these direct grants to be transformed into education credit vouchers that parents would then receive directly from government. Eventually there would be legislation to allow these credit vouchers to be topped up with cash and used at any of the self-managing schools which would be competing for custom in the marketplace.

According to the New Right, the way in which teachers' working conditions and pay are determined constitutes an obstacle to the development of a 'free market' in education and the ability of the self-managing school to operate effectively. The newly privatized self-managing schools will need to be able to appoint teachers on fixed-term contracts if they so wish, and to 'hire and fire' very much more easily than has been the case so far. The right argues that in a free market for education, 'teachers' salaries would no longer be determined on a national basis, but by each school. Schools might wish to institute different grades of salary for different qualities of teacher' (Omega Report, 1984, p. 7). This argument is made in almost identical terms by, for example, the Hillgate Group (1986, pp. 8–9) and by the 'No Turning Back Group' of right-wing Conservative MPs in their (1986) pamphlet, *Save Our Schools*, which argues that the governing boards of schools should be able to 'negotiate fixed term contracts of employment with the head and with the other teachers. . . . The head would be responsible, in consultation with the governors, for negotiating the terms of contract for all staff . . . and would have the authority to recommend appointments . . . [and] would have the authority to suspend and dismiss teachers' (p. 17).

For the New Right, what is important for the growth of privatized self-managing schools is the further development of market conditions both for school employees (the teachers) and for the paying customers (the parents). Such development cannot be achieved overnight, and cannot be achieved without the political force of central government. Many observers regard this as something of a paradox; the 'liberation' of schools from local political control and the creation of independent self-managed schools can only be achieved via an initial *centralization* of political control. Centralization is a mechanism which some on the right are prepared to tolerate, at least in the short term, in the hope that it will lead to eventual liberation. We will return to this issue later in the chapter when we examine the development of education in Conservative Britain in the late 1980s and early 1990s.

Non-Right Argument for School Self-Management

The New Right is not alone in addressing the question of the relations between the individual school and central and local government. In their book, *The Self-Managing School*, Caldwell and Spinks (1988) 'define a self-managing school as one for which there has been significant and consistent decentralisation to the school level of authority to make decisions related to the allocation of resources. This decentralisation is administrative rather than political, with decisions at the school level being made within a framework of local, state or national policies and guidelines. The school remains accountable to a central authority for the manner in which resources are allocated' (p. 5). Caldwell and Spinks present a detailed account of the mechanisms of school self-management. What constitutes the 'self' is not fixed in this context. Equally, the notion of 'collaborative' is open to interpretation and disputation. Adopting the phrase, 'collaborative school management', they set out possible 'alternative degrees of collaboration' which range from 'level 1: Head teacher alone decides policy without seeking information' (p. 59) through to 'level 8: Head teacher, staff and the community decide through a formal structure such as a school council or a board of governors' (p. 59). The authors express a 'preference and commitment to collaboration at Level 8' (p. 58). Like many similar texts on education management (see Ozga, 1992 for discussion), Caldwell and Spinks's account of school self-management is technically competent although somewhat pedestrian. At the same time their account is politically coy rather than naive. They acknowledge, briefly, that the policies being pursued by the Conservatives in Britain will lead to self-managing schools and that, 'What is proposed in Britain is potentially the most far-reaching development in any of the countries considered' (p. 9); but they have nothing to say about the politics of the New Right, or about the extensive criticism of right-wing education policy in Britain.

This apolitical approach to school self-management can be found extensively in the British literature on the local management of schools; budget devolution to the individual school, now widely practised in Britain and referred to as LMS (see Coopers and Lybrand, 1988). The argument is that LMS presents 'new opportunities' and a 'challenging environment' in which education is to be delivered. While there is usually a recognition that LMS does impose new demands on headteachers and school governors, the literature often presents an optimistic view, suggesting that the 'flexibility and choice' which budget devolution provides is very much welcomed by institutional leaders. Indeed, there can be no doubt that carefully planned and well resourced individual school self-management can appear very attractive, particularly to the administrative leaders of schools that are the winners in the education market. We shall return to the prospects for the losers in a moment.

In addition to those writing about the self-managing school in enthusiastic terms from an 'administrative' perspective there are other writers, some on the political left, who regard the idea of self-managed schools and even voucher systems as an acceptable way of involving parents more in their children's education, and as a means of delivering positive benefits to the needy. Indeed, over a decade ago the British educationalist and Labour Party supporter, A.H. Halsey, argued that education voucher schemes were 'too socialistic to be conceivable Tory policy' (Halsey, 1981, p. 346).

Halsey puts forward a number of suggestions which bear comparison with those favoured by the New Right, arguing for 'parent power plus direct grants for all' and for the abolition of local authority control of schools. He suggests that self-managed schools financed through both central and local taxation could make 'every school a direct grant school. School government could be simultaneously reformed along the lines recommended in the Taylor report, with more power to parents' (p. 347). Halsey accepts that in reorganizing education on the basis of individual self-managing schools rather than through local authorities, new inequalities would arise. But this 'would be more than compensated for by the release and creation of new energies for education from parents, teachers and children. And antidotes in reserve are national minima, the discretionary element in the direct grant formula, the inspectorate and the educational ambulance service' able to come to the rescue where minimum national standards were not met.

The significance of Halsey's proposals lies not so much in the detail but in the challenge they present, particularly to those on the left who are locked into thinking that provision via the local authorities is the only acceptable means through which to organize schooling. In fact, a nationally funded school system consisting of self-managed community schools could make available energy and enthusiasm which both the right and the left see as locked out of the schools by unacceptable professional practice and the effects of bureaucracy. However, right-wing attacks on teachers (see Demaine, 1988) are unlikely to encourage their cooperation in such an unlocking.

Halsey's arguments on direct grants are not accepted by the Labour Party. Nevertheless, in the late 1980s in its pamphlet, *Parents in Partnership* (Labour Party, 1988), and in a string of publications (see Demaine, 1992) leading up to the 1992 general election, Labour did commit itself more firmly than ever before to the idea of partnership between parents and schools, and to the recommendations of the Taylor Report. Indeed, *Parents in Partnership* suggests that parents are the 'cornerstone of a school's success and a pupil's progress' and that 'Labour wants to build a firm bridge between home and school.' The pamphlet delineates realistic forms of parental involvement which aim to supplement the formal mechanisms for election of parent and teacher governors recommended by Taylor.

In fact, Taylor's recommendations involve much more than a set of criteria for the formal election of governors. It is necessary to re-examine arguments for less formal mechanisms of parental involvement as well as the questions surrounding the formal election of governors and their responsibilities. Labour's pamphlet delineates possible forms of contact between parents and schools, pointing out that much could be gained by drawing on the experience and good practice of existing local education authorities and schools. It recognizes that at present many parents have little direct involvement particularly with the secondary schools which their children attend. The problem is to find ways of involving parents, not just as fund raisers or 'customers', but as partners with schools and with teachers in the education of their children. But parental involvement and 'democratization' can never provide solutions to all of the problems of racism, sexism, poverty, unemployment and inequality which face young people today. But that is hardly the fault of the schools or education policy; education is not some kind of panacea for all social problems and ills.

British Conservative Party and Self-Managing Schools

In the event the British Labour Party lost the 1992 general election, leaving the way clear for further Conservative education reforms at least until the mid-1990s. A White Paper published in the summer of 1992 signalled further steps along the path towards privatization embarked upon during the Thatcher-led administrations of the 1980s. The Conservative governments of the 1980s laid the ground for the privatization of schools through legislation leading up to and including the 1988 Education Reform Act. The provision for schools to opt out of local authority political control, the restoration of the direct grant system, the introduction of financial self-management (LMS) even for schools which did not formally opt out, and a limited form of 'open enrolment' amounts to a what Hywel Thomas (1990) refers to as a 'voucher economy' without the need to print the vouchers.

Many on the right had seen the education voucher as the main instrument of reform; a cutting edge with which to carve up the existing structure of educational provision. However, as the Conservatives pressed on with their program of reform in education, the voucher was no longer seen as an instrument of change. As well as differing from the New Right over the necessity to move to a fully fledged voucher system, there are other important differences between government and the New Right. These differences concern two very closely related matters: the issue of what the right refers to as 'the pace of reform' and the question of 'centralization', which we touched upon earlier.

The problem for the British government in the 1980s, recognized by Stuart Sexton, was that the 1944 Education Act had devolved most of the responsibility for education to the local education authorities (LEAs). The existing structure, which by the mid-1980s had been in place for some forty years and which had considerable support from Conservatives in local government, presented a considerable obstacle to reform. Nevertheless, during the 1980s Conservative central government sought to overcome some of these obstacles through legislation which clawed back responsibilities from the local authorities. This led to the charge of 'centralization' both from sections of the left and from sections of the right.

Although it is important not to overestimate the extent and capacity of centralization to bring about effective reform, it did provide the Conservatives with mechanisms through which to attempt to control the activity of LEAs, and in many cases, therefore, to attempt to steal political control from Labour councils. Understandably, centralization has been the focus of much criticism from the left. Of course, centralization is anathema to the libertarian New Right. Sexton, for example, argues that centralization of control of education is 'unsatisfactory and objectionable, especially in England where the whole concept is alien to our ideas of personal liberty and freedom' (Sexton, 1987, p. 7). Nevertheless, he regards central government policy as a necessary prerequisite to *eventual* liberty for the consumers in a market for education. Thus for 'pragmatic' sections of the New Right, central government provides a *mechanism* through which to liberate the schools from LEA political control.

As far as the education voucher is concerned, Conservative central government began to distance itself from the idea in the early 1980s following the damaging publicity surrounding the feasibility study carried out by Conservative controlled Kent County Council. Sir Keith Joseph, then Secretary of State for Education and Science, told the 1983 Conservative Party Conference that 'the voucher, at last in the foreseeable future, is dead' (quoted in Seldon, 1986). During the 1987 election campaign, playing down the idea of education vouchers, Mrs Thatcher had told an interviewer that 'something much more simple is required', suggesting instead that 'a headmaster [sic] would get so much money per pupil and he would be free to spend a proportion of that how he liked' (see English, 1987). Kenneth Clarke, Secretary of State for Education and Science until the general election in 1992, also dismissed the idea of vouchers, while promoting the idea of opting out and local management of schools.

In effect, Conservative governments have proceeded with a policy *towards* privatization by stealth (see Demaine, 1989). The Tories have been so concerned to keep vouchers and privatization off their explicit agenda for schools that the term 'commercialization' would perhaps more accurately describe the policy of gradually trying to bring market forces into education. Arthur Seldon registered the frustration of some sections of the New Right, arguing that the Conservatives 'have implemented half-measures, in education opting out by schools rather than parents, that will delay the best solution by a decade' (Seldon, 1988). His 'best solution' would involve further legislation to force most schools into the private sector proper. In fact, the 1992 White Paper published after the 1992 general election proposed making opting out easier rather than forcing schools to privatize. The Tories remain committed to the idea of a system of self-managing schools, albeit in the context of a system of central government funding. At this stage there is no suggestion of a formal voucher scheme or of top-up fee paying.

The Self-Managed Schools in a Marketplace of the Future

In that schools have always exercised a degree of self-management, the real issues concern the extent, the forms and the consequences of self-management. There can be no doubt that some headteachers regard further developments along such lines as beneficial to their own institutions. A developed market for education is likely to prove particularly beneficial to popular oversubscribed schools, but what are the prospects for the undersubscribed schools? In fact, the likely effects on undersubscribed schools are well illustrated by examining the prospects for the oversubscribed schools, precisely because the market establishes and extends the relationship between them.

The New Right suggests that under free market conditions over-subscribed schools would be faced with two main possibilities. The first would be to expand, and the second would be to adopt selection procedures; the two are not necessarily mutually exclusive. In the right-wing vision of the future, when schools are 'liberated' from local authority controls, and prohibition on the expansion of the individual school beyond prescribed limits is eventually abolished, the option to expand would depend upon assessment of specific conditions in which the schools operated. The governors of an individual self-managing school might not be persuaded, for example, that expansion was necessarily the best option. Indeed, 'giantism' is precisely one of the faults the New Right finds with the present comprehensive schools.

If expansion were ruled out, then selection would remain as a possible means of dealing with oversubscription, and the governors of a self-managed school might well calculate that it offered certain important advantages. Various forms of selection are possible, but two are particularly likely. Again, they are not mutually exclusive. One is selection by ability of the child to pass an entrance examination, and the other is selection by ability of the child's parent or guardian to pay a top-up fee in addition to the value of the voucher. Selection by ability of parents to pay fees would mean that the school would have money to employ more teachers and in doing so achieve smaller classes. With national scales for teachers' pay abolished, better off schools would also be in a position to employ better qualified teachers by offering higher salaries and favourable working conditions, including, for example, smaller classes and more resources. Selection by entrance examination would be likely to improve the school's future public examination results as it admitted more and more pupils with the ability to pass examinations. A reputation of achievement in public examinations would be all the more likely if selection by entrance exam were combined with selection by ability of parents to pay top-up fees, because it would help the school to provide those things which money can buy. Better off parents also seem able to make healthy contributions to school events designed to raise money for 'extras'. Such considerations might persuade the governors of some self-managing schools to opt for selection rather than expansion as a response to oversubscription.

We are now in a better position to view the likely future of the undersubscribed schools. They would be populated by children unable to pass the entrance examinations to the oversubscribed schools and by children whose parents were unwilling or unable to top up the value of the credit voucher. The market would have the capacity to produce a hierarchy of schools varying in the cost of places and the level of performance of candidates in entrance examinations. Schools with little or no revenue from top-up fees might be unable to afford to employ as many teachers as better off schools with the same number of pupils. They might have to rely on inadequately trained or less well qualified teachers than the better off schools, and on a supply of teachers unable to secure posts in schools paying higher salaries. Of course, this might not necessarily lead to less well off schools having uniformly 'worse' teachers than better off schools. Ideological commitment, geographical mobility and a variety of other considerations are involved in the distribution of teachers to posts. Nevertheless, it is not difficult to predict that a 'free market' would produce a range of schools closely related to the socio-economic status of their pupil intake, with 'sink' schools at one end of the range and expensive well provided ones at the other.

For the New Right one of the supposed benefits of introducing elements of a free market into public sector education is the effect it would have on teachers. The suggestion is that, fearful for their jobs, teachers in undersubscribed schools will improve their 'performance', and hence the market position of their school. If they did not make the necessary improvements, the school would lose viability as more and more parents exercised their 'right of exit' (see Hirschman, 1970). The beneficial effect, according to the New Right, is that 'schools will have to work in order to stay in business, and the worse their results, the more likely they will be to go to the wall' (Hillgate Group, 1986, p. 16). But this argument for introducing elements of a free market into public sector education supposes that teachers can indeed control the outcome of their work, in the sense of the level of educational performance of the school as a whole. However, educational research over the last forty years has shown that there is a relationship between the socio-economic status of children constituting the intake of the individual school and its aggregate performance in terms of public examination results. In fact, the housing market provides an important mechanism in this relationship and generally families and school are 'part of the same society and their respective places in society are, in general terms, determined by the same social relations' (Hussain, 1976).

While it *is* true that teachers can make a considerable difference to educational outcomes as far as individual children are concerned, the educational performance of the school as a whole is not reducible to the capacities of teachers. Teachers in undersubscribed schools might be severely limited in their capacity to respond to the market no matter how 'hard' or how 'effectively' they work. Indeed, teachers' effectiveness can only be judged relative to the specific circumstances in which they operate. The danger is that 'free' market conditions involving easier 'hire and fire' contracts might demoralize teachers working in difficult circumstances rather than forcing them to improve their performance.

Conclusions

I have argued that most schools already exercise a degree of self-management. Currently, in many countries there are arguments for extending the degree of self-management which schools are allowed by local and central governments. The New Right argues that schools should be freed from local and central government control to become private self-managing institutions. But the right are not alone in proposing reforms to the relations between individual schools and their local and national governments. The British Labour Party supporter, A.H. Halsey, has argued for doing away with local education authorities and developing a system of self-managed schools. The British Labour Party as such does not as yet go along with such argument but, rather, sees the way forward in terms of more accountability of schools to their local authorities and communities, and better partnership with parents.

In Britain the force to be reckoned with is the ruling Conservative Party, which has been in government since 1979 and will remain there at least until 1996. While there can be no doubt whatsoever that the Tories have been influenced by New Right policy arguments for education reform, it is quite clear that Tory policy differs in several ways from what is recommended by the right. The main differences involve the question of centralization, the pace of reform and the question of using the voucher as the main instrument of reform. The Tories have proceeded rather too slowly for the likes of Arthur Seldon, and they have chosen to use budget devolution (both LMS and direct grants) rather than vouchers as instruments of reform. But there have always been those on the right, such as Stuart Sexton, who have argued for a gradual approach; for the introduction of direct grants and budget devolution as a way of reforming the system, and leading only in the longer term to the introduction of vouchers.

There is nothing in the present reforms that would preclude the eventual introduction of vouchers, perhaps towards the beginning of the new millennium. For those who see the voucher as a useful instrument in enhancing the freedom of the self-managed school, it is not so much the voucher but the voucher top-up fee which is important. Top-up fees would make schools much more market-oriented, and some schools would be able to demand higher fees than others. For those who do not wish to see a further growth in inequality among schools, which voucher top-up fees would bring about, future prospects depend very much on national politics. If the Tories did eventually introduce top-up fees and vouchers, an incoming Labour government might be open to persuasion that it should manipulate such a system by making additional grants to schools in difficult financial and other circumstances. Indeed, such a system might be more effective in targeting schools in need than the practice of block granting to local authorities. But much depends on the politics of central government. Indeed, all non-fee-paying schools, including the opted-out direct grant maintained schools, are dependent on central government public expenditure politics.

References

BALL, S.J. (1990) *Politics and Policy Making in Education*, London, Routledge.
BARNS, J. (1981) 'Take Education Off the Rates,' *Journal of Economic Affairs*, 2, 1, pp. 28–30.
BEALES, A.C.F. (1967) *Education: A Framework for Choice*, London, Institute of Economic Affairs.
BOSANQUET, N. (1983) *After the New Right*, London, Heinemann.
CALDWELL, B.J. and SPINKS, J.M. (1988) *The Self-Managing School*, Lewes, Falmer Press.
COOPERS and LYBRAND (1988) *Local Management of Schools*, London, HMSO.
DEMAINE, J. (1988) 'Teachers' Work, Curriculum and the New Right', *British Journal of Sociology of Education*, 9, 3, pp. 247–64.
DEMAINE, J. (1989) 'Privatization by Stealth: New Right Education Policy,' *ACE Bulletin 28*, London, Advisory Centre for Education.
DEMAINE, J. (1990) 'The Reform of Secondary Education,' in B. HINDESS (Ed.), *Reactions to the Right*, London, Routledge.
DEMAINE, J. (1992) 'The Labour Party and Education Policy,' *British Journal of Educational Studies*, 40, 3, pp. 239–47.
ENGLISH, D. (1987) 'Maggie: "What We Still Have to Do": An Interview with Margaret Thatcher,' *Daily Mail*, 13 May.
GEE, R. and MADEN, M. (1988) *Managing Education in Partnership: The Case for Local Government*, London, Education Reform Group.
HALSEY, A.H. (1981) 'Democracy for Education?', *New Society*, 28 May.
HAYEK, F.A. (1960) *The Constitution of Liberty*, London, Routledge and Kegan Paul.
HILL, D., OAKLEY SMITH, B. and SPINKS, J. (1990) *Local Management of Schools*, London, Paul Chapman Publishing.
HILLGATE GROUP (1986) *Whose Schools? A Radical Manifesto*, London, Hillgate Group.
HILLGATE GROUP (1987) *The Reform of British Education*, London, Claridge Press.
HINDESS, B. (1987) *Freedom, Equality, and the Market: Arguments on Social Policy*, London, Tavistock Publications.
HIRSCHMAN, A.O. (1970) *Exit, Voice and Loyalty*, Cambridge, Mass., Harvard University Press.
HUSSAIN, A. (1976) 'The Economy and the Educational System in Capitalistic Societies,' *Economy and Society*, 5, 4, pp. 413–34.
KNIGHT, C. (1990) *The Making of Tory Education Policy in Post-War Britain 1950–86*, Lewes, Falmer Press.
LABOUR PARTY (1988) *Parents in Partnership*, London, Labour Party.
NO TURNING BACK GROUP (1986) *Save Our Schools*, London, Conservative Political Centre.
OMEGA REPORT (1984) *Education Policy*, London, The Adam Smith Institute.
OZGA, J. (1992) 'Education Management,' *British Journal of Sociology of Education*, 13, 2, pp. 279–80.
PEACOCK, A.T. (1983) 'Education Voucher Schemes — Strong or Weak?' *Journal of Economic Affairs*, 3, 2, pp. 113–16.
SELDON, A. (1982) 'West on Vouchers', *Journal of Economic Affairs*, 3, 1, pp. 44–5.

SELDON, A. (1986) *The Riddle of the Voucher*, London, Institute of Economic Affairs.

SELDON, A. (1988) 'Thoughts for the New Left,' *The Guardian*, 13 June.

SEXTON, S. (1987) *Our Schools: A Radical Policy*, London, Institute of Economic Affairs.

TAYLOR REPORT (1977) *New Partnership for Our Schools*, Department of Education and Science and Welsh Office, London, HMSO.

THOMAS, H. (1990) 'From Local Financial Management to Local Management of Schools,' in M. FLUDE and M. HAMMER (Eds), *The Education Reform Act 1988*, Lewes, Falmer Press.

WEST, E.G. (1982) 'Education Vouchers: Evolution or Revolution?' *Journal of Economic Affairs*, 3, 1, pp. 14–19.

3 Paradigm Shifts and Site-based Management in the United States: Toward a Paradigm of Social Empowerment

Gary L. Anderson and Alexandra Dixon

The current popularity of participatory, site-based management seems to be driven by its close association in the minds of many with democracy, empowerment and decentralized, local decision-making. Ironically, less than a decade ago the effective schools literature was touting school principals as the heroes of school reform. Effective schools had principals that were strong leaders who were responsible for everything from an orderly school climate to a school's high achievement scores. Principals who achieved positive change in their school, we were told, were those who were able effectively to promote — even through supportive coercion if necessary — innovation and change (Huberman and Miles, 1984). Now the image of the strong leader who makes the difference between an effective or ineffective school has given way to the facilitator who empowers by sharing decision-making power with a variety of stakeholders, or, in its strongest manifestation, the notion of schools without principals at all. This apparently dramatic shift in management theory exists in the context of an equally dramatic saga of school reform in the US.

This chapter attempts to shed light on three central questions regarding site-based management in the US context:

1 How does site-based management fit within the logic of recent educational reform movements?
2 Why has the move to site-based management gone largely unanalyzed and unchallenged in both the practitioner-oriented and academic education literature?
3 What are some of the contradictions and inconsistencies in the move to site-based management and local control?

To answer the first two questions we will review the current US reform movement and provide a conceptual lens which provides a more critical

ary L. Anderson and Alexandra Dixon

analysis that helps to explain the lack of serious intellectual challenge to decentralized decision-making from the educational community. To answer the third question we will suggest several conceptual limitations that are common to current discussions of site-based management.

Lest our critique of site-based management be construed as defending old models of control-oriented, top-down management, we hasten to add that we view the shift away from former modes of governance to be a positive development. The case we want to make is that microlevel (site-based) empowerment within a larger policy context of social disempowerment will contribute to an increasingly unequal distribution of educational resources. Although scepticism regarding site-based management runs high among many school practitioners, mandates continue to come from policymakers and administrators, encouraged by educational literature and a new generation of high-priced consultants that promote site-based management without any effort to place it in a larger social or political context. Through a brief review of recent US educational reform movements, we will attempt to contextualize site-based management and describe how the notion of empowerment has been appropriated by vested interests.

Recent School Reform in the United States

Reforming public education in America is a recurring event that periodically sweeps over schools in times of perceived economic and social crisis. It has been suggested that Americans are attracted to 'quick-fix' solutions to complex problems. This is particularly apparent in the case of educational reform. Slogans emerge from a broad range of political constituencies. Much of the current public discourse on educational reform is framed by military (McDaniel, 1989) and free market metaphors which depend on strategic planning, systems analysis, efficiency, accountability, discipline and 'unilateral education disarmament'. Concurrent with the trend that calls for top-down, authoritarian management are theories of enlightened management which include quality circles, shared leadership and cooperative learning (Barth, 1991) and restructuring proposals which include school-based management and teacher empowerment (David, 1989).

Historically, schools in America have been and continue today to be used to carry out a larger social and political agenda. Schools in the nineteenth century acted as sorting and selecting agents for colleges and universities and taught basic literacy to the rest of the population. By the turn of the century the public school system was radically altered to accommodate the socialization of immigrants and the poor, while still engaged in the process of preparing an elite group of students for post-secondary education. At the turn of the century less than 10 per cent of the student body graduated from high school. Influenced by two world wars and enormous demographic changes, the public perception of high school as the natural culmination of schooling led to graduation rates reaching 70 per cent by mid-century. In the 1950s the launching of Sputnik in the Soviet Union resulted in a nation-wide reform of the science and mathematics curriculum in America's public schools. While the perceived threat to the position of US military superiority that the launching of Sputnik brought about motivated the government to spend millions of dollars on a new science curriculum, the issue of school desegregation competed for attention. In 1954, in *Brown vs Board of Education*, the United States Supreme Court ruled that segregation by race would not be tolerated in the public schools. Major desegregation efforts took place. Educational policy in this period was driven by the dual concerns of international competitiveness and economic and racial equality. The structural changes that were used to desegregate schools were followed by a period characterized by social unrest in the 1960s and 1970s. Schools responded by creating a more liberal curriculum and greater access for minority groups. Emphasis was placed on bilingual education and entitlement programs in response to a perceived public demand for social equity. The practice of 'tracking' students into college preparatory programs and vocational programs, when it could be shown they were related to ethnicity or race, was outlawed (*Hobson vs Hansen*, Federal District Court). Graduation rates for minority students increased.

At the end of the 1970s the issues of social equity that galvanized school policy-making during the previous decade gave way to the perception that the position of American business in the competitive world market was eroding. This decline in economic competitiveness, along with falling test scores, led to the establishment of various commissions to study the role of education as a cause of the problem. A conservative Republican government began the process of defining decreased productivity, declining profits and unemployment as the consequence of inadequate public schools. In 1983 four major commission reports were issued.[1] These commissions received their support from the Reagan administration, from private foundations and from prestigious universities. Their focus on economic and technological interests was not surprising. In general, their recommendations included more time in school and more time spent on instruction (time on task), increased credit requirements for graduation, increased homework requirements, emphasis on computer literacy and science, and the establishment of a curriculum related to the job market. In addition, the reports proposed that schools emphasize 'back to basics' and attacked the current 'smorgasbord' of curricula offerings (National Commission of Excellence in Education, 1983). Altbach (1986) refers to the focus of the recommendations as '. . . concern for the role of education in equipping Americans for participation in a cut-throat global economic war'. This period (January 1983–October 1985) is often referred to as the first wave of educational reform and is generally characterized by a top-down, get-tough emphasis on raising standards (Murphy, 1990).

The first wave of reform was not altogether homogeneous. In addition to the various commissioned reports, school reform literature produced several research-based critiques of American education that stressed humanistic reform, teacher and student empowerment, cooperative and collaborative instructional and governance techniques, critical thinking, school climate concerns and dropout prevention (Goodlad, 1984; Sizer, 1984). These reform proposals countered much of the emphasis of the commission reports that viewed schools as the handmaidens of the economic interests of American business.

While a debate over public education raged during the 1980s, legislatures, state departments of education and school districts implemented new policies in response to the criticism presented in the initial reform reports. Most of the reform policies could be implemented without additional resources or redistribution of resources and without changing the school's basic authoritarian and bureaucratic structures. The reforms focused primarily on student behaviour and reflected a philosophy of 'more is better', more homework, more testing, more credits, more hours and more stringent discipline. States mandated wholesale competence testing, 'promotional gates' for student promotion, increased the number of graduation credits and created stricter rules for student conduct and attendance. Dress codes were revived, and student absences resulted in suspension. Little or no emphasis was placed on improving curriculum and equalizing instructional opportunity to counteract the increased burden placed on students to perform at ever higher levels. Traditional groups of low achieving students were faced with overwhelming expectations, and dropout and failure rates in districts with high proportions of minority and poor students increased.

As it became apparent that merely increasing standards and engaging in 'get-tough' rhetoric were not going to catapult America into the forefront of international economic competition, a second wave of reports and studies (1985–1988) shifted their emphasis to the restructuring of schools. Not the least of the reform initiatives was the adoption of various school-based management models of decision-making aimed at providing teachers and parents (students were seldom included) with a greater voice in school policy. Unlike earlier community participation movements, which had a grassroots emphasis (Levin, 1970), this community participation movement had its roots in free market ideology and had strong support from small business groups, chambers of commerce and financial capitalists (Stedman, 1987). The focus of school-based management in the 1960s and 1970s was to give more power to communities or offset state authority or increase administrative efficiency (David, 1989). The focus in the 1980s was to define schools as efficient institutions whose purpose was to prepare the next generation for global economic competition by garnering community and teacher support through a 'restructuring' that included site-based management or some form of participatory decision-making.

While the site-based management bandwagon continues full steam, there is an eerie lack of analysis in the US of why decentralized forms of decision-making are being so strongly promoted. Similar school reform movements are taking place in countries as diverse as Australia and Germany, Great Britain and Mexico. Although the reform movement varies with each country's unique circumstances, there are remarkable commonalities that appear to transcend partisan politics. Whether carried out by the Labor Party in Australia, the Tories in Great Britain or the Partido Revolucionario Institucional (PRI) in Mexico, school reform movements tend to promote the devolution of power to local schools and communities and privatization and market forces as allocators of educational resources (Watt, 1989; Cooper, 1990). The language of 'freedom' and 'choice' has replaced that of 'equality'. School districts in the United States are under enormous pressure to make schools 'competitive' by allowing parents to choose the schools that their children are to attend. The acceptance of what appears to be a democratic devolution of power in education through participatory site-based management and school choice has become so much a part of conventional wisdom that few educators question its premises.

Site-based Management and Shifting Paradigms

Paralleling the reform movement's shift from top-down to 'bottom-up' change strategies is a similar theoretical shift in the field of educational administration concerning what constitutes school administration and how we come to understand it as a social phenomenon. The theoretical watershed of this shift is often viewed as the Griffiths/Greenfield debates of the early 1970s, during which the positivistic orientation of the field was challenged from a phenomenological perspective. Later a critical theory critique was added to the phenomenological one (Anderson, 1990; Bates, 1984; Foster, 1986). These three theoretical perspectives — positivism, phenomenology, critical theory — continue to form the basis of theoretical debate within the field. These theoretical perspectives not only subtly influence the way in which we think and talk about administration; they also provide us with different lenses through which to understand our practice. We will argue in this chapter that one's analysis of site-based management will depend on which theoretical lens one uses to make sense of it.

The underlying philosophical assumption of each of these three lenses can be understood by using Burrell and Morgan's (1979) paradigmatic framework. This can be depicted as an axis whose ends are labeled 'subjective' and 'objective'. The objective paradigm incorporates the positivistic assumptions of a value-free science and practice. According to this paradigm, administration is a neutral, scientific technology whose methods have universal applicability, or at least require minimal situational adaptation. In this model leadership and expertise reside in the administrator who is viewed as a social engineer. Although practitioners' theories-in-use, as well as texts and research in education administration, are still largely premised on these assumptions, few in 1992 would openly espouse them.

The subjectivist paradigm represents the assumptions of a phenomenological, interactionist perspective in which organizational reality is constructed over time through social interaction. Organizations are viewed as social constructs, intersubjective creations that are constantly in the process of becoming. Administrators are one among many social actors who are involved in the daily negotiation of rules and norms that constitute organizational life. In this paradigm leadership and expertise are defused throughout the system, and their source varies depending on the particular issue.

Although there has been a gradual change in outlook in educational administration in the last twenty years from the objective end of the axis toward the subjective end, there has also been a tendency to combine the prescriptive, social engineering bias of the objective paradigm with the interactionist bias of the subjective paradigm. Thus, while interactionist (e.g., cultural, micropolitical, symbolic) analyses of school life characteristic of the subjectivist paradigm have become more central to the field, they have too often been appropriated by the control-oriented, managerial bias of the objective paradigm. Administrators are encouraged to *manage* the culture of the school, *manage* conflict and *manage* the discourse (i.e., meaning) of the school. Much as the discovery seventy years ago of the human dimension of organizational life was converted into a means for increasing production, so the subjectivist paradigm, in the hands of managers, promises to become a tool for tightening control in loosely coupled educational systems (Firestone and Wilson, 1985).

Partly for this reason, Burrell and Morgan (1979) divide the subjectivist perspective into two distinct paradigms. These paradigms are formed by intersecting the subjective/objective axis with a vertical axis that represents two extreme views of social theory (see Figure 1). At one end is a conflict perspective which views social relations as characterized by deep-seated structural conflict of interest. At the other end of the social theory axis is the order, consensus or status quo view of society. This perspective views society as a relatively stable structure, based on consensus of values among its members.

While both subjectivist paradigms formed by these axes agree on the constructivist, interactive nature of social reality, they differ in how they believe society is constructed and whose interests are served by a particular social construction. For the purposes of this chapter we have chosen to name the paradigms formed by these axes (1) individual efficiency, (2) individual empowerment, (3) social empowerment and (4) social efficiency.[2] As mentioned previously, we see movement at both the theory and

Figure 1. *Paradigmatic Predispositions*

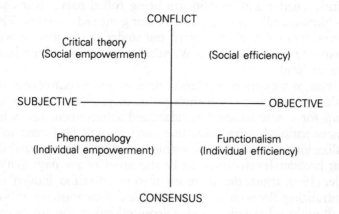

practice level from the individual efficiency paradigm toward an individual empowerment paradigm, and although, in our opinion, an individual empowerment lens is generally preferable to an individual efficiency lens, only when we move our lens upward into a social empowerment paradigm do the social contradictions of site-based management become apparent.

The Social Empowerment Paradigm and Site-based Management

We have chosen to use the term 'social empowerment' rather than 'critical theory' paradigm for two reasons. First, because the term 'empowerment' has entered management discourse with little analysis of its meaning, we want to establish a distinction between empowerment that empowers individuals and that which empowers social groups. Second, critical theory in education encompasses a diversity of social thought impossible to review in the space of this chapter.[3]

In the following sections we will briefly discuss several barriers to site-based management as a vehicle for social empowerment. For the most part, because of its paradigmatic bias, writing in the field of educational administration has failed to address issues of social empowerment, thus contributing to an uncritical acceptance of site-based management. Our purpose in the following sections is a modest one: to lay out the terrain for future analysis rather than provide an in-depth analysis of each issue.

Site-based Management in a Broader Social Context

Seldom is it pointed out in the business administration literature that at the same time that US workers are being 'empowered' in the workplace through participatory, site-based management, their unions are being busted, their salaries and benefits are being rolled back, their companies are being 'downsized' and their jobs are being moved overseas. This social disempowerment of workers carried out under the banner of workplace empowerment is like an Alice in Wonderland world in which language is turned on its head.

Likewise, as we exhort teachers to demand more control over decision-making that has an impact on their status as professionals, the nation is gearing up for a new national standardized achievement test which will drive a new national curriculum that teachers will be forced to follow. Decentralization at the local level within a context of centralized decision-making at broader levels seems to be the order of the day. Why?

Weiler (1990) argues that there are often manifest and 'hidden' functions for decentralizing decision-making. 'Hidden' functions are those which are not part of the official discourse of decentralization, but are, nevertheless, intentional rather than simply 'latent' functions.[4] Weiler claims that decentralizing decision-making has both a conflict management and legitimation function.

Weiler argues that in highly conflictual arenas such as educational policy, decentralization allows sources of conflict to be diffused throughout the system and provides additional layers of insulation between the state — or in the specific case of site-based management, the school district — and the rest of the system. Such a strategy is particularly helpful in the current era of cutbacks and 'downsizing'. In a recent case, the local school district in which the authors live allowed individual schools to decide how they wanted to cut back their budgets. Under the guise of local decision-making, the district administration was able to diffuse criticism for massive cutbacks. Thus, according to Weiler, the selective devolution of decision-making power can be an effective way to manage conflict.

A second 'hidden' function of decentralization, according to Weiler, is that in a time of legitimation crisis, the state (and its various governance units) gains added legitimacy by appearing to be sensitive and responsive to democratic expression and local needs. However, as Weiler (1990) points out,

> All real decentralization (in the sense of genuinely shared regulatory and allocative power among levels of governance) does imply a loss of control for the center. If it is true that decentralization also holds out the attractive prospect of compensatory legitimation at a time when legitimacy is in short supply, a major challenge for the modern state lies in reconciling these two conflicting objectives: retaining as much centralized control over the system as is possible without a severe loss in legitimacy, while at least appearing to be committed to decentralization and thus reaping the benefits in legitimation to be derived from that appearance.

The frequent wavering between centralized and decentralized modes of behavior — or, to be more exact, between decentralization rhetoric and centralization behavior — may well have to do with this difficult task of walking the fine line between the conflicting imperatives of control and legitimacy. (p. 442)

If Weiler is right, these two hidden functions of decentralizing decision-making at the district level may go a long way in explaining why participatory decision-making remains superficial and restricted to whatever the central authority chooses to allow. At a national level it helps to explain the apparent contradiction between the rhetoric of empowerment and the centralization of testing and evaluation.

Participatory Site-based Management: Collaboration or Collusion?

Studies of site-based management in the US have found that administrator/teacher/parent governance councils (or whatever name they go under) are quickly coopted by district and building administrators. Perhaps the most dramatic study is Malen and Ogawa's (1988) district-wide case study of site-based governance councils in Salt Lake City, Utah. These councils were given broad jurisdiction, formal policy-making authority, parity protection (e.g., equal voting power) and training provisions. Even under these highly favourable arrangements, Malen and Ogawa found that teachers and parents did not wield significant influence on significant issues in decision arenas.

Although in many cases the membership of site-based management teams and school councils is made up of teachers and parents selected by the principal, this is not always so. In the authors' local school district 50 per cent of the school management council must be made up of union members. Parents frequently 'volunteer', and principals must accept volunteers. Despite this obvious shift from administratively controlled access to union and community controlled access, the preliminary results of the decision-making show remarkably similar patterns of conformity to mainstream 'norms'. Recent decisions made 'collaboratively' by site-based management in the authors' district show high schools are moving toward more stringent and control-oriented policies involving student conduct. Permanent expulsion of students has recently been instituted in the district with the blessing of the high school management councils, while significant changes in curriculum and instruction, equity issues and fundamental restructuring of schools have gone untouched.

Although Malen and Ogawa (1988) make the point that parents and teachers exert less power than administrators on the decisions made by councils, there may be another way of explaining what happens in site-based management groups within the current political climate. Members, regardless of the conditions of their appointment, share a similar conceptual framework. They have similar interests, perceptions and bases of economic and social class. Middle-class parents have access to the school environment which is denied lower social class groups. Middle-class parents are related to schools by language and experience, while lower-class parents are not. Teachers also share this economic and political base. This difference in 'cultural capital' often leaves poor parents and their children out of the participatory process. As long as the arena for change does not involve the loss of power for administrators, teachers or middle-class parents, there is little conflict among the three groups within the participatory decision-making model.

Participation alone does not guarantee adequate voice to diverse constituencies. Participation continues to be limited, although not necessarily by administrative manipulation of power but by the hidden distinctions of social and economic class. The site-based management movement has yet to develop criteria for distinguishing collaboration from collusion in participatory decision-making.

Site-based Management and Unobtrusive Forms of Control

Political theorists from Gramsci through Lukes and Foucault have argued that power is seldom exercised in overt, observable ways. More often, according to these theorists, it is unobtrusive and embedded in the work process itself and the organizational vocabulary through which the work is defined. More and more in modern society control is exercised through a form of cognitive politics in which managers are expected to manage and mediate the meaning organizational life has for its stakeholders (Anderson, 1991). The devolution of decision-making power is relatively safe if meaning has been managed effectively since all organizational members will have internalized the same norms. This does not mean that dominant meanings will not occasionally be contested, but that bureaucratic discourse can be appealed to to derail conflict early on and to silence dissent by defining it as outside appropriate bureaucratic discourse (i.e., 'negative', 'not a team player', 'troublemaker', etc.). Norms of propriety and civility also function to mute criticism (Malen and Ogawa, 1988). But, according to Ferguson (1984), unobtrusive control goes beyond the subtle micropolitics of organizational life. She argues that we have created a bureaucratic culture in which power is embedded in the very ways we think and act.

> Power is not 'added on' to the activities at hand but rather is co-extensive with them; it consists of the multiplicity of power relations that are immanent in the discursive relations themselves. . . .

> Bureaucratic discourse invades and encompasses more and more of our personal and collective lives, presenting us with a metaphor for living that is reflective of the values and assumptions of the administrative disciplines. (pp. 60–1)

Bureaucratic discourse creates a kind of ideological control that is by far the most effective form of control for bureaucracies. A better understanding of how bureaucratic discourse functions as ideological control is necessary in order to understand why the devolution of decision-making does not necessarily result in a shift of power and resources.

Conclusion

Although the current wave of school reform includes site-based management, in practice it does not challenge the fundamentally conservative interests of existing governance structures. Two trends emerge and coexist. First, the local manifestations of site-based management do not challenge vested interests because membership in local school decision-making groups is determined by pre-existing social conditions that result from these interests. Decision-making is framed by the interests of like-minded participants. Second, top-down decision-making which emerges in national curriculum and testing schemes goes unchallenged because it fits within the widely accepted objectivist (functionalist) paradigm which asserts that scientific rationale is value-free.

The appearance of equity and democratic process is due to the largely rhetorical nature of discourse which continues to define equity as 'equal opportunity' for unequals,[5] and democracy as any form of participation. Much of the current site-based management movement is still modeled on entrepreneurial, free enterprise ideology with its emphasis on individualism fully intact. Conflict is effectively silenced within this framework because the norms in which the decision-making occurs reject the notion of competing or contradictory group interests. What is defined as 'fair' distribution of resources fails to take into account current unequal needs among schools. What is believed to be devolution of power to parents and teachers becomes shared power among already empowered individuals over less influential groups.

For participatory site-based management to become democratic and egalitarian, individual empowerment must give way to social empowerment. Unless group interests and inequalities of power among social groups become part of school reform discourse, we cannot expect site-based management to empower in the social sense of the word, and we cannot expect fundamental changes to occur.

Notes

1 The four reports are: (i) National Commission of Excellence in Education, *A Nation at Risk: The Imperative for Education Reform*; (ii) College Board, *Academic Preparation for College: What Students Need to Know and Be Able to Do*; (iii) Twentieth Century Fund Task Force on Federal Elementary and Secondary Education Policy, *Making the Grade*; and Task Force for Education for Economic Growth, *Action for Excellence: A Comprehensive Plan to Improve Our Nation's Schools*.

2 Burrell and Morgan call these sociological paradigms (i) functionalism, (ii) interpretivism, (iii) radical humanism and (iv) radical structuralism. We have taken the liberty of choosing terminology that is more appropriate to the analysis of site-based management. In this chapter we are only concerned with the first three paradigms. The fourth paradigm (social efficiency/radical structuralism), which is mainly informed by orthodox Marxist theory, has had little influence on management theory in the US.

3 For a more complete description of a critical theory paradigm and its application to educational administration, see Foster (1986).

4 Prawda (1992) makes a similar point in the Mexican contest, pointing out that a non-publicized (but widely known) function of Mexico's decentralization reform (called 'modernization') was to weaken the powerful Mexican teachers' union. In another case the 1988 Education Reform Act in Britain dismantled the Inner London Education Authority (equivalent to the Central Board of Education in New York City) and devolved authority to each of the thirteen boroughs. A manifest function of this move was to remove a bloated and inefficient bureaucracy. A hidden agenda was to eliminate an agency that was viewed as a hotbed of left-wing activity (Cooper, 1990).

5 An example of how this affected schools in the authors' district was that budget cuts, which are traditionally a central office function, were decided on at the schools and were an across-the-board percentage of each school's official budget. Schools' disparate resources were not taken into account. Rich schools traditionally get extra money from non-district sources (parents, businesses, etc.), whereas poor schools have limited access to additional resources. Consequently, across-the-board percentage budget cuts may appear fair, but in reality they penalize poorer schools more severely than richer schools.

References

ALTBACH, P.G. (1986) 'A Nation at Risk: The Educational Reform Debate in the United States', *Prospects: Quarterly Review of Education*, 16, 3, pp. 337–47.

ANDERSON, G.L. (1990) 'Toward a Critical Constructivist Approach to School Administration: Invisibility, Legitimation, and the Study of Non-Events', *Educational Administration Quarterly*, 26, pp. 38–59.

ANDERSON, G.L. (1991) 'Cognitive Politics of Principals and Teachers: Ideological Control in an Elementary School', in J. BLASE (Ed.), *The Politics of Life in Schools: Power, Conflict and Cooperation*, Newbury Park, Sage, pp. 120–38.

BARTH, R.S. (1991) Restructuring Schools: Some Questions for Teachers and Principals', *Phi Delta Kappan*, pp. 123–8.

BATES, R.J. (1984) 'Toward a Critical Practice of Educational Administration', in

T. SERGIOVANNI and J. CORBALLY (Eds), *Leadership and Organizational Culture*, Urbana, Ill., University of Illinois Press, pp. 260–72.

BURRELL, G. and MORGAN, G. (1979) *Sociological Paradigms and Organizational Analysis*, Portsmouth, N.H., Heinemann.

CARNEGIE FORUM ON EDUCATION, TASK FORCE ON TEACHING AS A PROFESSION (1986) *A Nation Prepared: Teachers for the 21st Century*, New York, Carnegie Forum on Education and the Economy.

COOPER, B. (1990) 'Local School Reform in Great Britain and the United States: Points of Comparison — Points of Departure', *Educational Review*, 42, 2, pp. 133–49.

DAVID, J. (1989) 'Synthesis of Research on School Based Management', *Educational Leadership*, 71, 1, pp. 45–53.

FERGUSON, K. (1984) *The Feminist Case against Bureaucracy*, Philadelphia, Pa., Temple University Press.

FIRESTONE, W. and WILSON, B. (1985) 'Using Bureaucratic and Cultural Linkages to Improve Instruction: The Principal's Contribution', *Educational Administration Quarterly*, 21, 2, pp. 7–30.

FOSTER, W.P. (1986) *Paradigms and Promises: New Approaches to Educational Administration*, Buffalo, N.Y., Prometheus Books.

GOODLAD, J. (1984) *A Place Called School: Prospects for the Future*, New York, McGraw-Hill.

HUBERMAN, A.M. and MILES, M. (1984) *Innovation Up Close: How School Improvement Works*, New York, Plenum.

LEVIN, H. (Ed.) (1970) *Community Control of Schools*, Washington, D.C., The Brookings Institution.

MCDANIEL, T.R. (1989) 'Demilitarizing Public Education: School Reform in the Era of George Bush', *Phi Delta Kappan*, 44, 2, pp. 15–18.

MALEN, B. and OGAWA, R. (1988) 'Professional-Patron Influence on Site-based Governance Councils: A Confounding Case Study', *Educational Evaluation and Policy Analysis*, 10, 4, pp. 215–70.

MURPHY, J. (1990) 'Preparing School Administrators for the Twenty-First Century: The Reform Agenda', in B. MITCHELL and L. CUNNINGHAM (Eds), *Educational Leadership and Changing Contexts of Families, Communities, and Schools*, Chicago, Ill., University of Chicago Press, pp. 232–25.

NATIONAL COMMISSION ON EXCELLENCE IN EDUCATION (1983) *A Nation at Risk: The Imperative for Educational Reform*, Washington, D.C., US Government Printing Office.

PRAWDA, J. (1992) 'Educational Decentralization in Latin America: Lessons Learned', Paper presented at the Annual Conference of the Comparative and International Educational Society, Annapolis, Md., March.

SIZER, T. (1984) *Horace's Compromise: The Dilemma of the American High School*, New York, Houghton-Mifflin.

STEDMAN, L. (1987) 'The Political Economy of Recent Educational Reform Reports', *Educational Theory*, 37, pp. 69–79.

WATT, J. (1989) 'Devolution of Power: The Ideological Meaning', *Journal of Educational Administration*, 27, 1, pp. 19–28.

WEILER, H. (1990) 'Comparative Perspectives on Educational Decentralization: An Exercise in Contradiction?' *Educational Evaluation and Policy Analysis*, 12, 4, pp. 433–48.

4 Culture, Cost and Control: Self-Management and Entrepreneurial Schooling in England and Wales*

Stephen J. Ball

> Change is not necessarily improvement . . . change may or may not be progress. (Cuban, 1990, p. 72)

Schools in the UK are currently faced with a reform package which includes not only a new national curriculum but also changes in school governance, management and funding, changes in the roles of local authorities, in student testing and school inspection, and in pedagogy and classroom organization and changes in teacher training, and teachers' conditions of work and employment. It is easier to capture the scope of change involved by listing those things that remain the same — but A-level examinations may be the only example. These changes are all facets of current Conservative government education policy; they are all externally imposed, virtually all have legal status. They are all happening at once. They all have dramatically short time scales for implementation. By general consensus, within the educational community they are all massively underfunded (Coopers and Lybrand Deloitte, 1992). Furthermore, the changes are frequently altered, amended and reoriented, often by ministerial fiat. Advisory committees are set up and then ignored. Development work is commissioned and then cancelled. Teacher representatives are excluded from consultations, consultation processes are deliberately short and responses are typically ignored. Separately and together these changes are bringing about profound shifts in the nature of teaching and the teacher's role, profound shifts in the relationships between schools and parents

* This paper reworks, extends and develops ideas outlined in Ball (1990a, 1990b, 1992a), Ball and Bowe (1991) and Bowe and Ball with Gold (1992). It is based on a symposium paper given at the 1992 AERA Conference, San Francisco.

and profound shifts in the nature of schools as work organizations. Not surprisingly, many teachers appear weary and wary, stressed and depressed, alienated and bitter. They are faced with threats to their autonomy and status, and livelihood in some cases, but are expected to respond constructively and intelligently to make sense of the uncertainties, incoherence and complexity of change. In a sense the more successful they are at coping, the more of themselves as professionals and their experience they must forego.

Together these changes assert a massive and complex technology of control over teachers' work in all its aspects. These changes are also tied together in complex ways. They interrelate and ramify in certain respects (some of which are indicated below), but they also contradict and confuse in various ways. In Cuban's terms both first-order quality control and second-order design reforms are in train. There is no evidence in either respect of the modesty on the part of reformers which he calls for (Cuban, 1990). Clearly, in terms of school organization and classroom practice, it is school managers and classroom teachers who must put the bits and pieces together — construct their own subjection. Individually and collectively, they must make sense of reform; and at organization and classroom level develop interpretations and practices which engage seriously with the changes and their consequences for working relationships and for teaching and learning. But this chapter is not about those aspects of reform (see Bowe and Ball with Gold, 1992).

As many commentators have noted, these different types of policy and forms of control have different provenances. This policy ensemble involves compromise, ad hocery and *bricolage*. But it is also riven with two strong and clear ideological thrusts (see Ball, 1990a); New Right free market liberalism is one thrust; nationalist authoritarian conservatism is the other. But, as suggested, the nature of change, the types of policies involved *are* different. The forms of control involved vary from reform to reform. They require different kinds of action and reaction. In general terms, the reforms and the forms of control they embody can be represented by three clusters: the curriculum, the market, and management. In particular, the market and management are tied closely together in the reworking of orientation and purpose in schools. Management plays a key role in *delivering* other changes.[1]

The introduction of market forces into the relations between schools, between schools and parents, and into the work of teaching means that teachers are now working within a new and different value context — a context in which presentation, image and impression management are as, or more, important than the educational process; and in which, in theory at least, control has been shifted from the producer (teachers) to the consumer (parents) via open enrolments, parental choice and per capita funding. In relations with parents, the use of performance indicators and tests places the achievements of students and the work of teachers in a new light. The market setting and the instrumentality it fosters produce a version of that confusion of relations between people with relations to things that Marx called 'commodity fetishism'. This is a confusion of social relationships with exchange relationships that is basic to the ideological thrust of Thatcherism and the hegemony of 'consumer' politics. In terms of relations between schools the key element of the market is competition (see Ball, 1990a, 1992b for more on the market).

Management

Even from the brief outline above the intimate relationship between the control exercised over teachers by parental choice and competition and the role of management should be clear. Management and the market are closely intertwined in UK government thinking, as DES *Circular 7/88* indicates.

> Local management is concerned with far more than budgeting and accounting procedures. Effective schemes of local management will enable governing bodies and headteachers to plan their use of resources — including their most valuable resource, their staff — to maximum effect in accordance with their own need and priorities, and to make schools more responsive to their clients — parents, pupils, the local community and employers. (p. 3)

The market both empowers and transforms the work of school management. The devolution of school budgets; the greatly reduced powers of LEAs; the breakup of national pay agreements for teachers; and the encouragement given to entrepreneurial innovation and income generation — all these contribute to an illusion of autonomy and flexibility for the manager. Together the market and the management reforms replace collective, bureaucratic controls, structures and relationships with individualistic and competitive ones. Schools are inserted into a new paradox; they are to be given greater autonomy within the constraints and pressures of market forces; they are to be able to exercise flexibility in order to be more responsive. The relative certainties of local democracy and bureaucracy are to be replaced by the relative uncertainties of enrolment-based funding. The point about both management and the market is that they are 'no hands' forms of control as far as the relationship between education and the state is concerned. Thus management is transformed into self-management with all the semantic and ideological confusion that that brings. Management and the market provide, in Kickert's (1991, p. 21) terms, 'steering at a distance' — a new paradigm of public governance. Steering at a distance is an alternative to coercive/prescriptive control. Constraints are replaced by incentives. Prescription is replaced by ex post accountability based upon quality or outcome assessments. Coercion is replaced by self-steering — the appearance of autonomy. Opposition or resistance are side-stepped, displaced.

> The refined subtle character of behavioural stimuli makes resist-ance difficult. The repressive tolerance of such a way of steering might cause a large latent aggression against that steering. Organ-izations and people cannot defend themselves against measures perceived to be unreasonable. There is no regulated way of pro-test, complaint or formal appeal. (Kickert, 1991, p. 26)

Thus, acquiring a market awareness and the skills of an on-task self-monitoring and individual accountability within the context of 'normal' school activities would, at least in theory, consolidate the basic principles of self-management within teachers' individual consciousness, decreasing the need for overt control. The individualization of consciousness oriented towards performativity constitutes a more subtle, yet more totalizing, form of control of teachers than is available in the top-down prescriptive steering of state Fordism.

> The Education Reform Act of 1988 and recent legislation aim to raise levels of pupil achievement in particular through the introduc-tion of the National Curriculum and improved self-management by schools. For governors, Headteachers and teachers, bringing together these changes will require, as part of the new partnership, strategies for managing development and change to make schools more effective. School Development Plans are a means of realizing this goal. (DES, 1989, p. 4)

Self-management is a key to the achievement of 'steering at a distance'; it articulates self-regulation with a microtechnology of control and ramifies the value and cultural changes set in train by finance-led decision-making and competition. In other words, it is a disciplinary practice. But as a discourse, management is productive rather than simply coercive. It in-creases the power of individuals — managers and managed in some respects — while making them more docile. Management is both a body of precepts, assumptions and theory, to be learned by managers, and a set of practices to be implemented, encompassing both managers and managed. It is in Foucault's terms an 'infinitesimal mechanism' of power with is own history and trajectory and tactics. It is such power relations at the microlevel of society that make possible certain global effects of domina-tion. This is a microphysics of oppression, not the long and coercive arm of the state at work but a bottom-up capillary process of local and unstable relations. This is a set of power relations which are produced 'from one

moment to the next, at every point', which are self-reproducing, imman-
ent. This power is not a thing that is possessed but practices that are
'exercised'. While 'the logic is perfectly clear, the aims decipherable . . .
there is none there to have invented them' (Foucault, 1979, p. 95).

But management itself (as theory/as practice) is not of a piece. It is
not a unitary perspective. There are at least two, perhaps three, discourses
of management in play within the reform process in the UK. They have
different effects. One is what might be called 'professional management';
this is articulated around a development planning perspective and relates
particularly to the production of school management plans — 'The purpose of development planning is to improve the quality of teaching and
learning in a school through the successful management of innovation and
change' (Hargreaves and Hopkins, 1991, p. 3). Three things should be
noted about this discourse at the outset: first, it provides a vocabulary
which links management directly to classroom practice; second, it articulates
with a teacherly 'professional' perspective on planning and purpose; and
third, it starts from a concern with managing change.

> We believe that when heads and governors see LMS as a spur
> to development planning (of which financial management is a
> component), they have taken a road to what will truly be self-
> managing schools — ones which not merely learn to manage change
> and finance but also learn the art of school improvement which
> leads to more effective teaching and learning. (p. 13)

A bold statement of faith! In many ways this is the acceptable face of
management. In as much that it begins from the professional end of the
planning spectrum, it is 'clean' (context-free) management insofar as it
treats the school in isolation and concentrates upon the business of *education*
rather than education as *business*. The Hargreaves and Hopkins book has
only one index entry for 'finance'. This approach is very process-oriented;
it is a value-free, content-free management (in the sense that good practice
is entirely a matter of process). It is the management of anything or nothing
(and this is profoundly disturbing). It divorces management practices from
values and from politics. The book also has only one index entry for
'values'. It is technically-oriented, rational and apolitical. There are no
index entries for 'conflict'. This is management in the best of all possible
schools. It is anodyne and reassuring and does a great deal to legitimate
management to the professional audience.

The second discourse I would term 'financial management'. It begins
from a concern with balancing the books, with maximizing the budget,
and with doing educationally what can be afforded. This is for many
practitioners the unacceptable face of management — but, we would
argue, a very real 'on-the-ground' approach. It is driven by context, by the
realities of per capita funding, 'rate-capping' (government imposed limits

on local government spending) and competition with neighbouring schools (see below). This is in stark contrast to the Mary Poppins world (a spoon-ful of sugar . . .) of management conjured up by 'professional manage-ment' texts like Caldwell and Spinks (1988). Here the task of budgeting is simply a matter of costing policies. In Caldwell and Spinks's five-point program for planning and budgeting in collaborative school management the cost of plans is only mentioned in item 4: 'identifying and costing resources required in the plan for implementation.' This is a far cry from the 'what we can afford' world of cuts in public sector spending in which most schools currently find themselves. There are no entries for either 'competition' or 'marketing' in the Caldwell and Spinks (1988) index.

There is a close relationship between the discourse of financial management and the third management discourse which I call 'entrepre-neurial management'. Here the market is to the fore; image, hype, PR, competition, diversification and alternative sources of income provide the lexicon.

> Stanley Goodchild [at the time Head of Garth Hill School in Berk-shire] was quoted as saying that 'we see the school very much as a business — where the business is educating young people'. Alter-natively, he said in the press release (sent out prior to the press conference at which Alan Watts was introduced to reporters):
>> We are sitting on a valuable resource which is not being used to full effect. If we are able to provide a service for local industry and commerce and at the same time increase the resource available for our students then I would be a very foolish Head not to take advantage.
> Press releases; press conferences — this is a new deal for state education.
>> Press Release. Royal County of Berkshire Date 4th September 1986 No 919
>> BUSINESS MANAGER APPOINTED AT BERKSHIRE SCHOOL Alan Watts who has spent his lifetime in senior management private industry, is next Monday (September 14) becoming what is believed to be the first ever Business manager at a local authority school. (Goodchild and Holly, 1989, pp. 246–7)

This third version is both the product and mechanism of what Keat (1991, p. 5) calls 'cultural engineering'.

> The task of constructing an 'enterprise' culture is (at least) two-fold. . . . First, a wide range of institutions and activities must be remodelled along the lines of the commercial enterprise, including its orientation to the demands of the consumer. Second, the

acquisition and exercise of enterprising qualities must be encouraged, so that the increasingly commercialized world will itself take on an appropriately 'enterprising' form.

Version 3 is most influenced by the values of enterprise and business, but experience of 2 is not unlike the real world of business, especially in the context of economic recession. In practice these discourses are not mutually exclusive, although their mixing is not easily achieved in every case. There are contradictions in principle, orientation and practice between 1 and 2, and in ethos and method between 1 and 3. The problem is that 1 is often not infrequently used to idealize the real use of 2 and 3. In a sense version 1 is a 'science of the abstract' and versions 2 and 3 are 'sciences of the concrete' (Hatton, 1988, p. 341). The differences between these versions cannot be reduced to matters of emphasis; and each version is supported and legitimated by a different sets of texts. Hargreaves and Hopkins (1991) and Caldwell and Spinks (1988) are perhaps the key texts for version 1.

Version 2 is underpinned by a set of technical manuals concerned with budgetary control, which tend not to be integrated with or cross-referenced to 1 or 3. An example of a version 3 entrepreneurial text is provided by Fidler and Bowles's *Effective Local Management of Schools* (1989). Here the relationship of management to planning and to organizational aims is very different from that envisaged by Hargreaves and Hopkins. Marketing professionals, Bowles argues:

> . . . would insist that marketing should be seen as integral to the management role of any enterprise operating in a competitive environment and be a total strategy starting from the aims and objectives of the organization, feeding into its information and decision-making systems and being closely connected to monitoring, evaluation and staff development activities. (p. 38)

In this conception of the manager and of the organization's relationship to the market, 'professional' judgments are regarded with profound suspicion. The 'mission statement' of the organization begins not with principles but 'by establishing clearly whose needs the school is there to serve. It has been too producer-dominated, too concerned with serving its own ends and imposing its own views on its clients. The present changes are designed to make the system more responsive, more answerable to the customer' (p. 40). Within this vision of the school, management mediates between a production technology and the customer. The manager's concerns relate to external quality control and internal cost control. The professionality so centrally positioned in the Hargreaves and Hopkins and Caldwell and Spinks texts is decentred here. Teaching and learning are defined by customers' needs, not by professional planning or judgment (although market-related funding might not have this effect in all schools

— see below). The aim is to drive all the 'natural ambiguities' which inhere in public service provision in complex and controversial areas like education (and health).

It might be argued that these discourses/versions of management should be seen as different aspects of the role of management in the school — allocated to different members of the senior management team or different aspects of the headteacher's total workload. But that is too simple. The values and cultures of institutions differ. The role and leadership styles attempted by heads differ; they are inflected and biased differently. Schools differ in terms of the extent to which any of these discourses becomes dominant and pervasive. The possibilities are very much related to a school's history and market position. However, few schools will be able to think about, or organize, themselves without use of, or reference to, these lexicons of control. As I have tried already to indicate, the reform process in the UK is not simply structural or technical; it is also cultural and ideological. On the one hand, as we shall see, management as practice is unstable and complex: 'Its success is proportional to its ability to hide its own mechanisms' (Foucault, 1979, p. 86). But, on the other hand, as a discourse of power and control, management is both a sophisticated technology and a pervasive commonsensical perspective.

Management is both means and end in the reform process. That is, management (as synonym for efficiency) is taken to be 'the one best way' to organize and run schools; and to the extent that management embraces enterprise and commercialism, it shifts schools away from the 'culture of welfare' towards the 'culture of profit and production' — that is, management does profound ideological work in relation to the conception and conduct of schooling. It is an end in itself. But management, and most particularly self-management, is also seen as a way of delivering other changes. It is a mechanism for ensuring the delivery of a national curriculum, and it ties classroom practice, student performance, teacher appraisal, school recruitment and resource allocation into a single tight bundle of planning and surveillance. It gives apparent autonomy to the manager while taking away apparent autonomy from the teacher. It drives a wedge between the curriculum and classroom-oriented teacher and the market and budget-oriented manager, thus creating a strong potential for differences in interest, values and purpose between the two groups. This gap is vividly present across our research on educational reform. The experience of this gap, the reworking of relationships within or across it, are subtle aspects of resocialization for those on both sides (see below).

The work of management in the resocialization of the managers and the managed and the construction of new roles and relationships for and between them is basic to the reform process and the achievement of new forms of control. The forms of self-management currently in play politically and textually are discursively distinct from either notions of empowerment (NASSP Bulletin, 1991) or interactive rationality (Saltman and Von

Otter, 1992). Self-management is the panopticon of modern educational organization.

Practising Management

I have laid out a stark scenario of change. I want to go on to illustrate some of the arguments with data from schools and use these data to elaborate some of the arguments. There are two main points to be addressed. First, there is a whole set of implications for organizational culture and relationships stemming from the professionalization of school management as self-management. Second, the rhetorics of reform in articulating a key role for management idealize and misrepresent the new freedoms and possibilities of devolution and school-based management. Using Kickert's terms, the 'distance' is stressed and the 'steering' is played down. These idealizations need to be carefully deconstructed, and the rhetorics of school development planning, financial management and entrepreneurship need to be tested empirically against the practice of management. Self-management in schools is being developed in the nexus between flexibility and constraint, autonomy and response. The political and professional literature attends primarily to flexibility and autonomy and has little to say about responsiveness and constraint.[2]

Culture and Relationships

Two major interrelated factors are evident in the 'new' cultural climate of UK schools. First, there is a clear division or 'gap' developing between school managers, oriented primarily to matters of financial planning, income generation and marketing, and classroom practitioners, oriented primarily to the demands of the National Curriculum and national testing. Notions like collaborative planning (Caldwell and Spinks) ideologically paper over the significance of such divisions. But this is a 'gap' of values, purposes and perspective.

> In discussions I've found that I was looking at the gap from the senior manager point of view. And I think there's another whole way of looking at it . . . [from the point of view of teaching staff] that they themselves should be now, and increasingly will in the future be having to appreciate some of the management issues we are facing. The gap is on both sides in other words. (Headteacher, Flightpath Comprehensive, research discussion day)[3]

One deputy head in our research captured the essence of the change in orientation that he was caught up in, when he explained: 'The Education

Reform Act . . . has really shifted the focus of the management team . . . from managing education to managing an educational institution' (Senior Deputy: Parkside Comprehensive). In other words, he now found himself operating as a generic manager with increasingly less of an educational orientation. He went on: '. . . all my non-teaching, non-contact time is taken up with going to meetings, or meeting people and organizing things, concerned with finance and resources, and not with promoting the grass-roots educational programme of the school.' Within this 'gap', this division of purposes and interests, there is considerable potential for tension and conflict, particularly in direct confrontations between financial planning and educational judgments about good practice (see Ball and Bowe, 1991). In these situations the 'steering at a distance' aspects of reform and the role of management in the 'delivery' of performativity are clear within the microphysics of the institution. The manager in effect stands for and does the work of the state in imposing financial limits and disciplines in the practices of colleagues. The development of a school management plan (SMP) is the key tactical device for mobilizing and imposing self-management across and through the organization — for achieving change and asserting control.

> What we've decided to do is hold seven open meetings from February onwards, but there's this anxiety in the Senior Management Committee about how the staff are going to respond to it. There will be six meetings on each of the main thrusts of the SMP, plus finance. But it's interesting to look at what the Head has put down as what these meetings will seek to do — 'provide an opportunity for staff to develop planning strategies with quantifiable achievable objectives in a timespan of one to five years'. The implication is that the SMP is in place, you need to know it's in place, so you now have to think about quantifying what you're doing. The next thing, raise questions about the school's aims and purposes in a year of unparalleled change imposed by government legislation with far-reaching implications for the future. That's admitting what we said earlier, that the aims and purposes, in a sense have been trivialized in this whole exercise. . . . (Senior Deputy, Flightpath Comprehensive)

Here performativity is the cutting edge of the planning process, the plan is 'an effect' rather than a process, with aims being subordinate to an externally imposed agenda (and financial limits). But this school is struggling to take seriously the mechanisms of reform. On the one hand, the Senior Management Committee had produced an SMP. The head intends that this provide the basis of objectives setting and target setting within the school — it will become a disciplinary instrument. All this is recognized as being instrumental rather than purposeful. That is, the plan is an instrument of management rather than a representative of collectively discussed aims and purposes, which have been 'trivialized'. As the Deputy says earlier in the same interview, 'we put the cart before the horse in bunging through this management plan.' On the other hand, the senior managers are clearly worried about the response of the teachers. Embedded in this worry is a new uncertainty about the roles and relationships of teachers and managers. Later in the same interview he said, 'the whole question of whether you over-burden people or patronize them is a major problem.' (See Wallace, 1991 on the role of SMPs in the reform process.) This *realeconomik* gives a particular thrust and intonation to the work of the self-managers.

The relationship between financial planning and the educational technology of the institution, although mediated by management, is ultimately constrained by the vicissitudes of the market and national and local government budget setting.

> I think there's no doubt at all that the finance and the quantitative approach is very much in the picture. I've always tried to keep it no more than in the middle ground. I don't think that the school should be driven purely by finance. If the school has stable numbers or slightly increasing numbers, I can see we can maintain that position, an almost idealistic position if you like. But I can see that once the school starts going into decline, then it is finance that is going to determine the quality of the product. But while we are stable I'd like to see us maintaining the quality as opposed to the quantity of education. (Senior Deputy, Parkside Comprehensive)

A further element of the cultural gap between managers and teachers anticipates the discussion of flexibility and responsiveness later. That is, the extent to which teachers' practice is oriented to the immediate needs of students becomes an aspect of the way the school markets itself to clients (see also Handscomb, 1992); that is, whether practice is driven by professional judgment or market forces (see Ball, 1992a). In this tension, the manager is caught between the client and the practitioner. This reorientation of the managers and the potential for distancing from the more immediate classroom concerns of teachers can be gauged from the following examples of new market relations in schools. They also point up the ideological and cultural changes produced within the current reform process. One of our research schools has obtained a commercial loan to build a sports hall (which includes a bar):

> with the express aim of it being available to the community, as a self-financing, hopefully, even profit-making enterprise. We are having to create a market for the use of this. And that's why I spent last Sunday on site as Licensee of the bar, from 12 o'clock

to 3 o'clock and found that the total takings for that period was
£4.28p. We'd nowhere near covered the cost of the barmaid or the
other people who were on site. It's in the classic position of any
small business that is starting up. You lose money the first year or
two years, before you start breaking even and making a profit.
And there are a whole range of facilities the school's got that are
quite marketable, if you can create a market for them. There is the
languages department, who can make their services available to
local industry for 1992 and all that in terms of the European market.
Or IT equipment for running courses and so on. It's a completely
new culture and it involves a certain amount of retraining of educationalists if you were to go down that road. (Headteacher,
Flightpath Comprehensive)

The second example is similar:

... it may well be that ultimately we'll get a different form of
spending and we'll also be funded more on an industrial basis ...
which takes us to another area, which is income generation, which
we now regard as essential. Especially the 9.2 acres we've just
been given and the development of that for recreational purposes.
I'm contacting various people to see if we can raise sponsorship or
loans to make that an all-weather surface, which we can let out
and generate income from. But in going into the marketplace like
that, we have to make sure that we are in an area of the market
which can guarantee income for many years to come. (Senior
Deputy, Parkside)

In effect, for the self-managers of the school, security and stability,
and thus survival, are beginning to become culturally and organizationally
founded upon, and oriented to, issues related to income generation —
both from student enrolments and elsewhere, rather than the production
process itself — teaching and learning. Security, stability and survival
cannot be simply equated with responsiveness. It is not axiomatic that the
market does, or can, produce responsiveness, especially when the impact
of individual consumers on the well-being of the whole institution is
minimal. 'Whether publically accountable or market driven, large organizations contain inherent pressures to pursue their own internal objectives
and self-interest in lieu of meeting what are diverse and often diffuse
consumer needs' (Saltman and Von Otter, 1992, pp. 99–100).

Flexibility and Autonomy

Much of the rhetoric of devolution and school-based management rests
on a celebration of the new freedoms available to individual schools, to

take control of their own futures, to make their own decisions about the distribution and use of their own resources — leaving aside the question of who experiences greater autonomy or gets to exercise greater flexibility. The question of autonomy and flexibility also has to be set in relation to the constraints of the education market, to cuts in funding and to the introduction of a National Curriculum. When the limitations and constraints involved are taken into account, autonomy may be less real than apparent. Heads may find themselves with a new, more demanding role, new, more difficult staff, governor and parent relationships and a lot of new responsibilities but little new freedom or power (see Arnott, Bullock and Thomas, 1992). The following comments both appear to deploy 'responding' as a key concept in expressing the feelings and experiences of headship.

> I don't feel that I lead the way I used to. I'm responding. I'm responding to the national curriculum. I'm also responding to the the LEA and they seem to be running like mad . . . we seem to be inundated with inspections and pressures that are coming through the LEA. My role has changed drastically. The main interest used to be curriculum innovation. Now I just run around servicing everybody else. (Headteacher, Overbury Comprehensive).

Here the headteacher seems to be on the receiving end of the reform process, its instrument rather than its agent. Here role is significantly changed as a result. The contradictions within the reform agenda and the overdetermination of the school are evident. This is a belt and braces, carrot and stick reform strategy.

> Now it strikes me that what has happened in the last two or three years is that whatever equilibrium you had established as a head, has now been disturbed by the sheer volume of stuff that is coming around, and one is actually responding to whole sets of initiatives and it is not until we are actually, as heads of institutions, able to stand back and regain some sense of that equilibrium and well-being that the institution as a whole will benefit. (Headteacher, Parkside Comprehensive)

Another example comes from a deputy head:

> . . . the kind of conflict that we suspected early on would emerge between a thrusting national curriculum, that is broad and balanced and all the rest of it. And the kind of things that schools actually do for certain pupils which allow them to go off at tangents, is there. And I feel that this is a genuine conflict. I dont think I'm attacking the national curriculum, I'm actually saying the national

curriculum is focussing on something that in the next few years will become increasingly problematic. (Flightpath Comprehensive)

It is tempting to suggest that these indications of an absence of 'real' autonomy point up the disciplinary role of self-management. *That is, self-management is a mechanism for delivering reform rather than a vehicle for in-stitutional initiative and innovation.* Again, the 'steering capacity' of the state is evident. But it is important to set the comments above against others which indicate the ways in which school managers *do* have a new sense of control, particularly in relation to financial flexibility.[4]

> I wouldn't be giving away extra incentive allowances because we haven't got the money to do it. And I wouldn't know where it would come from unless we turned the gas off or whatever. But even within the limited money that you've got, the flexibility of LMS has helped enormously, in that we have been able to take our Head of Library and put in an extra teaching day, with a point 2 allowance, for someone else, in order to enable her to develop learning resources, and appoint a learning resources assistant and appoint someone two days a week in the office. . . . (Headteacher, Pankhurst Comprehensive)

> . . . we're only 1 per cent down this year because we are cushioned. Now I love this word cushioned, next year we will have to lose between 2 and 3 per cent again. Had we had to take the real LMS shortfall we would have been £60,000 short. But neverthe-less there is flexibility there. You see, if you've got x amount of pounds for a learning resource assistant, then either you can add to it and have a sort of resources person on £16,000 a year or you say we'll have someone on grade 2 or 3. (Headteacher, Overbury Comprehensive)

> In the school as a whole we've got more than 20 people doing short term contracts or supply cover, things like that. All these cost savings are quite important. (Senior Deputy, Parkside)

The heads and deputies quoted here were not unaware of the cost dimension of their planning *as a constraint,* or of the tensions between a financial agenda based upon the most efficient use of resources and an educational agenda related to effectiveness in terms of student learning, for example, in terms of school size. (Crucially, flexibility is described and explained here in financial terms. The financial discourse is the predomin-ant discourse of school organization, not education.) The thrust of the Conservative government's commitment to the market is that 'successful' schools grow, and all schools are funded primarily on numbers of students enrolled. Concerns about the relationship between school size or class size and educational effectivity play little role in this unit-cost approach to school finance.[5]

Conclusions

As indicated above, one of the ideological and discursive tricks that self-management achieves is that a great deal of fundamental change (in teachers' work and workplace relationships, in decision-making processes, in the linking of reward closely to performance, in the disciplining of classroom practice) is not now seen as being done *to* schools but done *by* schools (with the proviso that it is in reality one group of people in schools managing another group). The school, the manager, the teacher and the student are all and each measured and compared by their performance, their output. They are rewarded or punished accordingly. The key points of control here are over the discourse of self-management and over the indicators of performance, rather than over practice. (Although, as indicated above, other aspects of reform attempt to intervene directly in practice.) Both, and particularly the latter, are subject to state control; the indicators of performance are the mechanisms of steering by the state (see Schools Bill, 1992 and Parents Charter, 1991).

The other fundamental transference achieved by 'steering at a distance' is that once the rhetoric of devolution is accepted, then it becomes possible to blame the schools for the faults and difficulties inherent in, or created by, the policies. This is crucial. Parental choice and market schooling provide two avenues for the displacement of the legitimation crisis in education. The state can distance itself from problems in education by blaming parents for making bad or ill-informed choices and by blaming schools for poor self-management, the misuse of their new autonomy. The schools are left to deal with the contradictions that policies create. All too often in policy research and in the texts of self-management, the focus of attention is entirely upon the strengths and weaknesses, faults and difficulties of individual schools. The role of policy-makers within the state in creating dilemmas and contradictions with which schools must deal is ignored. The state is left in the enviable position of having power without responsibility.

The uneasy professional double-bind created by this kind of policy nexus is nowhere more acute than when — as in the UK setting — devolution is accompanied by reductions in education budgets (see above). Schools find themselves 'starved of cash and playing with pennies', as one headteacher put it. It is tempting to see the devolution of budgets and self-management as ways both of getting those being cut to cut themselves and to think that it is for the best because they control their own decline. There is a shift of institutional focus from the cuts themselves to the ways of coping with cuts, a shift to dealing with what you can control rather than what you can't. Indeed, if the alternative is that someone else would control your decline, this may be the best of a bad job. But massive work of ideological and social control is done in the meantime; and the ideological role of self-management in relation to the state is never more clearcut.

Self-management provides a framework for a new institutional culture and for a process of resocialization; it interpolates a new kind of headteacher — although it is difficult to believe that there is a wholesale, unproblematic shift of subjectivity going on among senior teachers. Nonetheless, the new conditions and discourses of consciousness do construct new forms of consciousness and new patterns and possibilities of career. Mike Davies, Co-Director of Stantonbury Campus, writes about the new culture and its effects:

> . . . new teachers and those looking towards the furtherance of their career see that the 'top' jobs involve management activity, then it is hardly surprising that staffroom conversation is about management, systems and procedures, rather than about the excitement of the last lesson and the looking forward to the next. The ubiquitous way in which money and financial consideration can dominate management is a real coup for a government determined to stratify the system and deny that schools are for radical social change. (Davies, 1992, p. 5)

What Davies indicates is the potential profundity of the reform process, and the key role of self-management in those reforms. The dominant reality of the school as an organization, at least for its leaders and managers, is shifted and reconstructed. We should also bear in mind Foucault's key point that within microtechnologies of control (like self-management) those who exercise power are just as much captured and shaped as are those over whom power is wielded.

> In this form of management, power is not totally entrusted to someone who would exercise it alone, over others, in an absolute fashion, this machine is one in which everyone is caught, those who exercise power as well as those who are subjected to it. (Foucault, 1977, p. 156)

According to Davies (1992, p. 2):

> I cannot believe that hundreds of headteachers, whose professional and job satisfaction has come through working with teachers and children so that they can walk along the road towards empowerment and liberty, can so quickly swap all this for the keyboard, spreadsheet and bank balance. Post '88, we seem to have entered a new era of managerialism without ever being clear what it is that

we are managing. It may be over simplistic to characterize the many dimensions of the headteacher's role into two giant ledgers, but if we take one substantive column relating to being the 'leading professional' and the other being 'the managing director', then so much of our re-orientation since the end of the last decade has led us to serving the mythical customer with an unsatiable appetite for statistics and league tables and providing information for the Board of Governors.

Again, this highlights the headteacher as both beneficiary and victim of reform, both in and out of control. The head is freed and constrained within the management role, as well as being subject to other forms of control as indicated above. The conceptual and empirical simplicities of the devolution and school-based management literature (Caldwell and Spinks, 1988) are pointed up.

The textual apologists of self-management provide a professionalization and legitimation of self-subjugation in articulating an idealized technology for reworking the cultural and interpersonal dynamics of schooling. These texts are firmly imbricated in the construction of new forms of control, and concomitantly the reconstruction of teachers' subjectivities, relationships and careers, and thus also the possibilities of their efficacy and autonomy. The discourses to which they contribute reconstruction are complex and polyvalent, empowering and disempowering, intersecting and contradictory. Bear in mind that this chapter deals only with the 'will to power' — the attempt to bring off new forms of control through policies of school reform. Another paper is needed to explore resistance, interpretation and reconciliation and mutation (Corwin, 1983) of those policies (see Bowe and Ball with Gold, 1992).

Notes

1 Here I refer to the imposition of a National Curriculum, national testing and interventions into pedagogical decision-making. All three message systems of schooling are affected (Bernstein, 1971). In general terms, there is an increase in the technical elements of teachers' work and a reduction in the professional. The spaces for professional autonomy and judgment are reduced. Standardization and normalization are imposed upon classroom practice. The curriculum provides for standardization and testing for normalization — the establishment of measurements, hierarchy and regulation, around the idea of a distributionary statistical norm within a given population. This is based upon the possibility of monitoring the performance of both students and teachers and comparing them, and, going further, the linking of these comparisons to teacher appraisal and to performance-related pay awards (see Ball and Bowe, 1992, for more on the National Curriculum).

2 Here I will draw upon a small amount of illustrative data from two-year case

studies of four comprehensive schools 'implementing' the 1988 Education Reform Act. The research was supported by a grant from the Strategic Research Fund of King's College London.

3 I think what this headteacher is suggesting is that teachers should attend less to their own concerns and be more aware of what managers are trying to do in their best interests.

4 Flexibility is achieved at the cost of others' conditions of work and pay; the replacement of fully trained with less well qualified teachers; teachers with auxiliaries, full-time teachers with part-time or short-term contract staff.

5 Peter Downes, a headteacher with long experience of devolved budget holding recently produced an article which points up two rather different aspects of devolved financial management. The first is coping with cuts. Cambridgeshire LEA proposed cuts amounting to between £30,000 and £80,000 per school per year.

> The prospect of cuts of this size has come as a shock to Cambridgeshire Heads. As many of us have been managing our own budgets for nearly a decade, most of the possible savings have already been made. Zero expenditure on books, equipment and materials is totally unrealistic. If anything, heads of department are looking for increased funding as they re-equip for the national curriculum.

(Here is an example of two aspects of policy colliding within the remit of management.) Downes goes on to argue that at least the devolution of budgets provides insights into how budgets are constructed and allocated, insights which were previously unobtainable.

> By introducing LMS, the Government has opened the door of the secret garden of education finance. It can never be shut again. Heads or governors who now have the unenviable task of implementing difficult financial decisions imposed on them from afar, ought, I believe, to mount a campaign for access to central government financial information in a comprehensible format. I would probably say that half the size would be more effective in those terms [educational] but the reality is that you've got a large capital resource and the costs within that mean that you must operate nearer your maximum capacity to be cost effective. But the quality of the broader education may not be as good as one would like it to be. (Headteacher, Flightpath)

References

ARNOTT, M., BULLOCK, A. and THOMAS, H. (1992) 'Consequences of Local Management: An Assessment by Headteachers', Paper Presented to the 8th ERA Research Network Seminar, 12 February 1992.

BALL, S.J. (1990a) *Politics and Policymaking in Education*, London, Routledge.

BALL, S.J. (1990b) 'Management as a Moral Technology', in S.J. BALL (Ed.), *Foucault and Education*, London, Routledge.

BALL, S.J. (1992a) 'The Worst of Three Possible Worlds: Policy Power Relations and Teachers' Work', Keynote Address to the BEMAS Research Conference, University of Nottingham, 6–8 April 1992.

BALL, S.J. (1992b) 'Schooling, Enterprise and the Market', Paper to the AERA symposium, The Globalization of a Reform Strategy: The Role of the Market in School Reform, San Francisco, 20–24 April 1992.

BALL, S.J. and BOWE, R. (1991) 'The Micropolitics of Radical Change: Budgets, Management, and Control in British Schools,' in J. BLASE (Ed.), *The Politics of Life in Schools*, Newbury Park, Sage.

BERNSTEIN, B. (1971) 'On the Classification and Framing of Educational Knowledge', in M.F.D. YOUNG (Ed.) *Knowledge and Control*, London, Collier-Macmillan.

BOWE, R. and BALL, S.J. with GOLD, A. (1992) *Reforming Education and Changing Schools*, London, Routledge.

CALDWELL, B. and SPINKS, J. (1988) *The Self-Managing School*, Lewes, Falmer Press.

COOPERS AND LYBRAND DELOITTE (1992) *The National Union of Teachers: Costs of the National Curriculum in Primary Schools*, London, Cooper and Lybrand Deloitte.

CORWIN, R. (1983) *The Entrepreneurial Bureaucracy*, Greenwich, Conn., JAI Press.

CUBAN, L. (1990) 'The Fundamental Puzzle of School Reform', in A. LIEBERMAN (Ed.), *Schools as Collaborative Cultures*, Lewes, Falmer Press.

DAVIES, M. (1992) 'The Little Boy Said . . . "The Emperor, Still Isn't Wearing Any Clothes",' *The Curriculum Journal*, 3, 1, Spring.

DEAL (1990) 'Healing Our Schools: Restoring the Heart', in A. LIEBERMAN (Ed.), *Schools as Collaborative Cultures*, Lewes, Falmer Press.

DEPARTMENT OF EDUCATION AND SCIENCE (1988) *The Local Management of Schools, Circular 7/88*, London, DES.

DEPARTMENT OF EDUCATION AND SCIENCE (1989) *Planning for School Improvement: Advice to Governors, Headteachers and Teachers*, London, DES.

FIDLER, B. and BOWLES, G. (Eds) (1989) *Effective Local Management of Schools*, London, Longman.

FOUCAULT, M. (1977) 'The Eye of Power', in C. GORDON (Ed.) (1980) *Power/Knowledge*, New York, Pantheon.

FOUCAULT, M. (1979) *The History of Sexuality, Vol 1.*, Harmondsworth, Peregrine.

GOODCHILD, S. and HOLLY, P. (1989) *Management for Change: The Garth Hill Experience*, Lewes, Falmer Press.

HANDSCOMB, G. (1992) 'The Rhetoric and Reality of LMS: A Case Study of One Secondary School', Paper presented to the 8th ERA Research Network Seminar, 12 February 1992.

HARGREAVES, D.H. and HOPKINS, D. (1991) *The Empowered School*, London, Cassell.

HATTON, E. (1988) 'Teachers' Work as Bricolage: Implications for Teacher Education', *British Journal of Sociology of Education*, 9, 3, pp. 337–57.

KEAT, R. (1991) 'Starship Britain or Universal Enterprise', in R. KEAT and N. ABERCROMBIE (Eds), *Enterprise Culture*, London, Routledge.

KICKERT, W. (1991) 'Steering at a Distance: A New Paradigm of Public Governance in Dutch Higher Education', Paper for the European Consortium for Political Research, University of Essex, March.

NASSP BULLETIN (1991) 'The Challenge of Change in Reform and Restructuring', 75, 537, October.

ROSENHOLTZ, S. (1985) 'Effective Schools: Interpreting the Evidence', *American Journal of Education*, 93, pp. 352–88.

ROSENHOLTZ, S. (1990) 'Educational Reform Strategies: Will They Increase Teacher Commitment?', in A. LIEBERMAN (Ed.), *Schools as Collaborative Cultures*, Lewes, Falmer Press.

SALTMAN, R.B. and VON OTTER, C. (1992) *Planned Markets and Public Competition*, Buckingham, Open University Press.

SARASON (1971) *The Culture of the School and the Problem of Change*, Boston, Mass., Allyn and Bacon.

WALLACE, M. (1991) 'School Development Plans: A Key to the Management of ERA?', Paper presented to the 7th ERA Research Network Seminar, 7 February 1991.

5 Reinventing Square Wheels: Planning for Schools to Ignore Realities

Marie Brennan

I want to start this chapter with two related assertions: schools need to change; and societies need mechanisms for ensuring that schools change. These assertions are largely taken for granted as straightforward policy or political questions, except perhaps by students of reform movements and their fate in the education sector. The knowledge built up about how schools change and the problematic significance of school level change is rarely studied by those who decide, supposedly on behalf of the rest of us, what new educational policy directions will be and how they are to come into existence. In particular, as a consequence of the new styles of corporate management and economic rationalism that have swept Ministries of Education in the 1980s, those who were familiar with issues of planning and policy for school level change have been retrenched or displaced. Neutral managers, who (almost by definition) know nothing about the specific area of education, let alone have contacts in schools who could perhaps tell them about the problems of centre-periphery policy initiatives, have been put into place to avoid the educationally-oriented bureaucrats of the past whose task was to act as advocates for education.

In the latest version of the crisis of the state, education is one of the few remaining common institutions which appear to be controllable by more traditional means of government policy and bureaucratic activity. Schools are continually exhorted by the media, governments and bureaucracies to change in this or that direction. The flurry of politicization of education in the decade of the 1980s has not proved a flash in the pan, and seems to be continuing in the 1990s, with closer scrutiny of the role and efficiency of the bureaucracy, of school management, standards and accountability mechanisms. In this chapter I consider in some detail two rival approaches to school level change in the Victorian Education Ministry during the 1980s. The School Improvement Plan (SIP) and School Level Program Budgeting (SLPB) appeared at much the same time, but where school improvement has gone by the way, the descendants of the program budgeting initiative have gone on to encompass a whole approach to school level planning and management in Victoria. The success of the latter can only be accounted for by congruence with economic and political agendas which rely on speed and narrow versions of efficiency for their operation.

I pose these two initiatives as polar opposites for the purposes of analysis of their underlying assumptions. By doing so, I do not intend to caricature or oversimplify, nor to suggest that one is allied with the forces of good and the other a manifestation of all that is evil. Both were designed with similar interests in mind, and promulgated by a government interested primarily in how to achieve significant and longlasting educational reform. Nevertheless, the assumptions underlying both in relation to school level change, processes, focus and orientation to action are so different that the treatment I give them should thus appear justified. In the first section, I outline the conditions which gave rise to both initiatives and shaped their design. Then I consider specific emphases of each, particularly the difference of emphasis on planning and evaluation.

New Broom Governments

In 1982 a Labor government was elected in the state of Victoria after twenty-seven years in opposition. The new government had an extensive platform of change announced in their election policies, some items of which had been many years in development as a consequence of many years of critique of the previous conservative government and through active Labor Party branch involvement. The education platform led to the development of a series of *Ministerial Papers* which announced the new directions for the system of public schools and provided them with new structures to encourage greater participation throughout the system. School councils changed their membership to reflect better a partnership between parents and teachers, and their responsibilities were altered under the legislation to include school policy within broad state-wide guidelines in addition to finance and facilities management. The State Board of Education and Regional Boards of Education were established to ensure participation of parent, teacher, principal and system administration in policy and practice at all levels of the hierarchy. Curriculum goals and principles were also announced, and much effort went into developing materials and in-service activities to 'spread the word'. The scale and scope of the changes were massive, requiring nothing less than a major rethink of the place of schools in the society and the role of the education bureaucracy in assisting such change.

The School Improvement Plan, the second of the *Ministerial Papers* (1982), was developed in detail by a Ministerial Committee appointed after the election. It drew strongly on the long experience of a wide range of stakeholders in the state education sector, including parent and school council organizations, teacher unionists, federal and state special purpose program officers and evaluators, and departmental officers with a history of working on school reviews. These designers of SIP explicitly explored the mistakes and deficiencies of previous attempts to promote school level change, aiming to build on the specific curriculum, industrial and administrative historical context. As I have noted elsewhere, a number of prevalent approaches were rejected by the Ministerial Working Party (Brennan, 1992). These included rejection of the centre-periphery research, development and utilization models used in central curriculum branches and national projects of the 1970s, and the prespecification of topics, procedures and criteria of success for participating schools. For too long, Victorian educators had seen innovations hampered by designs that supported short-term programs, focusing on an individual or small group in the school, and requiring a great deal of work from those involved with little or no understanding of the processes of school change embedded in their procedures and goals. We also wanted to avoid putting all the emphasis on school level change without a corresponding need for systemic change.

The aims of the School Improvement Plan were set out as follows:

- To assist schools to reflect on their total practice (including curriculum, teaching/learning styles and organization) and to develop in ways that improve the learning experiences of all students.
- To encourage those processes of systemic decision making which provide resources and services to schools in ways that meet their identified needs and result in the delivery of co-ordinated support services to the school.
- To encourage and support collaborative practices between parents, students and teachers in schools, and between schools and the rest of the system.
- To encourage and support a cyclical process of school evaluation, planning, implementation and re-evaluation. (*Ministerial Paper 2*, 1982, p. 6)

Central and regional committees made up of the representatives of administrators, teacher unions, principal associations, parents and school council organization were established to promote the practices of school self-evaluation (Brennan and Hoadley, 1984), to assist schools to network and share their learnings (in a range of media) and to provide overall program evaluation and feedback to the system as a whole. The concept of participation so strongly present in all the *Ministerial Papers* was not only an issue of participation in formal decision-making structures but was also given a goal of improving the quality of education in schools. Schools were to be eligible for small-scale funding for the processes of participatory evaluation, covering all schools in the state over a seven-year period. Money was also made available for school networking through in-service activity and for publication of school documentation and other writing.

Education was only one government department that was to be the target of Labor's reform, although it was important, taking about a quarter of the state's budget. Massive changes were also planned for other areas such as health, housing, environment, agriculture and finance. The new government was, with some reason, worried that an entrenched bureaucracy would stonewall their initiatives, watering down their reform intent at best, while waiting for a new election to throw them out of office. They therefore organized reform of the bureaucracy, using a corporate management approach tied to their new Department of Management and Budget (DMB) as a way of monitoring that available resources were tied to their stated priorities (Victoria, Department of Management and Budget, 1983).

School Level Program Budgeting (SLPB) in the Education Department was introduced in 1983 as part of this state-wide approach to financial management and accountability adopted by the Department of Management and Budget. DMB employed as consultants to the Education Department Brian Caldwell and Jim Spinks, who had been part of a project about effective allocation of school resources in Tasmania and developed a system of school resource management at Spinks's school using program budgeting, the approach favoured by DMB. The term 'program budgeting' was eventually dropped by DMB after it became a source of criticism that the initial model was used by the military in the USA in Vietnam and subsequently found not to work. Nevertheless, the approach continued, and the Department's roles and functions were divided into separate 'programs' to which money (and formal reporting) was tied.

In the initial proposal, schools were to appear as the 'bottom line' of the Department's programs. That is, the Department might have programs reflecting functional areas such as personnel, finance, facilities, curriculum, special purpose programs, and schools would be expected to show both in planning and in reporting how their budget was tied to each of these Departmental programs. This would enable tighter reporting to Parliament and to DMB. After extensive arguments, both internally in the Education Department and with the DMB, it was finally agreed that schools could develop their own way of categorizing their programs since the program categories of the bureaucracy useful for carrying out their tasks would not necessarily correspond to the main kinds of tasks undertaken in schools.[1]

The initial impetus for school level program budgeting was thus oriented to DMB priorities of more efficient and controllable management of resources. Yet within the Education Department, SLPB had to be implemented within the context of the educational and structural priorities set out by the *Ministerial Papers*. These two sets of priorities were not always compatible, especially in generating tension between school-defined issues invited through participatory decision-making and the focus on reflecting state-wide priorities. Schools were asked to develop a set of programs reflecting their major tasks (Victoria, Department of Education, 1983, 1984). Each program would then be documented to include a brief policy statement (outlining purpose and description), a set of objectives and priorities, implementation strategies, targets and indicators for a timetabled major or minor evaluation, and a program budget of resources (Victoria, Department of Education, 1983, 1984). A school might have programs such as administration, pastoral care, language, maths, evaluation and assessment, home-school relations, science, environment and technology, the arts, physical education and excursions.

Victorian education was reform-oriented in particular ways that built on the political, industrial and economic history in the sector and the broader context. Schools were asked to take on greater responsibilities for educational policy, for addressing social justice issues, developing participation across the school community and relating to the rest of the system. However, mixed messages were being given by government and the central administration about the relative importance of these new directions, with the focus on management and efficiency tending to over-shadow many other dimensions of the implications for changes in curriculum, teaching, school organization and educational leadership. In the sections which follow, I will consider the School Improvement Plan and School Level Program Budgeting as microcosms of major debates-in-action both within schools and across the system. I will concentrate on their embodied views of the future, change and the role of educational administration by focusing on the different emphasis on evaluation and planning used in their elaboration and presentation to schools.

Planning to Manage?

The central disagreement between the models of school level change in SIP and SLPB lies in their different orientations to the concept and activities of planning and evaluation. 'Planning', as defined by Caldwell and Spinks, 'is simply determining in advance what will be done, when it will be done, how it will be done and who will do it' (1986, p. 26). This version of planning relies on the positivist concept of being able to predict the future accurately in order to control it.

The Caldwell and Spinks model, which they termed 'policy-making and planning for school effectiveness' (1986), sets out a number of steps for achieving collaborative school management:

goal setting and need identification;

policy-making;

planning;

budgeting;

implementing;

evaluating.

Planning is, however, more than a single step in their process; it lies at the heart of all the steps and the documentation processes that result from undertaking the recommended activities. Although these steps have been labelled as 'the collaborative school management cycle' (Caldwell and Spinks, 1986, p. 21) and presented in diagrammatic form as a circle, the steps described are in effect linear, requiring a certain sequence and limiting interaction between the elements. A set of steps to be carried out in sequence and then repeated in a five-year timetable does not fulfil criteria for a cyclical process, which should at least contain the possibility of reflexive interaction among the elements, redefining aspects of the process as it is being carried out. Setting out goals, followed by developing a policy statement, then a plan to implement the policy is the sequence required. Evaluation comes at the end after all the other steps have been carried out. Then the steps commence again.

A result of this linear process, what tends to become enshrined in the documentation for each step, is the knowledge and existing practices of those already empowered in the situation. This limits the extent and kind of participation, as I will discuss further below. Because of this tendency to enshrine existing practice in documentation, other, more localized processes of contesting power-in-use in a school are effectively disenfranchised. It is much harder for a teacher to suggest a change to the teaching of reading, even with the support of class parents, if this can be used as a way of accusing someone of disloyalty to school policy which is supposed to hold for five years unless or until the results of a major evaluation suggest otherwise. The timetable thus becomes a self-fulfilling prophecy unless a major crisis occurs.

The Caldwell and Spinks model of planning is mechanical and procedural; those following it can live in the illusion that their future is determinable-determined and controlled through the activities of planning. However, its assumptions about action in relation to the future are massively flawed. As Suchman argues, 'the circumstances of our actions are never fully anticipated and are continuously changing around us' (1987, p. ix). This is particularly true of schools, containing as they do so many disparate persons and expectations, and operating within highly contested contextual factors. The technicist view of planning is actually useless because changing circumstances are at best seen as an aberration rather than a necessary dimension of the usual 'state'. Because of the inevitability of changing circumstances,

> our actions, while systematic, are never planned in the strong
> sense that cognitive science would have it. Rather, plans are best

viewed as a weak resource for what is primarily *ad hoc* activity. It is only when pressed to account for the rationality of our actions, given the biases of European culture, that we invoke the guidance of a plan. Stated in advance, plans are necessarily vague, insofar as they must accommodate the unforeseeable contingencies of particular situations. Reconstructed in retrospect, plans systematically filter out precisely the particularity of detail that characterizes situated actions, in favor of those aspects of the actions that can be seen to accord with the plan. (Suchman, 1987, p. ix)

Thus for a bureaucracy to mandate school level planning of the kind described in Caldwell and Spinks is to work with an illusion of power and control. By confusing the reconstruction of hindsight with the capacity to predict and control, those who follow the technicist approach to planning can only repeat the states of knowledge from the past, often unsuited to changing conditions. Organizations remained trapped in ignorance of their own making. The time and energy consumed by the planning procedures confirm knowledge as limited instead of the possibility of producing further understandings. The narrow view of planning as organizing to get to a known destination or outcome cannot work — especially if what is being demanded is that schools change and that they help students to invent new futures. As a first step, those associated with schools need to acknowledge their own role in perpetuating and exacerbating educational disadvantage by supporting the status quo of power relations.

The goal for the Caldwell and Spinks model is one of reproducing what has been decided in other situations to be characteristic of effective management in which the allocation of resources is given central priority. Change is presumed to be known, and fixed, to be addressed by implementation of what has been researched previously in other schools. If nothing else, the amount and speed of politically driven policy redirection in the last decade itself attests to the problem of requiring schools to make certainties of relatively volatile and changing situations. The school planning documents themselves, though they may have contributed to some degree of shared knowledge for those taking part in their production, remain testaments to unachievable certainty of goals, resources and educational activity. The future, according to linear planning models, ought to be controllable and predictable, based on past knowledge. The struggle to assert this level of control in a school follows a kind of teleological determinism which can only spell failure of control when the unforeseen happens.

However, despite these criticisms of linear planning, it does not follow that all forms of purposeful action are similarly problematic. Schools do need to be organized, to allocate their (often decreasing) resources in effective ways that enhance the education of their students. A different understanding of planning as an orientation to shared practice is needed.

> It is frequently only on acting in a present situation that its pos-
> sibilities become clear, and we do not often know ahead of time,
> or at least not with any specificity, what future state we desire to
> bring about. Garfinkel (1967) points out that in many cases it is
> only after we encounter some state of affairs that we find to be
> desirable that we identify that state as the goal toward which our
> previous actions, in retrospect, were directed 'all along' or 'after
> all'. (Suchman, 1987, p. 52)

This approach to planning makes it less amenable to technicist managerial
orientations, because of its emphasis on local action as the primary resource
for organization. It is useful for schools to reconstruct their paths of development (or regression, as the case may be), but such a historical activity
should not then be used to masquerade as a management tool. Those
involved can certainly learn from their past experiences, but not in the
sense of controlling the future.

Evaluation as an Alternative Starting Point for School Change

In contrast to this strong emphasis on *planning* in SLPB, the School Improvement Plan promoted *participatory evaluation* as a route to change.
Participatory evaluation, as used in SIP, begins with the notion of inves-
tigation.[2] The situation is not presumed necessarily to be either known or
totally knowable. The version of evaluation promulgated by the Victorian
SIP emphasized participation as a means of understanding the different
perspectives that make up the multiple truths of 'the school'. It did not
presume that the 'truth' can be discovered elsewhere and implemented
at this site. Nor, however, did it suggest that only local knowledge is
important or valid.

Participatory evaluation was presented in SIP not only as a way to
discover what had been going on but as a way to orient to the future
through action. Evaluation was thus not to be summative but formative
in an ongoing and continuous way. Parents, teachers and students had to
learn what had been going on in the name of education not only from
their own perspective but from one another's perspectives. As Cumming
found in his overview of major approaches to evaluation (1986), SIP, in
comparison with other versions of prescribed school level evaluation, recommended no necessary starting point. The differences in starting points
were found to be attractive to schools which felt they could tailor the
organization of evaluation to their own history and current needs. The
approach favoured had a number of key principles rather than recommended steps. Evaluation was to be:

- action oriented
- group based rather than individual performance oriented
- focussed on the school as a whole as well as on classrooms
- emancipatory rather than technocratic
- participatory, involving parents, teachers and students in partnership
- school rather than externally controlled
- directed towards improvement rather than external account-ability
- ongoing and cyclical rather than event-oriented (Brennan, 1986, p. 59)

This list of preferred characteristics is instructive of the problems facing SIP: the previous evaluation experiences of schools. That schools would have to be convinced of — that it was necessary to spell out — these characteristics is a clear indication of practices that were individualistic, accountability-oriented, externally controlled separate events which ended with a document in the principal's office rather than any further action. These had been the prevalent models to date; inspectors or an external team conducted the review of either the teacher or the school. To move the weight of historically sedimented hierarchical, linear evaluation practices involved more than recommending a new set of procedures.

The ideas of 'school self-evaluation' were outlined in a short manual for schools (Brennan and Hoadley, 1984) and spread through in-service activity in the first instance, followed by the sharing of documented cases presented by schools which had participated in the initial year/s. The activities of evaluation were outlined, including priority setting, setting questions, gathering data, analyzing material and developing plans for action. On the surface these activities are similar to those involved in any evaluative work — or even to some of the Caldwell and Spinks activities. Where SIP was different, however, was in the kinds of relationships among the elements/dimensions of the specific activities and how they were to be carried out. Epistemologically, each activity was to be group-based, producing contested group knowledge about education. Politically and socially, the introduction of parents and students as partners of teachers was aimed to alter the power relations of the school, redefining 'school' away from equating with 'the staff'. Schools were encouraged to experiment and invent rather than to be organized along the same lines as before. Evaluation thus became a *means* related to the *end* of a more socially just public education system, not an end in itself.

There was continued need to debate and redefine school self-evaluation in the light of problems which emerged, whether across the state or within a small group of schools. The traditional form of outside expert evaluation as the 'commonsense' model continued to be prevalent, although the numbers of schools attempting participatory self-evaluation provided a growing pool of articulate opposition to the more traditional approaches too often presumed to be the norm.

If one considers the evaluation activities which best promoted partici- patory action based on a critical understanding of the current issues in the school, a number of points can be made from school experience. For example, starting by considering the kind/s of futures desired and ex- pected by parents and students for themselves was often a healthy way to break out of the straightjackets of current practice defining future possi- bilities. The discussion of broader issues affirmed the contribution of all parties — parents, teachers and students — as necessary for developing an orientation to the future not bound to one or other group's own expec- tations alone. Another strategy found useful by schools has been analysis of significant pieces of data by parents and teachers together, showing that participation not only could work, but was worthwhile in providing sig- nificant further questions, noting trends and, perhaps most important of all, delineating the gaps and silences of the school's current practices. Minimalism in data collection and maximum time for analysis proved maxims for many schools which passed on their learnings from experience. Having short-term, action-oriented taskforces with particular briefs helped to keep momentum going without establishing the ubiquitous 'commit- tee'. In-service for mixed teams was another strategy which appeared to equalize power relations through equal access to knowledge. Principals were not provided with training which they then passed on to staff who then involved parents and perhaps students. Rather, mixed teams from the school would be sent, whether the in-service was to find out other schools' experiences or to learn more about the evaluation process by focusing on their own school. Hearing another parent talk knowledgeably about their school's problems often gave courage to people worried about participation. Swapping advice about techniques (e.g., 'Don't waste time on question- naires') built the kinds of networks among schools that transcended the usual sources of information and organization.

Evaluation as used in the Caldwell and Spinks model and program budgeting more generally is based on a very different set of assumptions from those used in school improvement. First, it is placed at the end of the sequence of planning activities (although the authors suggest it can be built in throughout); second, it aims to see if goals have been achieved. Each program is to be subject to a minor evaluation each year. 'Minor evaluations are usually subjective in nature and focus on indicators of success' (Caldwell and Spinks, 1986, p. 133) and result in a report one page long. A fifth of the school's programs are timetabled for major evaluation each year, conducted so that the school/program group is in a 'position to decide whether purposes have been achieved and to what degree guidelines and plans are effective and efficient' (p. 119). The justi- fication of the approach to evaluation is provided in terms of its efficiency: since the management cycle steps have set out what is to be done (in policies) and how (in implementation plans) as well as its cost effectiveness (the program budget). Thus, it is argued, 'the base line information is already available' (p. 111) for measurement, saving time and energy on the evaluation task. The problem with this approach to evaluation is that purposes and goals, once written down, become the base line measurement criteria without themselves being brought into question. Such a process feeds an emphasis on formal decision-making forums where the policy group's task is reduced to making decisions on the basis of information — an overly rational and simplistic definition of planning, of evaluation and of the role of the participatory policy group.

Participation

For both planning and evaluation, the single largest problem has been to work out how to move from what has traditionally been individual activity to one which is shared. Planning and evaluation are usually tacit, carried out for particular puposes, often unconsciously but nevertheless a necessary part of living as humans. While they remain activities at least partly in the tacit domain, they are nevertheless highly socialized, reflecting at least the assumptions about the future, about the relations of individual and society, and the discourses of practice. The challenge for shared planning and evaluation is to avoid the hyperrationality that often comes with any reconstruction from hindsight, passing as an accurate description of the processes. Management and organizational theory, politics and economics can all be said to address the problem of mass organization. Yet planning and evaluation — even educational leadership itself — rely on models drawn from individual psychology or proceduralized bureaucracy as the dominant forms of the individual-society dualism supporting current organizational forms.

The argument about the line across Caldwell and Spinks's diagram of their 'cycle' to determine what counted as policy and what as implementation was a good case in point. On the surface this debate seems a relatively insignificant dispute about a diagram. However, at least part of what was being debated was the interpretation of participation enshrined in this management blueprint. With the focus on the new role for the school councils, many teachers feared that their own knowledge and experience would be devalued by the process of parental input, even if some of their own number were active members of the council. Some parents were also wary of being seen to 'take over' what the teachers knew best. Other parents seemed to see the new dimensions of their role as being about control of teachers.

The distinction between policy and implementation appeared as a necessary one to clarify. The school council members were not to usurp the professional role of teachers in making decisions about how best to teach. On the other hand, making the issue much more complex, policy and implementation cannot be so neatly separated through a definition or a line drawn on a diagram. A common example discussed at the time was that of the reading program in a primary school. If the school community, in investigating which students were being failed by the reading program of the school, found that certain groups were systematically in the lower achieving sections, then the evaluation logically required changes in the language teaching program. Since the school's policy description for the language program outlined the current teaching emphasis, the school's policy would need to change, as well as the teachers' practice in their classrooms. It would be impossible to draw a neat line and say that X was policy, and therefore under the aegis of the school council, while Y was implementation and therefore the responsibilities of the teachers. Policy and teaching are highly iterative, requiring regular examination to redefine both and their relationship.

Through the procedures developed by Caldwell and Spinks's model in Victorian schools, there was a greater emphasis on management and on the formal decision-making forum: the school council as management. The importance of the council and its committees was enhanced, even apparently legitimated, by the emphasis on management. The management emphasis enabled some people to feel that their new tasks could actually be 'managed' by the application of particular techniques. This outcome was a double-edged sword. On the one hand, the emphasis on local school council activism at a time when a large number of changes was occurring required a level of organization few schools at the time possessed, not to mention that school councils were unused to policy work or more than an advisory role. Thus the model of 'collaborative school management' appeared as a necessary path to take for many floundering in defining themselves within their expanded roles.

On the other hand, there were drawbacks to this emphasis. The current members of the council tended to remain largely those who had access to debates and the 'full picture', while others whom they represented were less able to interpret the significance of elements of the process with which they might become familiar. Participation in these circumstances was reduced in scope from a potential for empowerment of both teachers and parents (and students in secondary schools) to representation on a management body.

Thus, for all its claim to be a practical resource for 'collaboration' in line with *Ministerial Papers*, SLPB and the Caldwell and Spinks model moved away from participation in *educational* decisions and processes towards managerialism. Thus the ground was laid for cooption of the management methods for economic rationalism. The descendants of SLPB are now called 'whole school planning' or 'school development plans', a trend now apparent in most states as well as in international circles.

What was little understood at the time was that for participation to be more than an exercise in rubber stamping, accountability or even decision-making, both teachers and parents would have to modify their habitual practices in their relations. A 'partnership' model differs from the version of participation which is synonymous with one party controlling the work of others. In School Improvement, as well as the legislation and rationale for the changing role of the school council, the point of participation was not promoted as a focus on decision-making alone, nor as parents over-seeing the work of teachers.

Participation was a way of harnessing the multiple perspectives and expertise of the whole school community to develop new practices in schooling more appropriate for the changing times. Parents thus had a stake in new forms of schooling, not merely for their own children but for the cohort of students who were the future adults of the society. Teachers were to bring their specialist understandings and inventiveness derived from practice to contribute to reshaping the directions for the schools as a microcosm of the society of the future. Thus teachers were not to be put in the position of developing an idea and 'selling' it to parents who would bow to their professional expertise. Parents were not just telling teachers about the 'real world' in which teachers themselves were not presumed to live. Parental expectations of the role of schooling needed to be debated, alongside teachers and, wherever possible, students. A partnership that re-spected the differences within parental groups, among the teacher group and between the students would have more chance of developing a future that did not repeat the mistakes of the past. It would also redefine the meaning and practices of *public* education.

Promoting participation in public education was not meant to equate with localism, a return to the faith in 'grassroots' movements of the 1960s and 1970s. The local community of the school was important, especially since it was never homogeneous. However, partnership was also meant to apply to shared responsibilities among schools and their communities and between schools and other sectors, including universities and non-education agencies. Such a vision for participation was light years away from the inspectorial-divisional system and the highly contested interest group segmentation characterizing the educational politics which obtained when Labor came into power.

Yet important steps have been taken — in schools and by advisors/consultants and administration in regional and central offices. The invitation was best taken up by those schools and communities with a history of cooperation between parents and teachers (such as those active in the Disadvantaged Schools Program: Connell *et al.*, 1991). Other schools were accidentally surprised into participation by a crisis or political upheaval, or by attempts at participatory evaluation which were not expected to work. Participation, which was first understood to mean parents taking part in school activities, moved to include within its definition decision-making forum, educational directions and educational judgments. While many schools aim to keep parents as tame supporters of the status quo, mere receivers of legitimated information, enough other school communities have engaged in redefining their schools to make a weaker role for all partners less acceptable than before.

Managerialism Rules OK?

Implied in these contradictory approaches to changing schools and school systems are different ways of approaching the future. SIP attempted to work towards a future that was open-ended, available to be defined and produced through the interaction of different groups, dialectically related. Practices at central administration would be altered just as much as those at a school. SLPB was posited upon a different set of assumptions, with long-term consequences for reductionism in public education. Because it looks neat, tidy and rational, particularly in its focus on budgeting and management, the Caldwell and Spinks model appears as a buffer to the chaos and crisis manifest in the sphere of education. The concomitant emphasis on standardized documents may perhaps not promote account-ability per se but, rather, be necessary as a symbol of order, proving by their very existence that the state is still steering. Schools are 'under control'.

The irony is that having used the rhetoric of local decision-making, improved management and parental control of schooling to take educational matters largely out of central hands, governments and central bureaucracies may have 'exported the crisis', as Watkins suggests in this volume (see Chapter 8), a solution which cannot be used twice. If we follow the British, New Zealand or New South Wales approach, as appears likely, there will be no public education system left to steer. It is this paradox which may make the spaces for school communities themselves to develop networks, share knowledge and develop educative organizational strategies without centralized steering. Unfortunately, there will be few resources to assist with networking and other forms of activism.

In discussing the possibilities once made available through the School Improvement Plan, I do not wish to argue that its experience was without problems. A number of schools treated participatory evaluation as an event through which existing power relations were further entrenched; or participation as an end in itself, with little interest in educational outcomes. The central concept of partnership between schools and between schools and central administration reached only early stages. However, I have used it in this chapter as a way to point out that there are possible ways of approaching school level change that might engage in new futures, without being trapped in the 'island school' that is the necessary consequence of managerial foci masquerading as local decision-making or educational leadership.

SIP did not last in Victoria, although the first few years received enormous support from many school communities and from others in the educational bureaucracy. It also had its problems, though I believe that these were being worked out through interaction among schools and within the bureaucracy. However, corporate managerial approaches to restructuring major departments, characterized by the 'devolution' catchcry, spelled the end for official support for the school improvement initiative by the end of 1986. The existence of an alternative approach to school management that suited the devolutionary push gave added impetus to the use of the Caldwell and Spinks model. Their emphasis, despite many of its practical contributions to conceptualizing the organizational demands of a complex educational organization, reaches its logical consequence in deeming each school an 'island'. The 'divide and conquer' result of devolutionary policies has not yet reached its apogee in Victoria, but the main requirements and processes are in place.

They are still counterbalanced, however, by a history of practice that values the public education system and the connections it brings with others (schools, parents, teachers, students) who attempt to move beyond localism. In Victoria, although the older connections between teacher unions and parent groups have been fragmented with conflict in recent years, opposition to further dismantling of the public education system may yet result in closer activity once again. It is yet to be seen whether the influence of the problems in British and New Zealand education can be used fruitfully in the fight against their replication here.

Notes

1 There were, of course, many other arguments about program budgeting as a management tool. For example, in the program categories chosen for the Department, many activities logically fitted under at least two categories, making it difficult to plan and even more difficult to report on priorities. A more extended discussion of the problems of steering reform of bureaucracy using corporate management techniques such as this is beyond the scope of this chapter.
2 I use the term 'participatory evaluation' to distinguish this form from those characterized by MacDonald (1973) as bureaucratic, autocratic or democratic.

References

BRENNAN, MARIE (1986) 'Shifts in Control', *Working Papers in the Theory and Practice of Educational Administration*, Geelong, Deakin University.

BRENNAN, MARIE (1992) 'School Improvement-Again: A Tale Worth Retelling', *Unicorn* 18, 2, pp. 25–9.

BRENNAN, MARIE and HOADLEY, RUTH (1984) *School Self-Evaluation*, Melbourne, Victorian Government Printer.

Marie Brennan

CALDWELL, B. and SPINKS, J. (1986) *Policy-Making and Planning for School Effectiveness*, Hobart, Tasmanian Department of Education.

CONNELL, R.W., WHITE, V.M. and JOHNSTON, K.M. (1991) *Running Twice as Hard: The Disadvantaged Schools Program in Australia*, Geelong, Deakin University Press.

CUMMING, JAMES (1986) *Evaluating Your Own School: A Guide to Action*, Melbourne, Victorian Institute of Secondary Education.

MACDONALD, BARRY (1973) 'Evaluation and the Control of Education', in E. House (Ed.), *School Evaluation: Politics and Process*, Berkeley, Calif., McCutcheon.

Ministerial Paper 2 (1982) *The School Improvement Plan*, Melbourne, Victorian Government Printer.

SUCHMAN, LUCY A. (1987) *Plans and Situated Actions: The Problem of Human-Machine Communication*, Cambridge, Cambridge University Press.

VICTORIA, DEPARTMENT OF EDUCATION (1983) *School Level Program Budgeting: Strategy for Implementation*, Melbourne, Policy and Planning Unit.

VICTORIA, DEPARTMENT OF EDUCATION (1984) *Program Budgeting at School Level: Resource Booklet*, Melbourne, Policy and Planning Unit.

VICTORIA, DEPARTMENT OF MANAGEMENT AND BUDGET (1983) *Program Budget 1983–4: Overview Volume*, Melbourne, Victorian Government Printer.

6 The Evaluative State and Self-Management in Education: Cause for Reflection?

David Hartley

During the 1980s Western industrial societies have had to weather deep recession. Their governments have since come to two realizations: first, that the amount available to the welfare state as a percentage of GNP has had to be reduced (with all the attendant limitation of services and expectations which this entails); and second, that whatever the reduction in provision, it cannot simply be dictated from on high. It has to be managed with great tact, and in such a way that those affected by it come to be complicit in the very decisions which may ill serve them. These two realizations accord with what critical theorists refer to as a crisis of accumulation and a crisis of legitimation (O'Connor, 1973). When industry is in recession, less able to turn a profit, to accumulate wealth, it spawns many social problems, among them unemployment and the despair which attends it. Moreover, a market which contains many unemployed people is a market whose power to consume goods and services is weakened. The crisis of accumulation feeds on itself. Recession ensues. Those adversely affected expect the state to provide for them in their time of need, and if this expectation is not met, then they will come increasingly to question the legitimacy of the system. Meanwhile, those employed within the welfare state — teachers, health care professionals — face a contraction of their resources at the very time when they need them most. The state comes to be faced with a crisis of motivation within its welfare agencies. It appears now to have realized that overtly bureaucratic or administrative solutions are unlikely to succeed, and may indeed exacerbate the very problems which they purport to solve.[1] In addition to this need to strike a balance between accumulation and legitimation, modern capitalist society is marked by what Bell calls cultural contradictions. He argues that the three realms of capitalist society — the economy, the polity and the culture — are ruled by contrary principles. That is, for the economy it is efficiency; for the polity it is equality; and for the culture it is self-gratification

(Bell, 1979, pp. xxx–xxxi). In particular, the tension is between, on the one hand, efficiency, bureaucracy and the Protestant values of frugality, deferred gratification and asceticism and, on the other hand, a hedonism and narcissism which is continuously fueled by the advertising media. Deferred gratification is contrary to immediate gratification; bureaucracies marked by roles and specialism do not sit easily with a culture which seeks the self-fulfilment of the individual and which emphasizes the centrality of the 'whole' person (Bell, 1979, p. 14).

The stages of the argument hare are as follows. First, I shall consider the concept of the evaluative state (Neave, 1988), noting how, at one and the same time, the state seeks to direct policy, while appearing not to do so. In passing, I shall suggest that the emergence of the evaluative state itself marks an attempt to cope with an increasing motivation crisis within education. The state purports to achieve this through appeals to notions of choice, 'ownership' and self-management. In the second part of the analysis I examine, with reference mainly to Scotland, the notion of self-management at the level of the pupil, the teacher and the school, taking each in turn. I have defined each of these three levels because it is important to examine the concept of self-management at all three levels, each in relationship with the other.

So far as eliciting the consent of *pupils* is concerned, the 'best practice' is said to accord with the principles of progressive, learner-centred pedagogy. In this respect, I will suggest that, in the early 1980s, when youth unemployment was spiralling, the government intervened to head off what was perceived as a growing legitimation and motivation crisis. It did so through appeals to a learner-centred pedagogy, one aired first in the English Newsom Report (1963), and later developed in TVEI and the Scottish Action Plan (SED, 1983). To these have been added recently the Compacts Initiative, a Training Agency-sponsored endeavour which not only draws on learner-centred discourse, but which also inserts an even more utilitarian purpose, namely that of offering a 'guaranteed' job, or training leading to a job, to pupils who meet their 'targets'. Thereafter, I will consider corresponding procedures which are being put in place to manage the compliance of *teachers*, particularly those whose motivation and commitment are perceived as flagging. The state is set on remotivating them, giving them a sense of ownership of their professional development, catering to their needs. This begins with a process of self-assessment, of reflection. But this process of reflection is itself to be cast within the mould of a state-structured appraisal system. Nevertheless, the results of this self-reflection must, at the end of the day, mirror the state's own image of what shall constitute 'good practice'. If the teacher's performance is appraised as being sufficiently meritorious, then 'merit pay' will ensue.

I argue that the rhetoric of learner-centred education and reflective pedagogy have much in common. Both incorporate a liberal democratic discourse, with notions of freedom, needs, individual discretion, 'ownership' and self-management all well to the fore. Both attract quite different interpretations, ranging from the conservative to the radical. Finally, at the level of the self-managing *school*, it has to be said that Scotland has only in 1992 seen the first suggestions by the Scottish Office Education Department (SOED) for self-managing schools, these being contained in its consultation paper, *School Management: The Way Ahead* (SOED, 1992). In sum, the state has begun to 'enlist' the discourse of both 'active learning' and the reflective teacher movement to control both the cost and the outputs of pupils, teachers and institutions. In doing so, the state retains a 'ringmaster' function, setting, overseeing and 'rewarding' performance, but giving pupils, teachers and schools the opportunity of 'minding their own business'. The organizing concept which informs the analysis is that of the evaluative state.

The Evaluative State

The year 1991 marked the bicentennial of the publication of Bentham's *Panopticon*, a proposal for an architecture which would be so all-seeing that inmates would not know if they were being overseen or overheard. They therefore had to assume that they were. The *Panopticon*, though never built, marked a profound shift in the technology of social control away from external direction towards internal self-monitoring. Bentham's main educational work, *Chrestomathia*, published in 1816, sets out no fewer than thirty-eight 'principles of school management', all of them based on the assumptions of hierarchical observation, normalizing judgments and the examination.[2] In both schools and factories in the nineteenth century, Bentham's maxims of management held sway, culminating in the scientific management theories of F.W. Taylor in the first two decades of this century. During the twentieth century — particularly during the late 1920s — the more rigid regime of Taylorist management had been 'loosened' according to the principles of human relations management theory. This meant that there was an increasing reluctance on the part of managers to be openly directive. Compliance was now structured, tacitly, so that the worker exercised self-control, and appeared to be afforded a good deal of individual discretion.

This managerial style had its risks. The discretion which the worker exercised could, in theory, have led to a set of ends and means which were at odds with those of managers. It therefore had to be managed, but not obviously, not directly. There was another risk: during periods of economic downturn, 'harsh decisions', as the phrase goes, 'have to be taken'. The chances of tacitly managing the workers' acquiescence in these decisions often become decidedly slim, particularly if they lead to a reduction in their pay and privileges. In these cases management may have to resort finally to the use of directives.

The evaluative state is seen as an alternative to regulation by bureaucratic fiat (Neave, 1988, p. 11). Although Neave has analyzed policy on higher education using the concept of the evaluative state, it has wider application. It may be typified as follows. First, it focuses on product, not process. That is, it appears to devolve to institutions the discretion to decide on matters of institutional process and implementation, and saves its gaze for a scrutiny of the products which constitute the outcome of the process; more to the point, it makes a reward — be it a job, credential, merit pay or institutional funding — contingent upon the performance matching the criteria stated in the targets. The broad parameters are set by the state; the decisions on how to achieve them are now within the 'ownership' of individuals and their institutions. Increasingly funds will follow the achievement of targets, this achievement being measured through purportedly objective performance indicators. (This is known as 'output financing' in which 'input and throughput become the responsibility of the service provider and the Government allocates funds based on conditions which are related to the "outgoing flow of value"' (Witzel, 1991, p. 44).) But this 'ownership' and self-management do not mean control, only the appearance of control. The evaluative state devolves tactics, but retains strategy. It can therefore exonerate itself when its services (in, say, health and education) are not delivered satisfactorily; and it can rise above the conflicts which develop at the institutional level over implementation.

The Self-Managing Pupil

During the 1980s policy initiatives were introduced to enhance the motivation of young people, particularly those of low educational achievement. The rhetoric of these initiatives seemed to accord with that found in the progressive education movement of the mid-1960s. The 1980s' term, 'learner-centred', replaced the 1960s' label of 'child-centred'. The meanings of these two sets of vocabulary, however, are different. In the 1960s the justification for the child-centred education movement drew upon Piagetian developmental psychology, the romantic individualism of Rousseau and the emerging prominence of social phenomenology and symbolic interactionism. This justification did not turn on economic considerations. In contrast, the 1980s witnessed recession, high unemployment and a concerted effort to replace the romantic individualism of Rousseau with the competitive individualism of Thatcherism (Hartley, 1987). Yet the policies of the 1980s retained the same progressive discourse, thereby giving them an appeal even for those who did not find the new vocationalism to their taste. The focus in the 1960s on the 'individual' is not, however, wholly at one with the focus in the 1980s on the 'self'. Young people in the 1980s were expected to *reflect* on themselves, as a necessary stage in the journey to 'self-awareness' and to 'autonomy'. They recorded their own personal achievements, and they made explicit their personality profiles to themselves and to others. The 'ownership' and 'responsibility for' learning were theirs, not the teachers'. They were said to have a stake.

The interpretation of this learner-centred pedagogy has been mixed. (See, for example, Bates and Rowland, 1988; Broadfoot, 1991, pp. 252–3.) On the one hand, Rowland advocates student-centred learning because it gives learners a larger degree of control over their own learning, a necessity if one assumes, as he does, that the learning process is 'constructive': that is, the learner assigns meaning to experience rather than passively receives it. On the other hand, Fritzell's (1987) concept of 'negative correspondence' argues that the emphasis on 'expressive competencies' and 'self-realisation' gives the appearance of autonomy, but serves merely as a new mode of control. It is a matter, therefore, of radical pedagogy for conservative schooling. As mentioned, there are arguments that this constructivist theory of learning may have critical possibilities, not just of the self, but also of the system. For the latter to occur, however, radical pedagogy would have to transmit a radical curriculum. But this is hardly possible when the performance indicators and learning criteria are framed by central government, as is the case, for example, under the 16+ National Certificate in Scotland. To a small degree, therefore, it is a risky pedagogy for the state to endorse: while it is *pedagogically* radical, it is also possibly *politically* radical. To date, this risk has been seen as worth running, for this pedagogy gives few reasons for students to reject it, particularly if the mode of assessment is not demanding, and if the curriculum can be packaged in small, easily consumed modules. To return to the old didacticism would be a difficult U-turn to take. The risk, however, now seems set to be further minimized under the Compacts Initiative program, to which we now turn.

The Compacts Initiative has all the hallmarks of the evaluative state. It derives from a scheme initiated in Boston, but forms part of a wider partnership-in-education movement in the United States, where 70 per cent of schools reportedly have some form of 'education business partnership' (Employment Department, 1991c, p. 9).[3] In the USA the impetus for partnerships or compacts is reportedly in response to a crisis which derives partly from a 'national sense of youth at risk' from drugs, family breakdown, crime and high dropout rates from school, and partly from a 'sense of a nation at risk in economic terms' (Kirby, 1990, p. 3). Following a study visit to the USA, sponsored largely by the Training Agency, suggestions for establishing Compacts in Britain were drawn up (Kirby, 1990).

In general, the designation of Compacts schools has turned initially on whether or not they are in areas of social deprivation, and in this respect the scheme can be said to have egalitarian underpinnings. The initial focus has been on the secondary school, but it has been recommended that 'pupil participation should extend widely below age 14 — primary schools should be included' (Kirby, 1990, p. 5). Indeed, there currently exists a pilot Compact in a primary school in Hartlepool, York-shire. At the other extreme, adult Compacts were piloted in 1991 (Further Education Unit, 1991).

At the root of the Compacts Initiative is an undertaking by the pupil to set his or her own targets in relation to certain goals. This constitutes a pupil's action plan, one witnessed formally by both the pupil's parent and guidance teacher. These targets are arrived at on the basis of the pupil having completed a self-assessment questionnaire whose categories include attendance, time-keeping, behaviour, effort, homework, general attitude to school, cooperation, rules, work and work-related experience, and out-of-school activities. The pupil and the guidance teacher then discuss the self-assessment in order to set targets. In return, a group of employers guarantees to provide further training and/or jobs for those who achieve their goals. It is stressed that these goals and others 'will be negotiated, and will be individual and relevant to them.' While it is true that the pupil has 'ownership' of his or her targets, these are themselves set within categories *not* of their making. Indeed, the pupil is left in no doubt what is expected:

> **A COMPACT PUPIL**: works hard and is keen to learn; listens to staff; behaves well in all classes; does not waste time or distract others; returns homework on time; is well-mannered and co-operative; is honest; treats school property with respect; is a good attender and timekeeper; takes pride in his/her appearance and dresses according to school guidelines; takes pride in his/her work; is determined to get the most out of the school. (Extract from documentation from an urban comprehensive school in Scotland)

One conclusion to draw from this is that the Employment Depart-ment is 'buying into' the hidden curriculum, not, as was the case with TVEI, seeking to influence the formal curriculum as well. This may have something to do with the Employment Department's (1991c) report, expressed in its publication *Into Work*, that a large number of employers felt that young people were still not well equipped for the world of work once they had left school (Employment Department, 1991b, p. 8). Even those who had followed the TVEI program were thought by employers only to have been better prepared for the job application. TVEI did not, in their view, add much to their ability to do the job itself (Employment Department, 1991b, p. 33). Citing the Boston Compacts, Orrock (1991, p. 3) noted that neither 'employers nor educationalists felt that the cur-riculum was at fault; *the problem was perceived in terms of the need to increase the motivation of young people and so reduce the drop-out rate*' (emphasis added). Of course, the pupil is not compelled to 'opt in' to a Compact, but when the structure of the local economy does not promise a future job, then the onus is very much on the pupil to do so. Even so, while employers guarantee a 'job with training, or training leading to a job', this is in no sense a legally binding contract: it is but a good intention on the employer's part.[4] The discourse of learner-centred education has therefore been grafted on to what is clearly a narrowly utilitarian initiative, the Compacts Initiative. Even so, the expected academic benefits of Compacts have not yet been met. Recent evidence from the Boston Compacts program notes: '[. . .] our study of the effects of the Compacts efforts on the seven schools reviewed here reveals no noticeable correlation between business efforts and monies and overall improvement of student performance or school programs' (Farrar and Connolly, 1991, p. 27). In its own review of Compacts in America, the Training Agency noted that employers 'refused to re-sign at the end of the [Boston] Compacts's first phase' (Kirby, 1990, p. 5). While this is seen as a setback, it is not seen as the end of the matter: a second Boston Compact is under negotiation. Moreover, in its justification of the need for adult Compacts, the English Further Education Unit (FEU) glossed over these difficulties: 'The *apparent* success of the Boston Compacts [. . .] and the growth of school Compacts in a number of English cities, have resulted in growing interest in the feasibility of transferring the model to the adult sector' (FEU, 1991, p. 2; emphasis added). Indeed, the faith placed in Compacts in the face of contradictory American evidence is considerable. Orrock (1991, pp. 4, 6) notes that there is no incontrovertible evidence that the school Compacts have had a positive effect on young people. Yet he is ready to note the apparent success of the Boston Compacts.

The Compacts Initiative may usefully be interpreted against what Daniel Bell (1979) referred to as one of the cultural contradictions of capitalism. As stated earlier, he argues that the twentieth century has seen a steady weakening of the Puritan temper and the Protestant ethic. That is, the traditional values of deferred gratification, frugality and asceticism are in increasing contradiction with the emergent values of hedonism, narcissism and immediate gratification. The former are the requisites for *production* whereas the latter are needed for *consumption*; and whereas some of the former are transmitted through the high school, the latter are transmitted through the non-print media. Most individuals expect to be both producers and consumers, and their actions must express both sets of values. This is not easy to achieve. Evidence, both from large-scale American studies of high schools (Goodlad, 1984) and from small-scale ethnographic studies (McNeil, 1986), reveals schools which are highly bureaucratic and alienating for students. While middle-class students tend to adopt a position of deferred calculative involvement as a response to bureaucratic strictures, many minority students either drop out or reject the guidance counsellor's justificatory rhetoric for good behaviour. The drop out cannot pay for a life of continuous self-indulgence which advertisers say they need. In an age of ownership they own virtually nothing. They are without the means to prevent themselves from feeling demeaned.

Both learner-centred pedagogy and Compacts purport to rectify this acute social problem by defining it in terms of an individual personality matter, for this pedagogy speaks to self-esteem, to autonomy, to self-assessment and reflection, to having a sense of ownership of one's own life and learning, to being emancipated. Even if you cannot own goods, so the argument runs, at least you own yourself. In all this, however, young people are being asked to make an act of faith in believing that the lack of work or money does not diminish their dignity. What the Compacts Initiative purports to do, however, is to add hope to faith, for, at the end of day, the student who meets targets will be led to think that there is a guaranteed pay-off, a job; and throughout, the student will crucially have had a sense of ownership of his or her action plan. In a limited way the Compacts Initiative tries to reconcile both deferred and immediate gratification, direction and individual discretion. It seeks to revive the traditional work ethic in pupils without having to resort to the very pedagogy which traditionally produced it, namely a didactic pedagogy. Under Compacts, the pupil manages his or her own compliance, but this compliance is coldly calculative, not morally normative.

The Self-Managing Teacher

The concept of the reflective practitioner is now part of the commonsense discourse of teachers and teacher educators. In this respect it is on a par with the concept of student-centred learning. Indeed, both the constructivist approach to student-centred learning and Schon's conceptualization of the reflective practitioner have strong intellectual debts to pay to the social phenomenology of Schutz (1967) and to the symbolic interactionism of Berger and Luckmann (1966). But while the rhetoric of both is everywhere to be heard, their manifestation in practice is less common. There is a sense, too, in which both have become metaphors devoid of a context, and which admit many kinds of meanings. Just as active learning approaches to teaching young people have been regarded variously as conservative or as holding out the potential for radical change, so also has reflective pedagogy attracted similar analyses (Zeichner and Liston, 1987; Adler, 1991; Hartley, 1991a). For example, on the one hand, reflective pedagogy can focus only on narrow technical means, the ends of education remaining beyond the gaze of the teacher's reflection. The teachers reflect only on themselves, not on the structures of which they are a part. On the other hand, this process of rendering explicit what is for the most part a taken-for-granted practice can serve as a basis for a critical analysis of the moral and political ends of that practice, and this itself may provide a necessary endeavour prior to political change. In other words, both the active learner and the reflective practitioner have the capacity for either conservative or for radical action. I have argued above that, in the case of the Compacts

Initiative, policy-makers have sought to turn the hidden curriculum towards both utilitarian and moral ends. In so doing, they seek to elicit the compliance of the pupils by appeals to notions of self-assessment and ownership. A similar strategy now besets teachers. That is, the government has appeared to appropriate the discourse of reflective pedagogy (Hartley, 1991b, 1992; Smyth, 1991) and to have grafted onto it a justification for teacher appraisal, leading to another type of 'output financing', namely merit pay. I develop this point below with reference to Scotland.

In 1984 in Scotland the National Committee for the In-Service Training of Teachers (NCITT), a government advisory committee, introduced the idea of teacher appraisal. It did so as a way of identifying the professional development needs of teachers. It detached itself from the view that appraisal be linked to pay and promotion. The declared intention, therefore, was professional, not managerial: 'Staff development, as we have defined it, starts from the identification of individual needs. The process of identifying the needs of individual teachers is concerned with helping teachers who are basically competent to develop that competence further. *This process must be clearly distinguished from the appraisal of staff for other purposes such as promotion*' (NCITT, 1984, para. 5.5.4; emphasis added). At the time the NCITT confessed to little knowledge about how appraisal should be undertaken. Two years later, in the wake of a long and embittered dispute between Scotland's teachers and the Scottish Education Department (SED), the government's advisory committee on the pay and conditions of teachers (the Main Committee) gave further advice. It raised the issue of appraisal again, but cautiously: 'What reservations teachers have [about appraisal] appear to be concerned with the possibility of a direct link between their performance and pay (other than by promotion) through some form of merit pay; and with concern that the employers' real objective is to facilitate the dismissal of unsatisfactory teachers. We do not see any grounds for either concern' (Main, 1986, paras 6.13, 6.14). It went on to assert that: 'We would wish to see a major element of self-appraisal and assessment, so that the teacher is enabled to contribute to his assessment' (Main, 1986, para. 6.15).

This caution, however, was thrown to the wind when, in 1989, the SED issued its consultation paper, *School Teachers' Professional Development into the 1990s* (SED, 1989). Appraisal was placed at the core of the government's staff development program. National guidelines were to be established, and all schemes had to receive the sanction of the Secretary of State for Scotland. All this was given legal force in clause 64 of The Self-Governing Schools etc. (Scotland) Act. A line management model of appraisal was envisaged. The Secretary of State did not believe that arrangements which relied upon self-appraisal as their sole or dominant feature would be adequate (SED, 1989, para. 25). Needless to say, neither the General Teaching Council for Scotland (GTC) nor Scotland's largest teacher's union, the Educational Institute of Scotland (EIS), gave their firm support to what was seen as an unduly heavy-handed stance by the SED (EIS, 1990; GTC, 1989). Even the SED's own advisory committee on professional development warned of the 'threatening' tenor of the consultation paper (Scottish Committee for Staff Development in Education, 1989, para. 13).

Eventually the government paid heed. It changed its rhetoric. Teachers thereafter would be given a 'sense of ownership' of the appraisal process. But this was admitted to be no more than a managerial device. For example, in its draft guidelines for teacher appraisal, the SED noted: 'The style of management adopted for dealing with staff development and appraisal is critical. While the ultimate responsibility rests with management, school staff should participate in designing the arrangements so as to develop a sense of ownership. This is important for effective implementation.' When the final version of the national guidelines was published in January 1991, this 'sense of ownership' was replaced by 'an *appropriate* sense of "ownership"' (SED, 1991a, para. 24; emphasis added). The term 'appropriate' is not explained, nor is the reason why the word 'ownership' is set in quotation marks. The same document reaffirms (para. 2.15) that appraisal should not replace existing procedures either for promotion or for dealing with unsatisfactory performance, but would nevertheless 'make an important contribution to these procedures'.

Reflection and self-appraisal by the teacher were to be a preparation for the appraisal interview. An evaluation of past performance, a statement of future targets and a plan of future staff development activities were all to be made, recorded and signed by appraiser and appraisee. So far all this accords with the procedures to be followed by pupils in the Compacts Initiative: reflection on past performance; self-assessment; targets; self-management of an action plan; a sense of appropriate 'ownership'. What was missing, however, was what Witzel terms 'output financing', or, here, merit pay. This omission was shortly to be rectified, for in its *Parents' Charter in Scotland*, published in September 1991, the government asserted: 'The Government believes that the pay of teachers should reward them for good performance and for high skills. It wants to see more flexible arrangements in place to recognise the services and merits of individual teachers' (Scottish Office Education Department, 1991b, p. 12). In sum, the strategy of the evaluative state becomes clearer: in the case of the pupils in a Compacts school the 'output' is defined in terms of, and measured according to, government-sponsored specifications; in the case of the teachers the 'output' is defined in terms of national guidelines, again specified by government. In both, the 'ownership' of the effort which will generate the output is indeed the pupil's or the teacher's. As to the financing, for the Compacts pupil it is a 'guarantee' of a job; for the teacher it is performance-related pay. Moreover, the Scottish Office Education Department (SOED) in late 1991 appeared to distance itself from compulsory appraisal (Munro, 1991). This again is consonant with the Compacts

Initiative. There the pupil could 'opt in'; now it seems that the teacher can also 'opt in' for appraisal. But if neither the pupil nor the teacher chooses to opt in, then the pupil cannot be assured of a job, and the teacher cannot claim merit pay because his or her performance will not have been appraised. It is useful to recall Weber's prescient prophecy: 'The mighty cosmos of the modern economic order . . . the iron cage [in which] specialists without heart [are] caught in the delusion that [they] have achieved a level of development never before attained by mankind' (Weber, 1948, p. 182). However, the cage is no longer made of iron: cold, hard rationality has given way to a reflective therapy. The hard cell has been replaced by the soft sell. As with pupils and teachers, so with schools, to which we now turn.

The Self-Managing School

In Scotland school choice legislation dates from the 1981 Education (Scotland) Act. Under the Act — the so-called *Parents' Charter* — some 109,000 pupils had, by July 1987, been placed in state schools of their parents' choice. The Act also established the Assisted Places Scheme, the aim of which was to widen the range of educational opportunity for children whose parents would not normally be able to afford the cost of tuition in independent schools (Scottish Office, 1992).[5] The government's quest to empower the consumer took a further step with the 1988 School Boards Act which established a system of school boards on which parents would be in the majority. The powers of school boards were enhanced when, in 1989, The Self-Governing Schools etc. (Scotland) Act permitted them to apply to the Secretary of State to take their schools out of local authority control, or to 'opt-out', and to achieve 'self-governing' status (SGS), the equivalent to what is known in England as grant maintained status (GMS). By May 1992 in England and Wales only about 230 schools had opted out, but in Scotland none had done so, though one, London Street primary school in Edinburgh, had applied to do so, its request being refused on the grounds that it was applying to opt out simply to avoid closure.

In its quest to develop SGS schools, the SOED now appears to have admitted to a setback; and this is in spite of its wide dissemination of the publication, *How to Become a Self-Governing School* (SOED, 1990). It has now made a tactical withdrawal. That is, it is about to establish in Scotland the equivalent of local management of schools (LMS). In this respect, therefore, Scotland is well behind England and Wales.[6] Its reasoning appears to be that schools must have experience of managing their own budgets before they will have the confidence to opt out of local authority control. In its consultation paper, *School Management: The Way Ahead* (SOED, 1992), the government sets out, in a very general manner, its position on self-managing schools. Ironically, it cites the Labour-controlled Strathclyde Region's model of devolved management of resources (DMR) as a basis for its proposals (para. 1.5) and indicates a number of benefits, among them being 'the ability of each school to determine what its needs are and to act on these much more quickly'. It argues that there will be 'reduced bureaucracy' and 'savings in central administration costs at authority level for the benefit of direct expenditure on schools' (para. 2.2).

Strathclyde's DMR differs, however, in a number of important respects from LMS in England: whereas under LMS the budget is delegated to school governors, under DMR it is delegated to headteachers; whereas under LMS 75 per cent of the budget is generated from pupil enrolment, weighted by age, under DMR there is no fixed adherence to a formula based on pupil rolls; whereas under LMS schools must pay actual salaries from budgets based on average costs, DMR is based on the average regional salary; whereas under LMS promoted staff costs must be paid from formula-driven budgets, there is a separate provision to pay for promoted teachers; and whereas fuel costs under LMS are again based on a fixed formula, under DMR these costs are mainly based on actual consumption, with safeguards for emergencies (Henderson, 1992). Unlike the Strathclyde model, the SOED's position suggests a budget which is driven by a formula based on pupil numbers (para. 3.5), similar to that of the LMS scheme in England. An implementation date of 1995–96 is stated.

The SOED's proposals underline the concept of delegation to the school, personified by the headteacher, who will become more visibly accountable for its achievements (para. 2.5), these being measurable by performance indicators known as 'Relative Ratings and National Comparison Factors'. With all of this comes formula driven, output financing, and a convenient scapegoat — the headteacher — should the attainment and popularity levels of the school wane. By focusing on the delegation of *spending* to the headteacher, the government is able to avoid questions about the overall *funding* of the education service as a percentage of GNP. The headteacher must now, literally, do the government's bidding, knowing that strategic decisions about curriculum, assessment and the available resources still remain with the state.

To summarize: in its pursuit of the market model of education, the government's strategy has taken a clear course: first, to allow for choice *within* local authority managed schools (the 1981 *Parents' Charter*) and *between* these schools and the independent schools (the Assisted Places Scheme); second, to devolve to schools the control over their budgets (LMS in England; a DMR variant in Scotland); third, to 'enable' schools to 'opt out' of local authority control, and to be thereafter funded directly by central government (GMS in England and Wales; SGS in Scotland). In the scheme of these things England is further ahead than Scotland, where the appeal of Thatcherism is rather weak, to say the least. For the moment the SOED will tread softly, focusing on giving schools the confidence to manage their budgets, and only then to move them on to self-governing status.

Conclusion

Informed by the concept of the evaluative state, I have analyzed some emerging changes in education policy, drawing examples mainly from Scotland. Central to this policy is an intention to retain a liberal democratic discourse, one that emphasizes self-management, independent action and a degree of individual freedom or choice. But all this has been set to serve utilitarian ends which are not necessarily those of pupils, teachers or schools. They are the ends of the state. So far as pupils are concerned, with reference to the Compacts Initiative, the ends are economic (to meet a skills and manpower crisis) and moral (to prevent the erosion of the work ethic). As to teachers, the ends are also economic (to reduce the percentage of GNP spending on education, and to ensure that what *is* spent is within the specification of the state, not of the teaching profession) and managerial (to try to remotivate a profession whose esteem and resources have been diminished). Finally, proposals for self-managing schools are set to serve as a stepping stone to the full opting out of local authority control, all this providing choice for parents and self-management for schools. Once all that is achieved, then Chubb and Moe's (1987) call for a market in education will be heeded by the introduction of some form of voucher system, thereby forging a link between the citizen and the state, bypassing local government in the process. This emerging policy combines a subtle mix of discretion and direction, of autonomy and control, of progressivism and didacticism, of egalitarianism and vocationalism.

But will it succeed? In the short run it may be speculated that the discourse of self-management will prove attractive. The risk to the policy will be that the state is unable, or unwilling, to 'finance the output', be it in the form of a guaranteed job for the pupil, performance pay for the teacher or adequate funding for the school. The government is not unaware of this. For example, it notes 'the danger that compact graduates who do not find employment with the associated employer will sense failure and become demoralised' (FEU, 1991, p. 4). The fiscal overload for the state brought about by the increasing costs of monitoring may be such that it will be unable to meet its 'guarantees'. Any psychic payoff for pupils, teachers or schools which they derive from owning their own action plans, or from reflecting on and assessing their own needs, may quickly dissipate if quality is rewarded with no more than government calls for yet further reflection on personal performance and on organizational restructuring. Reflection and self-management may initially be therapeutic — and are intended to be so — but the image which they generate for pupils, teachers and schools could quickly become tarnished if the state fails to keep its side of the 'bargain'.

David Hartley

Within schools there will be an ever-increasing division between those who control files and finance, on the one hand, and those who educate, on the other. The former will work to stave off the financial bankruptcy of the school, while the latter toil to keep it educationally solvent. Freire's 'banking concept' will come to have an entirely new meaning. But these micropolitical divisions will be as nothing compared to the inter-school divisions that will ensue. Caught in the crossfire will be the children, especially those unfortunate enough to be born to poorer parents. But way above the fray the market-makers and their mandarins — honest brokers to a man — will monitor the movement of some kind of *Times Educational Index*, checking the balance sheets and accounts, downgrading one school's 'stock market' rating, taking out options on another and sadly closing their position on others. All this constitutes a financial audit. But what of the moral audit? It is not sufficient merely to invoke the democratic principle of liberty, or the freedom to choose, as a moral justification of these policies. When the pursuit of liberty — individual liberty — proceeds beyond the point when the public good is served, then the whole democratic basis of 'choice' education policy will be cast into doubt. Perhaps the academic standards of some children will be enhanced, but the overall academic standard of all our children is set to fall. The public good will not be served when inner-city children are left to languish in 'sink' schools, schools which are not of their making. For these children, it is chance, not choice, which will determine their educational fate. But at the end of the day the government may still claim to be able to exonerate itself, for it will surely suggest that all of these arrangements to do with self-management (at whatever level: pupil, teacher, school) are *optional*: if they are not taken up, then that is a matter for the pupil, the teacher or the school. Therein lies the 'choice'; therein lies liberty.

Notes

1 See, for example, Linda M. McNeil's (1986) ethnographic account of how the teaching of social studies in the United States comes to be caught between competing administrative and academic cultures within a school.
2 For a discussion, see Miller (1988) and Pitkin (1990).
3 The figures seem unreliable: in 1990 the Training Agency reported that America has 148,800 Partnerships involving 40 per cent of the nation's schools (Kirby, 1990, p. 3).
4 Under the Adult Compacts program (FEU, 1991), it notes, 'a contract is inappropriate but Statements of Intent . . . are a helpful way of formalising the agreement.'
5 For an analysis of the effects of the *Parents' Charter*, see Adler and Raab (1988). For a discussion of the Assisted Places Scheme in Scotland, England and Wales, see Walford (1988).
6 By 1 April 1992 all education authorities in England and Wales were expected

to have introduced local management of schools (LMS) schemes, as directed under section 36 of the 1988 Education Reform Act.

References

ADLER, M. and RAAB, G.M. (1988) 'Exit, Choice and Loyalty: The Impact of Parental Choice on Admissions to Secondary Schools in Edinburgh and Dundee', *Journal of Education Policy*, 3, pp. 155–79.

ADLER, S. (1991) 'The Reflective Practitioner and the Curriculum of Teacher Education', *Journal of Education for Teaching*, 17, pp. 139–50.

BATES, I. and ROWLAND, S. (1988) 'Is Student-centred Pedagogy "Progressive" Educational Practice?' *Journal of Further and Higher Education*, 12, pp. 5–20.

BELL, D. (1979) *The Cultural Contradictions of Capitalism*, New York, Basic Books.

BERGER, P. and LUCKMANN, T. (1966) *The Social Construction of Reality*, Harmondsworth, Penguin.

BROADFOOT, P. (1991) 'Review of S.J. Ball *Politics and Policy Making in Education: Explorations in Policy Sociology*', *British Journal of Sociology of Education*, 12, pp. 250–4.

CHUBB, J.E. and MOE, T.M. (1987) 'No School Is an Island: Politics, Markets and Education', *Journal of Education Policy*, 2, pp. 117–30.

EDUCATIONAL INSTITUTE OF SCOTLAND (1990) *EIS Response to Draft National Guidelines on Staff Development and Appraisal in Schools*, Edinburgh, EIS.

EMPLOYMENT DEPARTMENT (1991a) *Partnerships in America 1990: A Radical Agenda*, Sheffield, Employment Department.

EMPLOYMENT DEPARTMENT (1991b) 'Editorial: TVEI Eases Entry to Work', *Insight*, Summer.

EMPLOYMENT DEPARTMENT (1991c) *Into Work: An Initial Study of the Recruitment and Performance of School Leavers from the First 11 Extension Programmes*, Sheffield, Employment Department.

FARRAR, E. and CONNOLLY, C. (1991) 'Improving Middle Schools in Boston: A Report on Boston Compact and School District Initiatives', *Educational Polity*, 5, pp. 4–28.

FRITZELL, C. (1987) 'On the Concept of Relative Autonomy in Educational Theory', *British Journal of Sociology of Education*, 8, pp. 23–35.

FURTHER EDUCATION UNIT (1991) *Adult Compacts*, London, Further Education Unit.

GENERAL TEACHING COUNCIL FOR SCOTLAND (1989) *School Teachers' Professional Development into the 1990s: Response*, Edinburgh, GTCS.

GOODLAD, J. (1984) *A Place Called School*, New York, McGraw Hill.

HARTLEY, D. (1987) 'The Convergence of Learner-centred Pedagogy in Primary and Further Education in Scotland: 1965–1985', *British Journal of Educational Studies*, 35, 2, pp. 115–28.

HARTLEY, D. (1991a) 'Democracy, Capitalism and the Reform of Teacher Education', *Journal of Education for Teaching*, 17, pp. 81–95.

HARTLEY, D. (1991b) 'Education Policy and the Identification of Needs', *Oxford Review of Education*, 17, pp. 103–14.

HARTLEY, D. (1992) *Teacher Appraisal: A Policy Analysis*, Edinburgh, Scottish Academic Press.

HENDERSON, D. (1992) 'The Story of DMR', *The Times Educational Supplement Scotland*, 7 March.

KIRBY, K. (1990) *Education-Business Partnerships: Lessons from America*, Sheffield, Training Agency.

MCNEIL, L.M. (1986) *Contradictions of Control: School Structure and School Knowledge*, London, Routledge.

MAIN, SIR PETER (1986) *Report into the Pay and Conditions of Service of School Teachers in Scotland (Cmnd 9893)*, Edinburgh, HMSO.

MILLER, P.J. (1988) 'Factories, Monitorial Schools and Jeremy Bentham: The Origins of the Management Syndrome in Popular Education', in A. WESTOBY (Ed.), *Culture and Power in Educational Organisations*, Milton Keynes, Open University Press.

MUNRO, N. (1991) 'EIS Gauntlet on Voluntary Appraisal', *The Times Scottish Educational Supplement*, 15 November, p. 5.

NATIONAL COMMITTEE FOR THE IN-SERVICE TRAINING OF TEACHERS (NCITT) (1984) *Arrangements for the Staff Development of Teachers*, Edinburgh, SED.

NEAVE, G. (1988) 'On the Cultivation of Quality, Efficiency and Enterprise: An Overview of Recent Trends in Higher Education in Western Europe, 1986–1988', *European Journal of Education*, 23, pp. 7–24.

O'CONNOR, J. (1973) *The Fiscal Crisis of the State*, New York, St Martin's Press.

ORROCK, N. (1991) *Adult Compacts*, Unpublished mimeograph available from the Further Education Unit, London.

PITKIN, H.F. (1990) 'Slippery Bentham: Some Neglected Cracks in the Foundation of Utilitarianism', *Political Theory*, 18, pp. 104–31.

SCHUTZ, A. (1967) *The Phenomenology of the Social World*, London, Heinemann.

SCOTTISH COMMITTEE FOR STAFF DEVELOPMENT IN EDUCATION (1989) *SED Consultation Paper: 'School Teachers' Professional Development into the 1990s' Response by SCOSDE*, Edinburgh, SED/SCOSDE.

SCOTTISH EDUCATION DEPARTMENT (1983) *16–18s in Scotland: An Action Plan*, Edinburgh, Scottish Education Department.

SCOTTISH EDUCATION DEPARTMENT (1989) *School Teachers' Professional Development into the 1990s*, Edinburgh, Scottish Education Department.

SCOTTISH OFFICE (1992) *Assisted Places Scheme: A Brief Guide for Parents*, Edinburgh, Scottish Office.

SCOTTISH OFFICE EDUCATION DEPARTMENT (1990) *How to Become a Self-Governing School: Guidance for School Boards*, Edinburgh, Scottish Office.

SCOTTISH OFFICE EDUCATION DEPARTMENT (1991a) *National Guidelines for Staff Development and Appraisal in Schools*, Edinburgh, Scottish Office Education Department.

SCOTTISH OFFICE EDUCATION DEPARTMENT (1991b) *The Parents' Charter in Scotland*, Edinburgh, SOED.

SCOTTISH OFFICE EDUCATION DEPARTMENT (1992) *School Management: The Way Ahead*, Edinburgh, SOED.

SMYTH, J. (1991) 'International Perspectives on Teacher Collegiality: A Labour Process Discussion on the Concept of Teachers' Work', *British Journal of Sociology of Education*, 12, pp. 323–46.

WALFORD, G. (1988) 'The Scottish Assisted Places Scheme: A Comparative Study of the Origins, Nature and Practice of the APSs in Scotland, England and Wales', *Journal of Education Policy*, 3, pp. 137–53.

WEBER, M. (1948) *The Protestant Ethic and the Spirit of Capitalism*, New York, Scribner's and Sons.

WITZEL, M.L. (1991) 'The Failure of an Internal Market: The Universities Funding Council Bid System', *Public Money and Management*, 11, pp. 41–7.

ZEICHNER, K. and LISTON, D.P. (1987) 'Teaching Student Teachers to Reflect', *Harvard Educational Review*, 57, pp. 1–22.

7 The Politics of Devolution, Self-Management and Post-Fordism in Schools

Susan L. Robertson

Introduction

One of the notable features of second wave devolution reforms, if we accept Max Angus's (1990) argument that the federal initiatives during the 1970s constituted the first, is how very different they were in intent and purpose. Using borrowed rhetoric from the heady days of the Schools' Commission Innovations and Priority Schools Programs,[1] and appealing to the energies of the first wave reformers, devolution the second time around had a very different agenda for Western Australian schools. While each set of reformers talked about devolution and grassroots participation in decision-making within schools, a significant feature of the second wave of reform was a severing of educational means and ends, a shift toward measured output, and a dramatic reorganizing and tightening of the accountability structures for schools. In Western Australia these turbulent developments were punctuated by the most dramatic and momentous protests and strikes in decades by school administrators, teachers and students.

The shift toward devolved structures (and 'self-managing' schools), was not unique to Western Australia. Nor were the strategies used to engineer devolution into place: in almost all cases the strategies were top-down, and emerged from a commitment by the state and other vested interests fundamentally to transform the public sector. As Max Angus observed of the period: 'The core ideas spread like an epidemic across systems and state boundaries. Labor and conservative governments are following similar courses. There are as yet no discernible differences of a party-political kind: the ideology of devolution and its expression in management are basically the same across the system' (1990, p. 4).

It is clear that the political and economic context of the 1980s and 1990s in Australia, which gave birth to the second wave of devolution reforms, has been a determining factor in the shape of self-managing schools. As I will show later, corporatist political strategies and structures, corporate managerialism, and the emergence of a virulent economic rationalist ideology have combined to provide a very different environment for schools in the last decade of this century.

Nonetheless, a zealous band of increasingly faceless bureaucrats and economic rationalist inspired politicians (Pusey, 1991) has continued to deny the charge by educators that second wave reforms are undemocratic, inequitable, anti-educational and cost-cutting. Instead, the zealots point to central ideas embedded in the reform programs' discourse — 'devolution', 'self-determination', 'collegiality' — as demonstrations of a genuine commitment to a shared and democratic educational agenda.[2]

However, initial suspicions by stakeholders such as teachers and administrators have largely given ground to growing concern that the concept of a self-managing school is little more than an illusion. Could it be that the emperor's clothing is little more than an elaborate deception? There is emerging evidence in Western Australia, as in other parts of Australia and overseas, that the shift toward school-based self-management has done little genuinely to devolve significant power to teachers, school administrators, parents or students at the school-site. Indeed, it would appear that the self-management of schools is precisely that: the capacity to 'manage' specific resources and centrally determined policy at the school site within the context of increasingly contracting state revenues.[3]

How can we understand these shifts? In this chapter I will develop a socially critical view of devolution in Western Australia, arguing that such developments can be seen both as a consequence of and central to the production of a new set of social relations in Australia. I will suggest that this shift in the accumulation regime in Australia can be viewed as post-Fordist in nature, and is paralleled by the emergence of new hegemonic strategies that structure and shape daily school life. I will then examine the nature of the 'self-managing school'. The essential contours of this emerging organizational pattern will be traced by drawing upon work in Western Australian schools. In particular, I will highlight the tensions, resistances and contradictions that face teachers, school administrators and students in these emerging self-managing schools. Finally, I want to argue that devolution reforms do provide some scope and space for a rearticulation and reclaiming of the educational agenda by educators, in what is a strategic battle for hearts and minds. In essence the worst of times have carried within them the potential to create the best as well. I will conclude by exploring possibilities for a democratic set of practices which might act as a viable alternative in the future.

The New Production Rules of Post-Fordism and Public Sector Reforms in Western Australia

Educational reform and restructuring have occupied a central place in Western Australia since the early 1980s, paralleling an escalation in public criticism of educational provision and record levels of unemployment — especially among youth (around 25 per cent). At the same time, with the tax base underpinning the state shrinking due to (1) the increasingly private nature of capital, (2) changes in the distribution of wealth, (3) the rapid outflow of profits, (4) and corporate operations moving offshore (Soucek, 1992b, pp. 3–5), the state found itself in what can only be described as an unenviable situation. The state faced a fiscal and legitimacy crisis, unable to fund or respond to the growing demands made upon it.

The state's position was further complicated by its intimate (but now tarnished) relationship between key players within the corporate sphere: a complex set of scandalous relationships between the state and the corporate sector currently being investigated by both the crown and a state appointed royal commission. The scandal is widely known as WA Inc. Since the beginning of the Burke administration in 1983, political strategists had sought to create the conditions for an overt fusion of interests between the corporate sector and the state. The result was, in Maymen's words (1988, p. 18), 'the country's most efficient combination of business and politics'.[4]

On assuming power, the Burke administration enacted legislation which considerably enhanced the powers of government to operate in the commercial sphere, giving rise to 'an unprecedented interaction between government and business, and between company law and public law and policy in the Australian context' (Harmann, 1986, p. 248). Harmann cites three significant reasons for the increasingly corporatist nature of the Western Australian state. First, the state's dwindling tax base created an incentive on the part of the state to find additional financial sources. Second, to regenerate the flailing local economy, the state expressed a desire to expand and reshape the economy using public enterprises to supply finance or market access. This was no doubt welcomed by local corporate capital. Third, there was a desire to bring business practice into the management of government itself, as was increasingly the case with the federal bureaucratic restructuring. These corporate developments were distinguished by their considerable autonomy from the Minister, and their lack of accountability to Parliament.[5] Such developments, run by key figures from the corporate sector, not only considerably weakened the Westminister system, but had advantages for individuals within the corporate sector. For example, many of the directors, chairmen and executives for these state/corporate companies maintained an active private profile while at the same time undertaking their public tasks. It must also be pointed out such corporate executives had access to state policy-making forums, departments and personnel, as is typical in corporatist arrangements.

All three aspects of the government's strategy had very important ramifications for the state's financial status, ultimately undermining its capacity to deliver state services. For example, the state mediated a series of spectacular corporate losses, such as the Teachers' Credit Society and the Rothwells Bank. According to the chief executive of the Western

Australian Chamber of Commerce at the time, 'the Bond-Connell-Dempster group are doing what is right and good for them while the government is paying for it' (Maymen, 1988, pp. 18–19). However, throughout much of the 1980s the state's shield of the crown effectively thwarted the National Companies and Securities Commission's efforts to investigate growing public concern about the state and corporate sector activities.

It would be easy, but misleading, to create the impression that the Western Australian state's corporate activities during the 1980s were the sole cause of its increasingly difficult economic circumstances. Indeed, this is a view federal politicians have been only too happy to perpetuate, as it endeavours to stave off demands from the states for an increased share of federal revenues. Rather, as analysts such as Catley (1978), Crough and Wheelwright (1982), Robertson (1990), Smyth (1991) and Soucek (1992b) have all pointed out, Western economies have been faced with a prolonged crisis of accumulation emerging in the late 1960s and earlys 1970. This crisis, however, was qualitatively different from business cycle-type crises, which could be contained by Keynesian inspired allocative interventions within the current regime. As Soucek observes:

> [T]he neoclassical economists located the malaise of the flailing international economy in its inefficiency, low productivity, and lack of competitiveness. [This] diagnosis had become the the driving force behind global macro and micro-economic reforms. The former being expressed in a general thrust towards a deregulated free-market economic environment and chiefly in the deregulation of capital flows and the financial industry in general, the latter in the down-sizing of workplaces, privatization of the corporate capital, and the privatization and corporatization of state enterprises and the provision of some public services. (1992b, p. 2)

Since the early 1970s the Australian economy has been faced with a continuing dismantling and reshaping of its existing industries and social structures, within the context of global economic restructuring. This turbulent period in Australia's history has been characterized by deindustrialization, denationalization and deregulation (Smyth, 1991, p. 2). It has been a period of the rolling back of the welfare state and the rearticulation of the philosophy of entitlement under the banner of the Accord, with the argument that Australia can no longer afford the indulgences of the past.[6] It has also been a period when the conservative agenda of the New Right, armed with the logic of economic rationalism, has increasingly penetrated all aspects of public and private life. In short, it continues to be a war between the rights of property and the rights of citizenship.

One response by the corporate sector to the crisis of accumulation, and as part of the global restructuring, has been a shift toward greater market flexibility and competitiveness. This has entailed a major re-structuring of industries and the modern workplace, under the banner of microeconomic reform. Attention has focused on the nature of work in the modern technological workplace, pointing out the rigidities in labour organization and employment patterns. Some analysts have hypothesized these fundamental transformations of work as part of a newly emerging post-Fordist social formation, co-existing with others (such as Fordist) in a complex historical ensemble (Rustin, 1989, p. 61).

If this hypothesis is correct and there are fundamental transformations taking place in social formations such as Australia, and if we accept that there is a dialectical relationship between the spheres of production and those of welfare and politics (Dale, 1982), could we not expect to see similar post-Fordist structures and social relationships emerging as part of the reform agenda within education.

To explore this proposal, I want to turn first to a brief elaboration of Fordism and the post-Fordism hypothesis. According to Rustin (1989), Fordism can be defined as a system of mass production, mass consumption, the welfare state, and the integration of trade unions industrially and later on a corporatist basis.[7] These patterns of production largely defined modern industrialized economies such as Australia and the United States following the Second World War. An essential feature of the Fordist work-place is that the structures of control are largely built into the technology itself, for example, the pacing inherent in the assembly line. In other words, the structures of control are largely technical rather than ideological.

The post-Fordist hypothesis concerns the development of a new mode of regulation within modern capitalism and can be viewed as having two distinct elements. The first element points to changes in the nature of production and consumption, where mass production is seen as the bench-mark of the past. Technological developments, based upon the microchip, offer the possibility of reducing 'break-even points', where small and medium batch production (for market niches) can be more viable in what were mass production industries (for example, printing, education). Flex-ible work teams can be drawn together from a core and peripheral labour force attached to the organization, in an environment where there is a fusing of managerial and operational duties. The ideal worker in this type of environment is multiskilled, has a capacity to work cooperatively in groups, and is able to transfer and generalize knowledge from one problem area to another. Post-Fordism thus relies on the learning capacity of its workers in order to gain the competitive edge in an environment where machinery is a cost and labour is an asset. The mechanisms for control are increasingly ideological (such as group pressure), although technological innovation will provide the capacity for sophisticated surveillance of individual workers.[8]

This shift toward post-Fordist patterns of work organization, as part of a new post-Fordist accumulation regime, will present a new set of tensions and social relationships. According to Wood (1989), such trends will result in the proliferation of specialist production, with assembly line methods being modified for more integrated workplaces. Atkinson (cited by Wood, 1989, p. 7), however, argues that this explicit strategy on the part of employers to become more flexible will result in greater segmentation of the workforce, with a core workforce being multiskilled and functionally flexible, and a peripheral workforce being more disposable with fewer employment rights, facilitated through such practices as temporary employment, short-term contracts and part-time working.

The second element of the post-Fordist hypothesis focuses on the institutional regulation of economic growth and social conflict (Jessop, 1989). This area, according to Ball (1990, p. 125), describes a decline in collective bargaining, a decreasing role of the state, growing polarization and the consolidation of two nations. A broader version of the debate concerning the deterioration of the mass production model and the transformed workplace has also turned on the claim that bureaucratic organizations are no longer appropriate to the conditions of the late twentieth century. In essence, as David Gordon (1980) has argued, the social structures of accumulation of the old regime are no longer useful in furthering the capital accumulation process. Critics argue that Western economies now confront a choice between maintaining the rigid hierarchical division of labour, and the low-skill and low-trust relationships characteristic of Fordism, or shift to a system based upon adaptable technology, adaptable workers, flatter hierarchies and the breakdown of the division of mental and manual labour and learning. As a result, many organizations (public and private), in order to be competitive or efficient, have turned to devolved operational decision-making, flatter structures, encouraged collaborative approaches to decision-making, and increased the numbers of managers at the operational level. At the same time, centralized policy-making and sophisticated accountability and information systems act as important control mechanisms in the shift toward performance management.

Within Australia the reworking of the social structures as part of the new accumulation strategy resulted in an apparent uniformity of approaches to public sector reform across the various states of Australia, giving the appearance of an invisible hand. The Western Australian state's shift from bureaucratic to performance management found expression in the government's White Paper which was published in 1986 entitled *Managing Change in the Public Sector*. Not surprisingly, the White Paper closely parallels similar federal initiatives for bureaucratic reform: *Reforming the Australian Public Service* (Dawkins, 1983) and *Budgetary Reform* (Dawkins, 1984).

In the White Paper's Preamble it was argued that the restructuring of the public sector 'is designed to deal with an overriding problem . . . facing all Governments in the 1980's, namely that new or expanded services can no longer be provided by simply extending the tax base. . . . This means that additional services must be funded both at the expense of other services and by improving efficiency in continuing services' (Burke, 1986, p. 1). The White Paper is a blueprint for the implementation of the corporate managerial model within the state apparatus, replacing the old bureaucratic model. It begins by redefining old bureaucratic labels, such as 'public sector managers' and 'chief executive officer'. Many of these identities are reframed in the new corporate managerial discourse; a discourse which indicates a change in the identity of public administrators, and particularly what should guide their practice (Yeatman, 1990).

Responsibility for the formulation and implementation of public policy is also established in the White Paper, with the assertion that the lines between 'public sector managers' and government have become blurred. In essence, public sector managers must now *only* be concerned with policy implementation and not policy formulation (Burke, 1986, p. 5). This demarcation between ministerial responsibility and those of the bureaucratic apparatus effectively increases the ministers' power to direct the public policy process, and therefore the state's steerage capacity. In corporatist environments, however, closer ministerial involvement has also exposed the state to direct manipulation by vested corporate interests.

The lines of hierarchical control are clearly drawn through a detailed specification of tasks and relationships at each level (Burke, 1986, p. 6). This shift toward a flatter, less bureaucratic structure was accompanied by the slogans, 'let the managers manage' and 'make the managers accountable'. In essence, public sector managers must manage and be accountable for policy implementation within a regime that is defined by decentralized decision-making processes, performance-oriented management structures (identifying and monitoring standards, annual reporting), and where client need (defined in economic terms) and flexibility are seen as important. These would enable the measurement of efficiency and effectiveness as laid out in the Financial Administration and Audit Act (Treasury of Western Australia, 1986, p. 904).

The Politics of 'Better' Schools

The first phase in the shift toward 'better' secondary schools for Western Australia occurred with the implementation of the unit curriculum in 1987.[9] Emerging out of the Beazley Report recommendations, the unit curriculum proposals were an attempt to overcome the very real problems associated with streaming in secondary schools, and the career irrelevance of an overtly narrow range of subjects.[10] This reality had been intensified by escalating youth unemployment and reduced income support for the unemployed, forcing a rapidly expanding number of reluctant students back into school.

By 1987 piloting the unit curriculum was well under way in a number of voluntary high schools. While this broadening of the curriculum base from four core components to seven was welcomed by teachers and students, it is also immediately evident that the model required considerable financial support for the escalation in student counselling. However, this fiscal support was not forthcoming from the Ministry. Teacher support for the unitization of the curriculum dwindled and frustration levels grew daily, as the Ministry failed to support the flagging energies of teachers.

These changes to the curriculum must be set against more dramatic change taking place in the structure and organization of the 'old' educational bureaucracy. In October 1986, and in line with the restructuring of the public service outlined above, a blueprint was announced for the structural reorganization of the Education Department using the corporate managerial model. In particular, the bureaucratic 'mandarinate' was replaced by the appointment of a new technical intelligentsia in charge of the corporate bureaucracy.

On 22 January 1987, with teachers and school administrators still on summer vacations, the newly established Ministry of Education released its proposal for reform entitled *Better Schools in Western Australia: A Programme for Improvement*. The report proposed the devolution of administrative responsibility to enable school self-management over a period of five years. The report, however, outlines a very particular conception of schools: as management rather than educational units. Within this newly cast framework, a 'good' school is defined in managerial terms, while 'self-determining' is understood as the devolution of administrative responsibility to the local level. In particular, it is the crafting of management, as a scientifically applied technique, that is seen as pivotal in the facilitation of quality. Given this equation, high standards were expected to result through mechanisms for monitoring performance. In the same vein community participation was welcomed to manage the school's limited resources and to endorse the school's management plan. In essence, devolution and the creation of the self-managing school appear to mean the restructuring of the centralized bureaucracy into smaller collegially managed units, responsive to centralized policy-making and hierarchically accountable to the new corporate head office.

It was a gamble as to whether the proposal for devolution would be immediately welcomed by teachers and school administrators, a number of whom had been enthusiastically involved in local innovations and school development as part of the first wave reforms during the 1970s. The reform had appropriated the discourse of democracy: 'school development', 'self-determination', 'community participation', 'collegiality', 'school-based decision-making'. However, the facts that (1) key stakeholders were not invited to participate in the discussion to formulate *Better Schools*, (2) tight accountability structures were embedded in the reforms, (3) schools appeared to be given greater responsibility and less power, and (4) there was excessive attention to outcomes as opposed to processes, all raised the scepticism and anger of interest groups, particularly the State Schools Teachers' Union of Western Australia (SSTUWA). That things were not what they appeared to be was clearly the case, especially with regard to school autonomy. Writing in 1990, the Executive Director of the School's Division, Dr Max Angus, observed:

> Some teachers took the slogan 'self-determining schools' to mean literally that — unlimited autonomy without regard for system-wide parameters and agreed standards. Subsequent attempts by the Central Office to define policy parameters have been regarded as an infringement of the school's responsibilities.

The reaction to the *Better Schools* reforms by the SSTUWA and professional associations was swift. Their immediate objection was the lack of consultation in drafting the report, and what appeared to be an elaborate attempt at hiding the cost-cutting of state services. Indeed, the ensuing reforms in education, far from holding the line on expenditure, produced what many educators had long suspected was a prime motive for the restructuring in the first place: massive cuts in educational provision, which by 1991 amounted to 3 per cent in real terms as an expression of budget expenditure (Soucek, 1992a).

The SSTUWA called upon its members to refuse to implement the *Better Schools* proposals, not to take part in drawing up school development plans, and to do nothing in their own time (Black, 1987, p. 5). After considerable pressure by the SSTUWA, the Minister for Education reluctantly agreed to a moratorium. However, relationships between the Ministry and the SSTUWA and professional associations deteriorated over the year. The SSTUWA advanced the view that the reforms had significantly intensified teachers' labour. It moved quickly to mount a campaign over an issue that would be politically strategic: class size. In the opening weeks of 1988 the union targeted 'flagship' schools involved in the unitization of curriculum to mount their campaign of protests and strikes. On 15 February 1988 newspaper headlines reported that '50 Schools Faced Classroom Chaos' (Wainwright, 1988). Teachers refused to allow class sizes to exceed charter size. Disgruntled students were simply turned away. In the days that followed, the crisis deepened, with students joining the strike action. The failure of the Minister to contain the industrial action finally led to his replacement. However, this was not sufficient to mediate the conflict, and 1989 was marked by a period of industrial action over the state's reform agenda unprecedented in Western Australian education history.

The 1989 Teachers' Strike

It can be argued that one of the consequences of educational restructuring to enable the self-managing school was a radical intensification of teachers' labour. The new structures to promote self-management, accountability and curriculum relevance to the working-life needs of students meant many teachers were increasingly drawn away from the classroom and toward administrative tasks. These administrative responsibilities were the result of the emergence of a plethora of new management committees as well as a growing concern with marketing the school. Lesson preparation and marking, some of which could be done in non-contact school time, were increasingly having to be done at home. The unitization of the curriculum exacerbated the demands upon teachers with extensive rewriting of curricular programs and the escalation in student assessment, all within the pressures of a ten-week delivery mode.

In Western Australia teachers' salaries and working conditions are a matter of agreement between the union and the Ministry. However, pay rises are determined through national wage case arbitration procedures. In 1989 the state government was to argue for an immediate wage rise of 3 per cent, to be followed by an additional 3 per cent in six months. There was, however, provision for an increase over and above the nationally adjusted levy increase and within the existing wage-fixing guidelines. To qualify for such a rise, the relevant union needed to argue a special status case, and justify the proposed pay claim in terms of increased productivity.

In 1989 the SSTUWA argued for an extra 15 per cent, precisely on the basis of a special status derived from an increase in productivity consequential to the structural changes in educational provision that had occurred over the previous two years. Specifically, teachers claimed that a 10 per cent increase in productivity had already occurred, and a further 5 per cent productivity was anticipated in the immediate future. Significantly, prior to July 1989 the Ministry had given every indication of support for the teachers' claim of special status. However, this support was withdrawn, and teachers found themselves facing a hostile Ministry as well as the Industrial Relations Commission (IRC).

There was little doubt that teachers were long overdue for a pay rise, over and above the nationally determined figure of 6 per cent. For example, support for the teachers' position came from the Trades and Labour Council, the Independent Schools Salaries Officers Association, the Australian Teachers' Federation, the Shadow Education Minister and from sections of the public. However, what teachers failed to understand was the state's own fiscal crisis — precisely the reason for the restructuring in the first place.

The conflict between teachers and the government was set in motion when the SSTUWA set a deadline for the Ministry of Education's approval of their 15 per cent claim. At a special meeting 400 delegates voted for possible courses of action: one-day strikes, district strikes, rolling strikes and picketing. Both sides held firmly to their positions, and any attempt at communicating became totally useless. The Ministry's strategy from then on was to deal with the issue through the IRC, and through a series of compulsory conferences which aimed to block the strike action. The situation was further inflamed when the Ministry's Chief Executive Officer sent letters to all school principals asking them to report all teachers involved in industrial action, and when the Minister for Labour asked the federal IRC to exempt Western Australian teachers from the national wage case on the grounds that the SSTUWA was guilty of a breach of wage-setting guidelines. The latter request was subsequently denied by the federal IRC. Nevertheless, the stage was set for a first salary strike by teachers in sixty-nine years.

Following the strike, the teachers' strategy was to place bans on all restructuring changes for which the members had not been adequately compensated. This included, for example, out-of-school-hours meetings for school management groups. However, the IRC ordered the SSTUWA to stop all industrial action, and warned that the union could face fines and even deregistration. The union interpreted this move as denying the basic rights of workers, and that they could not use industrial action to protect the working conditions for members. Nevertheless, despite the IRC order banning the union from industrial action, teachers showed their defiance and voted for a package of rolling stoppages. Six weeks into their rolling action, teachers decided to step up their campaign. Furthermore, they threatened to withhold students' marks from the Secondary Education Authority to prevent final year school leavers receiving their Tertiary Entrance Exam scores. The Ministry's response was to threaten, once again, with a deregistration of the union, if the ban on industrial action issued by the IRC was not obeyed. The union's answer was to confirm that rolling strikes would go ahead. Furthermore, the union executive directed teachers to work to rule: the ban called for a 320-minute teaching day for forty weeks. Such a move highlighted the considerable commitment by teachers to extracurricular activities, and was a strategic public statement about the work of teachers.

Amid claims and counterclaims by both sides, the Annual Conference of the SSTUWA decided to push ahead with a work to rule campaign, rolling strikes and stop-work meetings. As a consequence, the Ministry delivered a two-pronged ultimatum: the IRC would take steps toward the deregistation of the SSTUWA; and the Ministry would withdraw its pay offer of 6 per cent. At the same time the IRC declared the union executive election void and ordered changes to the union's election rules.

It was at this stage that teachers in Queensland were offered a substantial pay rise ($38,000), above that still proposed by the Western Australian Ministry for Education ($36,000). The Australian Teachers' Federation subsequently used the Queensland offer as a national benchmark, arguing for a similar pay rise in all states. To resolve the now damaging dispute, the Western Australian government agreed in principle with the notion of a national benchmark for teachers' pay. However, a compromise formula that would bring Western Australian teachers' salaries to $37,020 was well below what teachers might otherwise have expected. Nonetheless, and with reluctant resignation, teachers finally accepted the government's offer, bringing to an end a prolonged industrial campaign. In essence, the only significant gains were a redirection of pay away from principals to classroom teachers, and the negotiation of a Memorandum of Agreement concerning the implementation of the *Better Schools* reform agenda. The impact of the turmoil on teacher morale was, however, devastating. One survey reported up to 50 per cent of teachers saying they would not willingly choose to work in the profession again. It was indeed the worst of times!

Self-Managing Schools and Post-Fordism

The implementation of devolution and the creation of self-managing schools has not been plain sailing. Indeed, implementation politics has seen the short-circuiting of a number of potential careers. Teachers and school administrators have contested and resisted some aspects of the reforms, some actively and others passively, in the hope that it would all blow over. Others have exploited the confusion and chaos and sought to shape their own school environments, for better or for worse.

But the question remains. What evidence is there as to the essential features of the self-managing school? There has been little systematic re-search into the changing nature of teachers' work and the organization of self-managing Western Australian schools as a consequence of devolution. Rather, studies have focused upon disparate aspects of school change, such as school-based decision-making, the changing role of the superintendency (Chadbourne, 1990) or teacher stress. This failure to 'call in the evidence' is partly a result of the increasingly tentative relationships between schools and academics: a reluctance largely a consequence of greater teacher stress at work, a concern schools have about potential bad press and therefore poor marketability,[11] and diminishing resources to do extensive ethno-graphic research.

One research project (Robertson and Soucek, 1991) has turned its attention to teachers' and school administrators' perceptions and experi-ences of the devolution effort, and attempted to understand the precise nature of the changes: changes the authors claim that are distinctly post-Fordist. The researchers gathered their data through extensive interviews with teachers and administrators in an average suburban working-class secondary school in Perth. The intention of the project was to determine teachers' perceptions and experiences of the unit curriculum and devolu-tion reforms in Western Australia, and whether and how their work and the school had changed as a result.

What was clear from the study is that the teachers in the school did not look at the past through 'rose coloured glasses'. In fact there were many things that both teachers and school administrators disliked about the old highly bureaucratic regime: the excessive rules, imposed rigidities, the lack of opportunity for change, inflexible resourcing and staffing, boundaries, the promotion by seniority and an irrelevant curriculum. Many of the teachers spoke of the need for reform, for new ways of doing things and were happy to embrace change. The school had willingly trialled the implementation of unit curriculum as one of the pilot schools. They also note that the school had been supportive and fully involved in the strike actions of 1988 and 1989.

But these changes had entered them into a new regime of uncertainty, as the shape of the self-managing school began to unfold. Teachers talked of knowledge and secrecy, politicking, bargaining and the advancement of personal careers. Learning to use this new system of power, now located firmly within the school, required different skills and time. The new regime of power also exacerbated status differentials between subject areas, with some areas increasingly marginalized and viewed as less legitimate because of the nature of knowledge taught (such as industrial arts). The outcome was, according to the teachers involved, less favour and financial support. In short, they had to fight for their subject areas' survival in the school.

Nonetheless, the scope to be entrepreneurial, to take a risk, had been created, and some teachers quickly grabbed the chance. This had included the setting up of new courses and projects likely to promote the school's image (or, as one teacher put it, 'the glitz and sugarplum'), and the opportunity for individuals to be appointed to some of the school's important decision-making groups. However, it was clear that risk-taking had to exist within an agreed vocational emphasis on industry, technology and future employment.

The first wave of uncertainty for the school began with the implementation of the unit curriculum at the school. Endless collegial meetings and deliberations gave teachers a taste of what was to come. However, many of the teachers commented that they were happy to support and develop the curriculum changes in what appeared to them a 'whiff' of professional confidence. The changes represented the first opportunity systematically to embrace an apparent autonomy over curriculum offerings in the high school. However, the uncertainty factor raised its head when it became apparent the ministry was not able to resource the reforms. It was also a reform that had embedded in it major tensions. While apparently directed toward meeting the increasingly diverse curriculum needs of students (and to that extent was seen as student-centred), it was at the same time both highly tailored and modularized into consumerable packages and excessively assessed. These features worked to compartmentalize school learning and teaching, as well as to develop an intense sense of alienation between the student and the teachers. Ten-week modules turned into eight, with students failing to appear after the last round of assessments. The pressure to assess dominated the routine, and under-mined any opportunity to foster longer-term problem-solving and process skills. This had the effect of exaggerating the reductive, technocratic and fragmented nature of much school knowledge. The school complained about the lack of curriculum support and new resources from the ministry because of the financial crisis. This sense of stagnation was compounded by the demise of the subject superintendent. In frustration, several of the teachers were willingly turning to the national curriculum, despite the implications for self-determination.

The second wave of uncertainty occurred with the implementation of the *Better Schools* reforms. For some teachers this period could only be described as an 'absolute disaster'; others welcomed the opportunity to become involved in the corporate life of the school. In the main, the growing alienation which emerged around the unit curriculum tended to neutralize strong feelings about *Better Schools*, where much of the detail of the initiatives simply tended to wash over them. Yet these reforms had resulted in major changes in the prevailing ideology within the school and in the social relations of their work (more intense, more corporate in orientation, more managerial, more technical).

A series of trends could be identified emerging within the school. The first was a shift toward entrepreneurialism and market choice as accepted practice, albeit within a context that favoured industry and tech-nology. For example, IBM had invested heavily in the school in computer technology, while one of the airlines offered scholarships to participate in the aviation program. Both these areas were tied to market niches: first as a way of attracting students; second as a way of linking the school to employment opportunities. Future employment and links with industry were major foci. Whole courses of industry-oriented, tailored and systematic study had emerged within the school, such as art and fashion linked to the clothing industry; a special flight was linked to the aviation industry; and cricket to sport as a vocation. In other words, as Ball observed of similar developments in the United Kingdom, 'schools are increasingly viewed as commercial production units, the notion being, therefore, that schools can and must learn from industry' (1990, p. 120).

This same pattern of development was increasingly occurring in other schools, where links with industry were significantly shaping the curriculum of schools, or where market niches tied to future employment were being exploited by the school. Many of these courses push at the boundaries of the Fordist type of mass production school organization. They were spe-cialized yet flexible market-oriented educational packages. This is not to suggest that the courses were all bad, although they must be viewed as attempting to occupy educational and employment niches and as fitting into the new market driven industry-oriented entrepreneurialism of post-Fordism. From the school's point of view it was merely attempting to solve problems of its own future survival due to the declining enrolment of students. They sought to boost their flagging population by recruiting students to innovative programs from outside the school community. However, this practice tended to foster a new type of elitism within the school — two nations — those students who participated in the new (vocational courses) and those drawn from the local (working-class) community (who would typically leave school without a job), causing growing conflict and rupture within the school.

The school also operated in an environment of uncertainty. However, this was often the result of taking the centralist rhetoric at face value. In other words, self-determination did not really mean what had once been understood by the term. It meant self-management within the context of the new centralist power structures (state and federal). It was not always clear, at least from the school's point of view, where the boundaries were drawn. Numerous examples were cited of initiatives or decisions which had to be withdrawn because they conflicted with centrally made determinations (not always of a policy nature). In commenting on the ambiguity and frustration of this period, the Executive Director of the Schools Division, Dr Max Angus, observed:

> . . . attempts by the Central Office to define the policy parameters have been regarded as an infringement of the school's responsibility. The Central Office is caught in a class Catch 22: the more reticent it remains regarding the delineation of the policy framework the more it encourages the position that self-determining schools can ignore systemic accountability; on the other hand, the further it proceeds with the delineation the greater the criticism that *Better Schools* is fraudulent and designed to limit the authority of schools. (1990, p. 12)

This confusion as to who could make decisions about policy and the management of schools was complicated by the plethora of policy initiatives emerging as a result of the restructuring of the economy (pathways, post-compulsory schooling, national curriculum, testing and standards). Teachers complained that areas that were important to the school, such as the student behaviour management program, were left to slide as new energies were required to respond to the state's hastening educational agenda. This created a climate of policy uncertainty within the school, having a dramatic impact on teachers' work and the nature of the school. It could be speculated that as the crisis within the economy intensifies within Australia and the education system is forced to respond, policy (and therefore practice) uncertainty will become a prevailing feature of teachers' lives in school. The sense of 'paddling hard to stay afloat' has done little to engender confidence in the teaching profession.

A further trend was the intensification of labour for teachers within the school, and the growing burden of administration or management.

Teachers were increasingly managing (often not very successfully) students as they attempted to deal with the unit curriculum. They were also constantly assessing students, in order to meet the new accountability requirements. In addition, they were increasingly involved in the corporate life of the school, with numerous committees being formed to handle devolved managerial responsibilities. They reported little time to talk to colleagues, few opportunities for genuine curriculum development, long hours, typically minimalist relationships with students,[12] weekends of work, of their being ignored, and of the pressures to develop the credentials that would allow them to be promoted within the system.

This raised important tensions for teachers. If they participated in the corporate life of the school, this participation typically undermined their commitment to the classroom. If they remained committed to kids and the classroom, they missed the promotional raft as it swept by. Yet a significant number of the teachers talked about the pedagogical (as opposed to managerial) relationship as central to what it meant to be a teacher; a relationship they could see under pressure and slipping by. There was increasingly little time for personal and professional reflection, for getting to know students and their needs, for developing a sense of pedagogic purpose. The ultimate losses with the strike, at least for some teachers, compounded the sense of alienation. In short, the school had begun to take on the shape (with many contradictions and not without conflict) of a post-Fordist workplace: niche-oriented, managerial, client-oriented, packaged choices, flexible and vocational.

Creating a Discourse about Genuine Self-Managing Schools

It ought not to be a surprise that schools have been given little more than an opportunity to 'manage' a dwindling set of fiscal resources within a context that has become increasingly typified by tightening centralist controls over policy, curriculum form and content, evaluation and standards. For, indeed, that was the intention for them all along. As I have argued, the collapse of the old Keynesian settlement and the construction of a new regime of accumulation had resulted in a very different configuration of interests and set of social relations. The initial scepticism and anger displayed by schools as the devolution reforms were hoisted on them so undemocratically has been vindicated. The rhetoric of self-determination, collegiality and school development has had a hollow ring. Self-managing schools, as they are typically presently being constructed,[13] carry within them the danger of engaging teachers in endless debate and a futile routine about means and not ends, at an enormous moral and social cost.

At one level the self-managing school is a political and administrative solution to the more intractable problems confronting the state: dwindling resources, flagging motivation, the rolling back of state obligations especially with regard to citizenship entitlements. At anther level evidence is emerging that the transformation of the old bureaucratic mass production mode of schooling to that which is niche-oriented, flexible, vocational and client-oriented has been facilitated through the process of devolution and shift toward school level self-management. Around Australia this pattern is becoming increasingly dominant, spurred on by the constant stream of policy from a centralized state education apparatus. The harnessing of schools to the economic project of the nation, under the banner of self-determination and self-management, will in the long run increasingly drain teachers of the interest, energy and capacity to respond to local problems.

The question is, how can we reclaim the educational discourse from the morally and socially blinkered economic rationalists; those vested interests that have so energetically hitched education to the future of the Australian and world economy? A new discourse about schools and their role in the broader community needs to emerge which has embedded within it the politics of possibility. Such a discourse needs to exploit difference and diversity of voice and difference and diversity of moral and ethical values. This new discourse also needs to examine ways of connecting means and ends, and to resist, debate and subvert those policies and practices which attempt to sever this fundamental link. It is only then that teachers will be able to counter strong tides which will disengage them from the fundamental relationships upon which critical pedagogy is built.

Notes

1 These programs were sponsored by the Commonwealth Schools Commission. The Commission was established by the Whitlam administration in 1973 and operated until 1988.

2 John Smyth has offered an excellent critique of the cooptation of discourse by the current restructuring movement in his article, (1991) 'International Perspectives on Teacher Collegiality: A Labour Process Discussion Based on the Concept of Teachers' Work', *British Journal of Sociology of Education*, 12, 3, pp. 323–46.

3 Increasingly policy affecting schools is being determined at the federal level and in conjunction with corporate interests, as with the Finn (1991) and Mayer (1992) reports.

4 With the benefit of hindsight, it would appear that both sides were particularly efficient in lining their own pockets with state funds.

5 Specifically Government Holdings, Exim and WADC. The majority shareholder is Treasury.

6 The Accord, an agreement struck in 1983 between peak interest groups drawn from big business, the state and trade unions to work toward economic recovery within a negotiated framework, has had a major impact on Australian political and social life.

7   Named after the United States car giant, Henry Ford. Ford was the architect of the modern production line which successfully integrated Taylorist principles of time and motion management along with a greater division of labour to create production efficiencies.

8   These patterns of work organization and social relationships are currently highlighted in the Finn report (1991) examining post-compulsory schooling and in the Mayer Committee's report (1992) which looks at the development of workplace competences within schools.

9   In 1984 the Burke administration announced a Committee of Inquiry into education in Western Australia to be chaired by Whitlam's Education Minister during the 1970s, Kim Beazley. The Beazley Report, as it became known, advocated wide-ranging changes to curriculum and the organization of schools including the unitization of the curriculum. This was to overcome the problems associated with streaming and career irrelevance of an overtly narrow range of subjects. This meant a broadening of the curriculum base from four core components to seven. Each component was built from a range of units, with each unit having a defined set of objectives and established assessment points and procedures.

10 This report, know after its chairman, was the result of deliberations by the Committee of Inquiry into Education in Western Australia (1984) [Chairman: K. Beazley], *Education in Western Australia: Report of the Committee of Inquiry into Education in Western Australia*, Perth, Western Australian Government Printers.

11 All the more critical when schools are attempting to get a competitive edge.

12 Some even admitted they wrote reports on students they did not know.

13 I am not wanting to suggest that schools are not attempting to become self-determining, or that these are not creative and energetic teachers; rather, that the current self-managing framework for teachers works to create an illusion about the state of affairs in schools today.

References

ANGUS, M. (1990) 'Making Better Schools: Devolution the Second Time Around,' Paper presented to the American Educational Research Association Annual Meeting, Boston, April.

AUSTRALIAN EDUCATION COUNCIL REVIEW COMMITTEE (1991) *Young People's Participation in Post-compulsory Education and Training*, Canberra, Australian Government Publishing Service.

BALL, S. (1990) *Politics and Policymaking in Education: Explorations in Policy Sociology*, London, Routledge.

BLACK, M. (1987) 'Teachers Ban New System', *The Western Mail*, 7 February, p. 5.

BURKE, B. (1986) *Managing Change in the Public Sector: A Statement of the Government's Position.* [Parliamentary White Paper], Perth, Western Australian Government Printer.

CATLEY, B. (1978) 'Socialism and Reform in Contemporary Australia', in E.L. WHEELWRIGHT and K. BUCKLEY (Eds), *Essays in the Political Economy of Australian Capitalism: Volume Two*, Sydney, ANZ Book Company.

CHADBOURNE, R. (1990) *Issues Facing and Shaping the Role of District Superintendents during a Period of Radical Change*, Perth, IIPAS.

COMMITTEE OF INQUIRY INTO EDUCATION IN WESTERN AUSTRALIA (1984) [Chairman: K. Beazley] *Education in Western Australia: Report of the Committee of Inquiry into Education in Western Australia*, Perth, Western Australian Government Printers.

CROUGH, G. and WHEELWRIGHT, T. (1982) *Australia: A Client State*, Ringwood, Vic, Penguin.

DALE, R. (1982) 'Education and the Capitalist State: Contributions and Contradictions', in M. APPLE (Ed.), *Cultural and Economic Reproduction in Education: Essays on Class, Ideology and the State*, London, Routledge and Kegan Paul.

DAWKINS, J. (1983) *Reforming the Australian Public Service: A Statement of the Government's Intentions*, Canberra, Australian Government Publishing Service.

DAWKINS, J. (1984) *Budgetary Reform: A Statement of the Government's Achievements and Intentions in Reforming Australian Government Financial Administration*, Canberra, Australian Government Publishing Service.

FINN, B. (1991) *Young People's Participation in Post-Compulsory Education and Training*, Report to the Australian Education Council Review Committee (Finn Report), Canberra, Australian Government Publishing Service.

GORDON, D. (1980) 'Stages of Accumulation and Long Economic Cycles', in T. HOPKINS and I. WALLERSTEIN (Eds), *Processes in the World System*, Beverley Hills, Calif., Sage Publications.

HARMANN, E. (1986) 'Government and Business in Western Australia, 1983–85: Legal and Political Aspects of the New Hybrid Enterprises', *Australian Journal of Public Administration*, 35, 3, pp. 247–62.

JESSOP, B. (1989) 'Conservative Regimes and the Transition to Post-Fordism: The Cases of Great Britain and West Germany', in M. GOTTDIENER and N. KOMNINOS (Eds), *Capitalist Development and Crisis Theory: Accumulation, Regulation and Spatial Restructuring*, London, Macmillan, pp. 261–99.

MAYER COMMITTEE (1992) *Employment-related Key Competencies: A Proposal for Consultation*, Melbourne, Mayer Committee.

MAYMEN, J. (1988) 'Behind Closed Doors', *Australian Society*, 7, 10, pp. 17–21.

PUSEY, M. (1991) *Economic Rationalism in Canberra: A Nation Building State Changes Its Mind*, Cambridge, Cambridge University Press.

ROBERTSON, S. (1990) The Corporatist Settlement in Australia and Educational Reform, Unpublished doctoral thesis, University of Calgary.

ROBERTSON, S. and SOUCEK, V. (1991) 'Changing Social Realities in Australian Schools: A Study of Teacher Perceptions and Experiences of Current Reforms', Paper presented to the Annual Meeting of the Comparative and International Education Society, Pittsburgh, 14–17 March.

RUSTIN, M. (1989) 'The Politics of Post-Fordism: Or the Trouble with "New Times",' *New Left Review*, 175, pp. 54–77.

SMYTH, J. (1991) 'Higher Education Policy Reform in Australia in the Context of the Client State', Paper presented to the Annual Meeting of the Comparative and International Education Society, Pittsburgh, 14–17 March.

SOUCEK, V. (1992a) Making Sense of Better Schools: A Discourse Approach to Educational Policymaking, Unpublished Master of Education thesis, Curtin University of Technology.

Susan L. Robertson

SOUCEK, V. (1992b) Post-Fordism: An Economic-Rationalist Attempt at Making or Unmaking Capitalism? Unpublished manuscript.

TREASURY OF WESTERN AUSTRALIA (1986) *Financial Administration and Audit Act: Regulations and Treasurer's Instructions*, Perth, Treasury of Western Australia.

WAINWRIGHT, R. (1988) 'Fifty Schools Face Classroom Chaos', *The West Australian*, 15 February, p. 1.

WOOD, S. (1989) 'The Transformation of Work?' in S. WOOD (Ed.), *The Transformation of Work?* London, Unwin Hyman.

YEATMAN, A. (1990) *Bureaucrats, Technocrats, Femocrats: Essays on the Contemporary State*, Sydney, Allen and Unwin.

8 Pushing Crisis and Stress down the Line: The Self-Managing School

Peter Watkins

Introduction

Recent post-Fordist visions of industrial relationships have stressed the interplay of a powerful, central governing body feeding off numerous smaller units which are satellites, subsidiaries or subcontractors to the powerful central unit. Scott (1988), for instance, suggests that this tendency marks a process of vertical disintegration where a formerly large-scale organization proceeds to discard units of the organization which are then recombined in a seemingly loose network. Such networks do not, however, mean a reduction of the governing body's power. Indeed, it is enhanced as modern information technology enables the constant surveillance and control of these myriad smaller units by top management, without the assistance of an army of middle managers. Further, resources, financing, policy, monitoring and assessment are firmly in the hands of top management. Loton (1991), the Chairperson of the Business Council of Australia, has strongly lobbied that schools should follow this pattern being implemented in the business world. Separate schools should, by and large, manage themselves but within strict parameters of policy, curriculum, student evaluation and teacher appraisal which should be determined in an even more highly centrally prescribed fashion at the national level. This chapter argues that such moves are part of a general strategy to displace the stress of the current economic crisis of capitalism down into smaller organizational units. Similar to the relationships in the business world, in schools there would be an element of dependence on the central power for political, financial and legal help; there would be domination, with schools being closely monitored and assessed with regard to both 'standards' and teacher and student 'performance'; and there would be a degree of competitive isolation as the sense of solidarity held by teachers is gradually broken down by an enforced competitive individualism as not only schools but also teachers are forced to compete with each other in the so-called 'marketplace'. These trends do not herald any new post-Taylorist panacea, as some post-Fordist advocates would suggest. Rather, it can be shown that they mark an even closer return to the technical rationality of the principles of scientific management. The move towards the self-managed school can thus be seen in terms of Habermas' view of the life-world which, in late capitalism, has taken on a one-sided rationality. Habermas (1984a) terms this one-sided rationality the colonization of the life-world where contemporary economic rationalism and the financial imperatives of late capitalism attempt to stifle the critical capacities of people and their scope to act.

This chapter outlines the post-Fordist vision of industrial relations, then discusses the dependent nature of those relations, especially between powerful and less powerful organizational units. However, the nature of the dependence implies the reality of domination, with, in particular, key aspects of education being increasingly centralized, standardized and subject to greater surveillance. Yet at the local level the push is for an ethos of competitive individualism both between schools and between teachers within schools. Finally, there will be an attempt to explain these recent trends in the administration of education through theoretical insights to be found in recent works by Habermas.

The Post-Fordist Vision of Industrial Relations

The current quest throughout the capitalist economic system for greater flexibility has focused, as one of its central planks, on the promotion of flexible labour relations and work practices (Piore and Sabel, 1984; Watkins, 1991). Coupled to this promotion has been the evolution of more flexible administrative practices which have engendered a process of vertical disintegration whereby, it is argued, many of the time consuming, mundane administrative functions can be done more efficiently by decentralized, smaller organizational units. Such a scenario, often termed post-Fordist, contrasts with the so-called Fordist model where organizations are highly integrated, often utilizing mass production methods to satisfy a mass consumer market. Scott (1988) suggests that there are a number of factors leading to disintegration. It may occur if the organizational and economic environments are unpredictable. Instability, through turbulent labour relations, may also lead to disintegration. The entry into highly specialized niche areas may also be a factor. Similarly, the requirement of production in small-scale volumes may be important. Nevertheless, Scott argues that such disintegration enormously enhances flexibility in the deployment of capital and labour for it permits producers to combine and recombine in loose, rapidly shifting coalitions held together by external transactional linkages (Scott, 1988, p. 176). The advocacy that educational systems should follow a similar path has, inherently, clear parallels. For instance, how better to deal with the militant teacher unions than to push the responsibility and stress of negotiating wages and conditions down onto the administration of the individual schools? In addition, the disintegration of the system might also mean the disintegration of the unions who will have to deal with a myriad of small self-administering school units.

Conservative bodies like the Business Council of Australia are strongly lobbying that education should mirror the administrative changes taking place within the business world. So that the education system can respond adequately to the demands and needs of the business sector, the Business Council has asserted that the management structure of education should be set within clearly laid out nationally defined objectives and within a rigorous, nationally determined system of 'accountability' for teacher and student performance. However, in other respects, in post-Fordian terms, the education system should disintegrate. The Business Council (Loton, 1991) has forcefully demanded that, within the strictly enforced parameters outlined above, by the year 2000 all school systems within Australia should be operating with decentralized managing structures, with schools established as self-managing units responsible for many of the tasks formerly held at the centre.

Loton (1991) has outlined the thinking behind this advocacy. He has asserted that the management lessons of business need to be applied to education systems so that their performance orientation can be improved. He further argues:

Large corporations have responded to increasing competitive pressure by pushing decisions away from the centre. This enhances responsiveness to the constantly changing demands of the marketplace and speeds up reaction time to those changes.

What this means is that responsibility for meeting agreed performance targets is vested in divisions and individual operating centres. These centres must then be given the requisite authority to meet the targets.

In no way does this result in operating centres having license to do as they please. Thorough reporting procedures ensure this does not occur. (Loton, 1991, p. 15)

Thus while the central education offices at both state and federal levels will arbitrarily, with the help of powerful interest groups, set goals, targets, instruments of surveillance and the extent of resource and financial help, the self-managing school will be left to sort out the problems. In this way the economic and fiscal crises facing business and governments will have been effectively displaced to the local school context. With the demise of most of the middle management in education, the regional advisers and consultants, for instance, Norman (1992) suggests that also gone will be the organizational networks and memories which provide continual support to teachers. He argues powerfully that the glib distinctions and tidy little boxes that corporate executives bundle into self-managed schools are recipes for inflexible irrelevance. As for the instruments of surveillance and measurement of 'standards' so dear to the Business Council, Norman (1992) bitingly perceives that they stay with most of the troubles of Thatcherism in the United Kingdom, while costing large amounts of money for any, at best highly dubious, effect.

The insights of Norman, who has linked the move towards the self-managed school with the conservatism of Thatcherism, can also be applied to the post-Fordist view of change in the business world. The fostering of small specialized production units exercising creative entrepreneurial activities; personalized salary negotiations between management and employees; and the consequent withering away of unions and union power (Piore and Sabel, 1984) have likewise aroused perceptions of the closeness between the neo-conservative and post-Fordist visions of the world. In reviewing the literature, Tailby and Whitson (1989) point out that the similarities between post-Fordism and the neo-conservatism of Thatcherism are obvious. They claim that numerous case studies of the rationalization of industrial organization indicate that there may have been some benefits for management. 'But the outcome for workers has been job losses, more oppressive supervision and higher levels of stress' (Tailby and Whitson, 1989, p. 7). The same outcomes for teachers and middle education managers would appear to apply with regard to the similar neo-conservative changes being pushed onto education systems in Australia.

Dependence

However, while there may be disintegration into smaller organizational units, there still exists a strong tie of dependence between the central and small units. This can be aptly illustrated by the example of Japan, the country most cited as indicative of the post-Fordist vision. Although the myriad Japanese small firms are theoretically independent, in reality they are dependent on one of the giants. In explaining this dependence, Wolferen points out that: 'much is made of the family metaphor. The "parent firm" helps the subcontractor with supplies and technical assistance, including investments in machinery. . . . But the "child firm" must accept its role of shock-absorber in periods of economic downturn' (Wolferen, 1989, p. 1781). Littler (1982) has outlined the historical background of this dependent relationship through the development of the Oyakata system. This was a patriarchal practice based on the father (oya)-child (ko) relation which survives today in the family ethos which governs the cultural context in which both large and small organizational units are embedded.

In post-Fordist terms there can be said to exist, between the two layers of administration, a relationship of vertical dependence. In this vertical dependence the smaller unit acts as a shock absorber in deflecting major local social, fiscal and industrial crises away from the centre. For instance, in periods of fiscal cutbacks blame and community hostility are focused on the stringent conditions imposed by the local administrators in responding to the crisis. The major body remains insulated from any anger cutbacks might engender. Similarly, when industrial disputes arise over wages and conditions, the central body provides expensive legal backing, but at a distance, to put down the industrial unrest. Thus, for its part, the central unit, the state in the educational context, offers financial, administrative and legislative resources in return for the smaller units absorbing much of the stress emanating from the various crises. As a consequence, Tailby and Whitson (1989) argue that the state and its intervention in the restructuring of industry remain a vital factor. This is especially evident with conservative governments which have the weakening and exclusion of unions as a major goal in any post-Fordist industrial scenario.

Dependence also occurs at the microlevel with employees left dependent on the paternal/maternal goodwill of senior administrators. In terms of the self-managed school, teachers will be greatly dependent on the way the principal decides to distribute the bulk funding coming from the central body. The principal may feel a need to promote certain subjects, for instance, music, by paying the staff in that area a much higher wage than teachers in other areas. Again, the principal may have a special project that has to be funded out of the bulk grant. One solution, often promoted to cater for such needs, is the appointment of more junior staff, who are cheaper than the older, more senior staff who are then passed over in such a situation. Similarly, with any reduction in the bulk funding, the teaching staff in the self-managed school become dependent on the principal in deciding on who stays and who goes.

This last point gains even greater strength with the realization that another aspect of post-Fordist internal labour markets is their polarization (see Watkins, 1989). For instance, in a recent study of the effects of technology and privatization on British Telecom, Clark (1991) found a decided polarization of the workforce. He concluded that there had been a pronounced polarization in maintenance work tasks, jobs, careers and in the distribution of skills between junior and senior technicians (1991, p. 142). A similar scenario is envisaged in the teaching labour market of the self-managed school. Not only do such influential bodies as the Schools Council (1990) forecast such changes, but other advocates such as Ashenden (1990) and Dimmock (1991) have promoted the segmentation of teaching staff in schools. Dimmock, for instance, suggests that in the self-managing school will be found 'a cadre of highly trained advanced career teachers . . . assisted by teachers' aides, who will assume responsibility for preparation of materials and learning packages, servicing equipment and routine administration and record keeping' (1991, p. 4). The determination of the ratios between the two segments, the definition of one from the other and their wage differentials will make teachers extremely dependent on the school's senior administrators in the carving up of the school's bulk grant.

The work of teachers, what they teach and what students learn — the curriculum — are also becoming the centre of major restructuring evolving over the control of the curriculum. A major shift is taking place whereby the construction and assessment of the curriculum are moving away from the local level and school curriculum committees to the national level. In particular, the rise to power of the Australian Education Council has signified a major shift regarding key curriculum policy issues. These have been taken out of the hands of professional educators and placed nationally in the hands of politicians and corporate managers who are now the dominant players.

National Domination

Considine, in a recent paper (1990), suggests that the current attempts to restructure public institutions along corporate management lines at both state and national levels are a response to the ruptures and tensions which are now manifest throughout the English-speaking world. A turbulent environment has come about through continuing economic crises, the restructuring of the labour market, the strength of sectional mass movements and persistent ideological attacks on the public sector. Considine argues that corporate management is essentially 'a framework designed to "circle the wagons" and ration supplies' (1990, p. 177). The major concern is to bring greater discipline and control to the systems through limiting goals, focusing on what are perceived as key programs, and reducing waste through tying work to achieve narrowly prescribed outputs. Considine concludes that the result is 'increased central control and greater homogeneity' (1990, p. 177). The essence of the strategy is to obtain more from public sector workers at less cost.

Important in the more specific move to bring greater control and discipline to the education 'industry' has been the Australian Education Council (AEC), which comprises the ministers for education of the Commonwealth and the states. While initially relatively insignificant, the AEC has recently gained great power as the Commonwealth government has sought to gear the curriculum nationally to the economic and social restructuring it is attempting to implement. The importance the AEC sees for itself in this agenda is set out in the report, *Common and Agreed National Goals for Schooling in Australia* (1991). For instance, some of its main activities entail establishing national goals for schooling, initiating a national project on the quality of schooling, mapping out the national issues an Australia-wide curriculum should be addressing and setting up a new agency, the Curriculum Corporation, to facilitate this process. Peppered throughout the report, however, are references to corporate plans, concerns to foster greater efficiency and effectiveness and linking education more tightly to the needs of industry. This occurs even though it has been convincingly shown that notions such as efficiency have been socially constructed (Fligstein, 1990) so that, over time, efficiency has taken on a range of meanings reflecting the ability, and ultimately the power, of dominant groups to shape the definition of efficiency. Fligstein points out that modern corporations have only become increasingly efficient because at each phase of their development efficiency has been redefined. These insights are important not only because they cast new light on notions like efficiency but because they can give a wider understanding of how the curriculum and the management of education are being redefined in Australia. Accordingly, Lingard (1990) argues that the emergence of the AEC as a major policy player, with its promotion of economic rationality, human capital theory and a national approach within a more tightly managed framework, sits firmly within the structure of corporate federalism. But he points out that the dominance of the managerialist and economic agendas has marginalized and indeed overwhelmed other approaches and other areas of policy. Equally important, though, is the point that the growing power of the AEC signifies a major shift in who decides how education is administered in Australia, away from educationalists and toward politicians and the business community. Indeed, the latter's strength can be seen in 1991 with Finn of IBM heading the Committee of Review of Post-Compulsory Education and Laver of BHP being appointed to chair the National Board of Employment and Training.

In Britain a similar situation seems to have arisen. Hartley (1990) has likewise noted that in recent reports on education, economic rationalist theory and the language of Taylor's scientific management predominate. Saturating the documents are words such as 'standardisation, monitoring, itemizing, differentiating, testing for quality control, accountability, machinery, systematic, packaging, skills, tasks, aims and objectives — all set within a highly centralised hierarchy' (1990, p. 71). The continual use of words such as these constitutes, in the Gramscian sense, a war of manoeuvre. The language of economic rationalism and scientific management takes on the appearance of being normal and natural, while other approaches are forgotten or considered 'impractical' in times of economic crisis. At the forefront in such a 'war' are bodies such as the Business Council of Australia which, as indicated earlier, lobby the government to gear education along the lines which they perceive industry is managed. Accordingly, the Council wants a comprehensive system of performance and accountability measures giving 'valid' and 'reliable' assessments of student and teacher performance (Loton, 1991). While suggesting that school systems should operate with decentralized management systems, the Business Council wants them tied to a national curriculum framework with common tasks and performance standards, especially in the core areas of

English, mathematics and science. The Business Council concludes that 'this should be accompanied by a rigorous system of accountability for performance targets based upon a clear set of educational objectives for the systems themselves and for the nation' (Loton, 1991, p. 15). This quite overt instrumentalism is concerned to foster a new flexible individualism which is able to respond to the rapid fluctuations being generated in both the production and consumption spheres of the economy (see Watkins, 1991). Schools by themselves can no longer be guaranteed to produce an appropriate workforce, so the curriculum and the management of education must properly be seen as national concerns. Schools, then, will be subject to more centralized control and direction, which will be coupled to closer scrutiny of the way in which teachers work (see Schools Council, 1990).

Yet such strategies are being linked with the decentralization of many quite difficult administrative tasks. Within the framework of centralized policy, finance and assessment detailed above, school administrations are being conditioned to a decentralized environment. In such an environment, school administrators not only individually compete with other schools for 'consumers', but they promote individual competition among their staffs as teachers compete for a slice of the school's bulk funding. It will be argued that such practices are much akin to the traditional principle of scientific management, acting to weaken the power, solidarity and influence of workers' unions by isolating them in an environment of competitive individualism.

Competitive Individualism

Following the precedents set in Great Britain and New Zealand, the conservative political parties in Australia are seeking to move authority and finances to the school level, with the principal and the school council being key players in their distribution. In this context the principal would be given maximum authority, including the ability to hire staff, with complete control over staffing at the school level. Gude, the Minister for Industrial Relations in Victoria, has conceded that, there will be individual bartering between the principal and individual teachers in a school over conditions and salaries. With such individual negotiating taking place, every school, and within them every teacher, could end up with separate, individual conditions of employment. As Gude has made evident, 'We'll have individual contracts . . . there are only so many dollars in the education budget, it's important that they're spent efficiently.' In relation to teachers it is important that they 'are rewarded properly for the work they perform, and that's all we seek to achieve' (*VSTA News*, 26 June 1991). Gude went on to explain that the personal, individualized contracts negotiated with permanent members of the teaching service were a means by which the outstanding teachers who went beyond what was expected of them could be rewarded. For any future conservative government there was no doubt that the current system of uniform conditions and salary packages had to be changed. As Gude explained, 'it's not a question of taking money off the non-performer so much as that we are wanting to reward those who put the extra effort in' (*VSTA News*, 26 June 1991). A similar scenario has been outlined at the federal level by the conservative opposition. In their 'Fightback' policy document they envisage that each school and each teacher will go through the process of negotiating individualized salaries and conditions. The apparent autonomy conferred on such self-managing schools would, however, be strongly curtailed by the central determination of resources, policy and evaluation.

The establishment of incentive components of individually negotiated salary arrangements closely parallels the principles of scientific management as espoused by Taylor. He argued that 'in order to have any hope of obtaining the initiative of his workmen the manager must give some special incentive to his men' (1972a, p. 33). Taylor suggests that this incentive can be incorporated not only into the promotion system but also through higher wages for individual workers. Accordingly, incentives in an individualized wage form could come about 'in the form of generous piece-work prices or of a premium or bonus of some kind for good or rapid work' (1972a, p. 34). Through such a process Taylor hoped to capture the 'initiative' of employees, which consists of their goodwill and acceptance of management, their willingness to work hard, and the placement of their ingenuity in the service of management. These aspects of the individual worker's performance, tied to the increasing control of management, would make scientific management more efficient than past methods. In these terms Taylor was able to claim that 'we are not dealing with men in masses, but are trying to develop each individual man to his highest state of efficiency and prosperity' (1972a, p. 43). Accordingly, similar to the proposals which are inherent in the conservative vision of the self-managing school, every worker should end up with a completely distinct and individual wage packet.

Taylor claimed that the extra bonus received by workers was a vital aspect of scientific management in that, by this means, workers came to accept the right of management to manage while being conditioned to 'carrying out orders' (in Boddewyn, 1961, p. 105). Linked to the concept of highly individualized rewards was the point that Taylor felt that an essential part of scientific management was a concern to concentrate on the individual worker. In line with this philosophy, he directed his efforts toward scientifically measuring how much each employee in the firm could accomplish. He believed that the fostering of personalized pay rates and productivity goals were important factors in the undermining of any group or union solidarity that would emanate from uniform conditions and salaries. He wrote that 'personal ambition always has been and will remain a more powerful incentive to exertion than a desire for general welfare'

(1976, p. 17). Accordingly, an essential part of his policy was the individualizing of the workplace to stimulate each employee to give maximum effort. He bitterly condemned any form of solidarity which resulted in uniform conditions whereby 'misplaced drones' were able to loaf around yet still get the same money as more energetic employees (1972a). Similarly, Gilbreth, Taylor's disciple who was important in establishing and spreading scientific management to other countries such as Japan (Watkins, 1992), argued strongly that the individual should be the only unit of analysis in the workplace. This meant that tasks should be measured, assessed and rewarded on an individual basis. Indeed, the traditional methods of organizing work were castigated for treating all employees as the same and not paying sufficient heed to personal ambition. To foster the ambition of each employee, Gilbreth encouraged them to compete not only against other workers but against themselves in the workplace. A constant analogy which was used to stimulate workers in this direction was the competition associated with various sports such as athletics, golf, etc. (Bluedorn, 1986). Such scientific management principles are perpetuated today not only in many workplaces but with such events as the 'Skill Olympics'.

By the adoption of personalized salary packages, negotiated in a 'scientific', 'rational' manner with management, educational systems may not be merely incorporating the 'best practices' of organization and management from the business world but simply recycling the best practices of eighty years ago, albeit in a more subtle and sophisticated form. This constant rationalization of the ongoing world of people in the name of economic or administrative efficiency has been termed by Habermas the 'colonization of the life-world'. As this is an argument which holds much substance, I will use it to gain some theoretical insights into the self-managing school.

The Rationalization of Educational Management

In the ongoing fiscal crisis facing Western capitalist economies, crucial economic decisions and approaches are being substantively influenced by ideologues who are located outside the sites of local, community activities. Speculators, sitting in front of their screens in New York or Tokyo, have no interest in promoting democratic and participative decision-making. Their main interest is to maximize their profit as investors in the various commodity or money markets. To enhance this profit, the economic rationalists, holding sway in the financial, corporate and government sectors, continually are seeking ways to cut back on public expenditure. The state, in generally endorsing such reductions in expenditure, must be careful, however, not to alienate the community to the extent that any public hostility is sheeted home to it. Thus the state must attempt to determine various financial, resource and surveillance policies, while leaving the 'nuts and bolts' of implementing these policies to local administrators. Thus through this crisis of accumulation there eventuates a constant erosion of the local, communal essence of life by a stream of economic and administrative decisions which owe more to the economic rationalist's textbooks than to any concern for local decision-making (see Pusey, 1991). Habermas (1984b) terms this invasion by economic and bureaucratic administration systems into communal decision-making as the 'colonization of the life-world'.

The introduction of the self-managing school should be seen as a way to resolve the demands for increased local consumption of resources at the cost of increasing private capital investment. There has been a tension between these two economic tendencies because increases in social consumption at the local level via increased rates of taxation will reduce the amount available for capital investment. The self-managing school goes some way to solving this problem by splitting the local community on the way the amount handed down for local consumption will be doled out. Through this strategy the state still hopes to present an appearance of being a good economic manager to the corporate and financial sectors, while avoiding any serious legitimation problems by pushing forward the local administrators to deal with any crises and stress. Nevertheless, in this way the economic problems of capital accumulation are constantly resonating with the values espoused in the local, political sphere. Habermas (1989) claims that this interaction in the end undermines the normative steering of socially cohesive relationships. In this the dominant factors are the steering media of money and power embodying purposive-rational views which act to decouple the everyday actions of people from the normative contexts of the life-world. Thus the concept of a self-managing school, in competitive isolation from its neighbouring schools, is driven by the quest for money, power and status on which, in the present economic rationalist environment, its survival depends. In this context Habermas argues that the one-sided rationalization of communicative action has been brought on by 'the penetration of forms of economic and administrative rationality into areas of action that resist being converted over to the media of money and power because they are specialized in cultural transmission, social integration, and child rearing' (1989, p. 330). The highly competitive, entrepreneurial nature of the self-managing school contributes to the undermining of any pockets of resistance which might be present in the contemporary environment.

In Habermas' terms the increased colonization of the life-world reflects the displacement of moral-practical elements by bureaucratic and monetary considerations. Through this process, Habermas explains:

> The communicative practice of everyday life is one-sidedly rationalized into a specialist-utilitarian lifestyle. . . . As the private sphere is undermined and eroded by the economic system, so is the public

> sphere by the administrative system. The bureaucratic disempower-
> ing and desiccation of spontaneous processes of opinion — and
> will-formation expands the scope for mobilizing mass loyalty and
> makes it easier to decouple political decisions from concrete,
> identity-forming contexts of life. (1984a, p. xxxii)

Political decisions which limit the amount local communities can spend
on educational services, the scope and content of their curricula, and
methods of evaluation are reified and relocated into the upper echelons of
centralized 'experts' and corporate managers who pontificate on education
in terms of the money market and the economy. Dunleavy (1984) has
emphasized the role of these 'experts' in the formation of policy in general. With the fashionable hold of economic rationalism in teaching institutions (Pusey, 1991), education and its relationship to the economy
are being centrally guided by econocrats, giving rise to a situation 'where
policy over large areas seems to be dominated for long periods of time by
professionally promoted "fashions" which are nationally produced . . .'
(Dunleavy, 1984, p. 77). Thus both Labor and Liberal parties in Australia
cling to the panacea of deregulation and the 'market' along with the fetish
to reduce taxation and expenditure in the public sphere. All this is done
under the ideological shadow of the current economic fashion of economic
rationalism.

For Habermas the 'life-world' is the prereflective network of assumptions, expectations, relationships and 'the interpretive work of preceding generations' (1984a, p. 70). But in modern capitalist society the
life-world takes on a one-sided rationality (1984a, p. 340) due to the
hegemony of the value sphere of science which, because of its power to
control and dominate, supplants other value spheres. Habermas terms this
one-sided rationality the 'colonization of the life-world' whereby institutions 'function as the basis which subjects the life-world to the constraints
of material production and thereby mediatizes it' (Habermas in Wellmer,
1985, p. 55). With the colonization of the life-world the reification of the
economy and the 'market' bring on a loss of meaning, anomie, alienation
and personality disorders, damaging communicative structures necessary
for social integration and the development of autonomous personalities
which are needed for human emancipation. As Habermas puts it:

> The encroachment of forms of economic and administrative
> rationality into life-spheres that in fact obey the independent logic
> of moral-practical and aesthetic-practical rationality leads to a type
> of *colonization of the life-world*. By this I mean the impoverishment
> of expressive and communicative possibilities which . . . remain
> necessary even in complex societies. These are the possibilities that
> enable individuals to find themselves, to deal with their personal
> conflicts and to resolve their common problems communally by
> means of collective will formation. (Habermas, 1984b, p. 20)

The increasing colonization of the life-world by the economic and centralized bureaucratic imperatives of the modern capitalist state has meant a reduction in the critical capacities and the scope for human agents to play a crucial role in social life. The colonization of the life-world curtails and redefines activities within the communal sphere merely to responding to problems of technical instrumentality. For instance, the question of how to provide adequate staffing in the self-managed school becomes how shall we staff the school with the declining bulk grant, within the existing centrally determined industrial relations climate and the limits imposed by the prevailing economic ideology? In facing these difficulties, the self-managing school becomes a buffer absorbing the impact of the motivation and legitimation crises facing capitalist societies in their pursuit of instrumental rationality.

But from this tendency towards the colonization of the life-world Habermas sees resistance developing. The economic and administrative imperative imposed nationally by central bodies promoting the instrumental rationality of late capitalism has within it the potential for the emergence of progressive opposition. In particular, Habermas points to the progressive new social movements as examples of people who are activated by the deterioration of the quality of their life rather than by problems of profit and capital accumulation.

While there may easily be a tendency to overestimate the potential of such opposition in giving people some respite from the demands of the economic and political-administrative systems of action, Habermas still sees any level of opposition to economic and administrative colonization as important.

> Regardless of how unrealistic these notions may be, they remain important for the polemical significance of the new resistance and retreat movements which are reacting to the colonization of the life-world. This significance is hidden in the self-image of the participants just as it is in the ideological depiction of the enemy when the rationality of the maintenance of the status quo in economic and administrative systems are identified with each other; that is, whenever rationalization of the life-world is not carefully distinguished from the increasing complexity of the social system. (1981, p. 37)

In refining this argument, Habermas sees such groups, for instance, concerned with the environment, local quality of life and poverty in the world, as embodying the potential for moving society to a position where the instrumental rationality of the econocrats and corporate managers is more evenly balanced by the communicative rationality concerned with recognizing the agency of people as well as providing for them the potential to interact in more democratic and harmonious ways. The resistance taking place, even now, to the implementation of the self-managing school

(*VSTA News*, December 1991) shows a willingness to contest the industrial relations branch of economic rationalism. 'In this way state and economy [can] be sensitized to the goals established by participatory decision-making processes' (Dews, 1986, p. 17) and can be prompted to modify their initial position. Indeed, Pusey (1991, p. 241) has argued that the rationalist attempt to 'liquefy, dissolve and instrumentalize every aspect of the lifeworld' will probably collapse under the pressures of its own logic, becoming just another market failure.

Conclusion

This chapter has looked at the proposed formation of self-managed schools in the light of the general restructuring of industry which is often termed post-Fordism. The way the administration of schools was to be restructured in the self-managing school has much in common with the general restructuring taking place in the economy. In this restructuring, be it called post-Fordist or something else, a number of discernible features are present which could just as easily be ascribed to the suggested restructuring of school administration. First, there is an element of dependence at both macro and micro levels. Second, there is a relationship of domination, where the smaller units are largely subordinate to a more central, national body. There is isolation brought on by the competitive individualism where not only the small units compete among themselves but the people making up these small units are forced to compete with each other for a share of the financial cake. Further, much of the restructuring is based on the classic rationalist principles of scientific management.

To gain some understanding of the theoretical implications of the restructuring taking place, Habermas' work was suggested as a good starting point. Habermas suggests that the economic and administrative rationality which underpins these changes marks a one-sided rationality that colonizes the life-worlds of people. Society's sense of community, compassion and justice are lost in the rationality portrayed in the everyday economic and administrative imperatives by the economic managers. Habermas, however, argues that people do not submit to such one-sided rationality easily but are willing to resist the economic rationalists where it becomes obvious that such rationality is destroying the well-being of society.

References

ASHENDEN, D. (1990) 'Award Restructuring and Productivity in the Future of Schooling', *Victorian Institute of Educational Research Bulletin*, 64, pp. 3–32.
AUSTRALIAN EDUCATION COUNCIL (1991) *Common and Agreed National Goals for Schooling in Australia*, Melbourne, Curriculum Corporation.

BLUEDORN, A. (1986) 'Special Book Review Section on the Classics of Management', *Academy of Management Review*, 11, pp. 442–64.

BODDEWYN, J. (1961) 'Frederick Winslow Taylor Revisited', *Academy of Management Journal*, 4, pp. 100–7.

CLARK, J. (1991) 'Skill Changes in Maintenance Work in British Telecom', *New Technology, Work and Employment*, 6, pp. 138–43.

CONSIDINE, M. (1990) 'Managerialism Strikes Out', *Australian Journal of Public Administration*, 49, 2, pp. 166–78.

DEWS, P. (1986) 'Introduction', in J. HABERMAS, *Autonomy and Solidarity: Interviews*, ed. by P. DEWS, London, Verso.

DIMMOCK, C. (1991) 'Schools for Quality Learning', *Australian Council for Educational Administration*, 5, pp. 1–4.

DUNLEAVY, P. (1984) 'The Limits of Local Government', in M. BODDY and C. FUDGE (Eds), *Local Socialism? Labour Councils and New Left Alternatives*, London, Macmillan.

FLIGSTEIN, N. (1990) *The Transformation of Corporate Control*, Cambridge, Mass., Harvard University Press.

HABERMAS, J. (1981) 'New Social Movements', *Telos*, 49, pp. 33–7.

HABERMAS, J. (1984a) *The Theory of Communicative Action, Vol. 1*, Boston, Mass., Beacon Press.

HABERMAS, J. (1984b) *Observations on 'The Spiritual Situation of the Age'*, Cambridge, Mass., Harvard University Press.

HABERMAS, J. (1986) *Autonomy and Solidarity: Interviews*, ed. by P. DEWS, London, Verso.

HABERMAS, J. (1989) *The Theory of Communicative Action Vol. 2*, Oxford, Polity.

HARTLEY, D. (1990) 'Tests, Tasks and Taylorism: A Model T Approach to the Management of Education', *Journal of Education Policy*, 5, 1, pp. 67–76.

LINGARD, R. (1990) 'Corporate Federalism: The Emerging Context of Schooling Policy-Making in Australia', Paper presented to the Australian Sociological Association Conference, December.

LITTLER, C. (1982) *The Development of the Labour Process in Capitalist Societies: A Comparative Study of the Transformation of Work Organizations in Britain, Japan and the USA*, London, Heinemann.

LOTON, B. (1991) 'Education and Australia's Economic Future', *Business Council Bulletin*, June, pp. 12–15.

NORMAN, M. (1992) 'Should We Be Banking on the Brians?', *VCEA Bulletin*, February, pp. 1–2.

PIORE, M. and SABEL, C. (1984) *The Second Industrial Divide: Possibilities for Prosperity*, New York, Basic Books.

PUSEY, M. (1991) *Economic Rationalism in Canberra*, Melbourne, Cambridge University Press.

SCHOOLS COUNCIL (1990) *Australia's Teachers: An Agenda for the Next Decade*, Canberra, Australian Government Publishing Service.

SCOTT, A. (1988) 'Flexible Production Systems and Regional Development', *International Journal of Urban and Regional Research*, 12, 2, pp. 171–85.

TAILBY, S. and WHITSON, C. (1989) 'Industrial Relations and Restructuring', in S. TAILBY and C. WHITSON (Eds), *Manufacturing Change: Industrial Relations and Restructuring*, Oxford, Blackwell.

TAYLOR, F. (1972a) 'The Principles of Scientific Management', in F. TAYLOR (Ed.), *Scientific Management*, Westport, Conn., Greenwood Press.

TAYLOR, F. (1972b) 'Testimony Before the Special House Committee', in F. TAYLOR (Ed.), *Scientific Management*, Westport, Conn., Greenwood Press.

TAYLOR, F. (1976) 'Profit Sharing', in D. DELMAR and R.D. COLLINS (Eds), *Classics in Scientific Management*, Alabama, University of Alabama Press.

WATKINS, P. (1989) 'The Polarization of Society: Flexibility and the Restructured Workplace', *Education Links*, 36, pp. 7–9.

WATKINS, P. (1991) *Knowledge and Control in the Flexible Worlplace*, Geelong, Deakin University Press.

WATKINS, P. (1992) 'Restructuring Australian Educational Administration: Japanese Management Strategies, Taylorization and Best Practices', Paper presented at the Commonwealth Council of Educational Administration, Hong Kong, August.

WELLMER, A. (1985) 'Reason, Utopia and the Dialectics of Enlightenment', in R. BERNSTEIN (Ed.), *Habermas and Modernity*, Cambridge, Polity Press.

WOLFEREN, K. (1989) *The Enigma of Japanese Power*, London, Macmillan.

9 Managerialism, Market Liberalism and the Move to Self-Managing Schools in New Zealand

John A. Codd

The New Zealand school system has recently undergone the most radical restructuring in 100 years. This has involved a decentralization of certain decision-making functions combined with increased self-management at the school level. The legitimating rhetoric proclaimed that these reforms would produce greater flexibility and responsiveness, but in reality they have produced a structure in which managerial decisions are more effectively controlled. There are clear parallels here with the 1988 British Education Reform Act which has been described as a structural change from corporatism to a new form of contractualism (McLean, 1988). It represents a fundamental transformation of educational administration and an extension into the domain of education policy of the same logic that informs market liberalism and economic rationalism.

Traditionally, educational administration in New Zealand has embodied values of consensus and social justice. Decisions generally have been founded on sound and widely accepted educational principles, rather than political or economic expediency. Thus, when a team of OECD examiners evaluated the system in 1982, they were able to comment that: 'Consensus is still valued in the world of education. Education is not seen as an activity above, or uninfluenced by politics, but as requiring to be pursued in accordance with more or less intrinsic purposes, having to do with the growth and development of individuals, rather than as an instrument for the attainment of political or social goals' (OECD, 1983, p. 22). It is indeed ironic, therefore, that the central thrust of the recent restructuring policies has been towards the attainment of a particular set of political and social goals. Intrinsic educational purposes have been cynically disregarded. As Grace (1990) has argued, the New Zealand reforms have largely been an attempt to reach a new political settlement. His analysis shows that: 'The restructuring of primary and secondary schooling in New Zealand between 1987 and 1990 was the site for a struggle of contesting political, ideological, and educational principles. The outcome was a complex compromise. The question for the future was not only whether the settlement would work in practice, but just whose agenda would shape its working in practice?' (Grace, 1990, p. 184). The question is most pertinent, although is it arguable whether a new settlement has yet been reached. Rather than a complex compromise, what we have is a precarious balance between conflicting forces. Essentially, it is a conflict between instrumental values of economic management and intrinsic values of educational democracy. This is not a new conflict (Callahan, 1962). There are historical precedents, although not to any significant extent within the New Zealand experience.

Whereas the reform rhetoric promised more democratic community involvement, increased parental choice and schools that would be better managed, more effective and more equitable, the reality is very different. The recent New Zealand educational reforms have produced a brave new educational world in which schools have become independent, self-managing units, competing with each other for staff and resources, where teachers are to be rewarded according to what they produce, and where children are to be regularly assessed in relation to nationally specified learning objectives.

This chapter examines deep-seated contradictions within these reforms and the conflicting political forces by which they have been produced. It argues that there is a fundamental conflict between a democratic imperative for more community participation in decision-making and an economic imperative for stronger mechanisms of accountability and centralized control. These conflicting imperatives for devolution and control are a direct consequence of the crisis that has beset the New Zealand state in recent years. It is a dual crisis of political legitimation and economic management, the culmination of a deterioration throughout the 1970s and 1980s of the post-war political settlement combined with steadily worsening conditions of economic decline and fiscal instability (Codd, Gordon and Harker, 1990).

The Political Context of Restructuring

During the 1980s most advanced industrial societies have witnessed a strong resurgence of economic and political liberalism. It is a movement which began in Western capitalist states as a response to the economic difficulties of the 1970s and now, in some ways, has its counterpart in the recent democratization of the Eastern bloc. The central tenet of this movement is the subordination of state intervention to the operation of market mechanisms as a more effective way of promoting economic growth and a more efficient means of allocating and using scarce resources (King, 1987). The maximization of individual choice within a deregulated social environment is given priority over state imposed responsibilities, duties and obligations. Property rights are given priority over social citizenship or welfare rights, and economic efficiency is given priority over human need in the allocation of resources. This 'new' market liberalism is no more than a revival of classical liberalism with its doctrines of individual freedom, public choice and minimal government (Barry, 1986).

A resurgence of market liberalism, accompanied by adherence to monetarist economic policies, occurred in the United States under the Reagan administration, in Britain under the Thatcher government and more recently in New Zealand under the Lange-Douglas government (Easton, 1989; Holland and Boston, 1990). In each case the main effect has been to 'roll back' the state (deregulation, privatization), to foster a climate of competition (the so-called 'enterprise culture') and to set aside most of the traditional concerns for social justice in the political reform agenda.

In New Zealand the advent of market liberalism and economic rationalism coincided with the election of the fourth Labour government on 14 July 1984. From this time Treasury became the most powerful bureaucratic influence in state policy-making. This involved what Jesson (1988, p. 42) has called a 'policy coup' in which monetarist solutions were presented as the only viable responses to the immense economic problems faced by the fourth Labour government. Treasury produced the blueprint for Labour's program of monetarist reforms in a volume of briefing papers to the incoming government entitled *Economic Management*. Jesson (1988, p. 42) comments as follows:

> *Economic Management* does not state its assumptions clearly, but it is obviously based on this separation of ends and means, the social and the economic. This has the effect of enormously reducing the government's role. Economics is regarded as a technical matter that is outside the area of political choice, and virtually all areas of society are treated as belonging to the economy. *Economic Management* has policies on virtually everything, and these are treated as matters of economic orthodoxy that are beyond political debate. Political choice then becomes a residual matter, of tidying up inequities and malfunctions of the marketplace.

During 1985–87 this was to become the dominant ideology guiding state policies in New Zealand. The proposition that a marketplace free of government intervention will work to the benefit of all, and the related proposition that excessive government spending was the prime cause of the economic crisis, came to be held as self-evident facts rather than articles of faith. By 1987 these doctrines of economic rationalism were being applied to education policy. Hence the Treasury's brief to the government that year contained a graphic account of an educational system that was relentlessly squeezed between fiscal and political pressures. The monetarist analysis posited a crisis in which state policy-makers, faced with absolute limitations of resources, could no longer meet public expectations and political demands for further extension and improvement of educational provision. As the Treasury brief (1987, p. 15) pointed out: 'In recent years a number of pressures on the state system have become discernible. They are not just pressures for more and better of the same (such pressures always exist), but for different types of education service and, in some respects, a different kind of education structure.' Given these pressures, within a context of severe fiscal constraints, the monetarist agenda called for policies that would effectively reduce educational expenditure and fragment existing structures and patterns of interest representation. The report of the Taskforce to Review Education Administration (Picot Report) would provide legitimation for such a policy in the shape of a White Paper entitled *Tomorrow's Schools*.

The Picot Report, named after the businessman who chaired the Taskforce, was released on 10 May 1988, with proposals for an extensive restructuring of the education system. The public was 'persuaded' by a skilfully orchestrated media presentation that the major Picot proposals were both necessary and beneficial. An incredibly short period (six to seven weeks) was given for submissions, and on 7 August the Minister released the White Paper, *Tomorrow's Schools*, and announced that it would be implemented by 1 October 1989.

The main thrust of the restructuring has been to reduce the size of the central bureaucracy, to abolish regional education boards, and to convert each learning institution into a self-managing unit having its own elected Board of Trustees. Thus the new educational structure entails a devolution of decision-making in a wide range of administrative areas, including resource allocation, staff appointments, support services and staff development. Boards of Trustees are given some discretion in these areas, but control is firmly invested in central state agencies, including the Ministry of Education, the Education Review Office and the Qualifications Authority. This control is maintained through tightly circumscribed limits on local autonomy and contractual forms of accountability.

Removing formal administrative structures from the local and district level has produced a situation in which schools and other learning institutions are encouraged to compete for students and for resources. At the same time highly centralized control is exercised through legal contracts, in the form of institutional charters, and regular review and auditing processes. In this way the state can more effectively control educational expenditure in the form of bulk grants, while shifting responsibility for the way funds are spent to the institutional level.

The policy of bulk funding has been undoubtedly the most strongly contested feature of self-management. Within the new structure, individual schools receive annual 'operational grants' from the Ministry of Education. Based on a complex formula, these grants cover such areas as school maintenance, teaching resources, in-service training and relief teaching. Although schools are able to supplement these grants with local fund-raising, their capacity to do so has varied widely, with resultant inequalities of provision (Wylie, 1992).

One of the consequences of devolution has been increased politicization at institutional and community levels. This has been accentuated with recent moves by government to extend bulk funding to cover teachers' salaries, to place all teachers on individual employment contracts and to introduce a scheme of merit pay based on performance appraisals to be conducted at the school level. These moves have been vigorously resisted by the vast majority of teachers, principals and school trustees (Gordon, 1992).

Another consequence of this devolved structure is that pressures for increased expenditure in education can no longer be as readily applied through established channels at the national level (Codd, 1990). The new structure effectively removes most of the institutional routes by which claims have been made on central government for qualitative improvements in education. Teacher organizations, for example, can no longer press for reduced class sizes, more professional support, curriculum resources or in-service training. Responsibility for these matters resides in each institution.

Not only have these reforms changed the fundamental structure of the New Zealand education system, but they are now transforming the practice of educational administration in two major ways. First, under the influence of economic rationalism there is a concerted effort to impose a managerialist ideology on all schools and other learning institutions (e.g., bulk funding, individual employment contracts, merit pay, etc.). Second, under the influence of market liberalism, educational administrators are being forced to surrender their traditional commitment to social justice in order to pursue the goals of competition and increased individual choice (e.g., privatization of services, dezoning of schools, etc.). The following sections of this chapter will consider each of these influences in more detail.

The Ascendancy of Managerialism

While much of the rhetoric surrounding the reforms has invoked such concepts as partnership, collaboration, participation and professional leadership, the political forces behind the restructuring have been strongly imbued with an ideology of hierarchical managerialism. These forces have come indirectly from the large corporations, through the Business Round Table, and more directly from the control agencies of government, namely the Treasury and the State Services Commission.

The contradictions between the underlying agenda and the legitimating rhetoric have been evident from the outset. One such contradiction concerns the role of the principal. In an unequivocal statement about research evidence on successful educational leadership, the Picot Report (1988, pp. 51–2) emphasizes 'the collaborative relationship between principal and staff', proposing that both 'participate regularly in reviewing the quality of the institution's educational performance', and commenting that 'the way decisions are arrived at is just as important in the life of an institution as the decisions themselves.' In reality, however, the new administrative structures have specifically precluded principals from adopting such a model of professional leadership, based as it is on processes of democratic participation and shared responsibility.

When *Tomorrow's Schools* was announced as government policy in August 1988, the Minister of Education referred to it as 'an affirmation of the Picot proposals' (p. iv). In one sense this was indeed the case. There is very little of substance in *Tomorrow's Schools* that was not drawn directly from the Picot Report. There is, however, a definite change of emphasis, with much of the Picot account of collaborative management and leadership dropped from the policy statement. It is stated in *Tomorrow's Schools* that the principal 'will be the professional leader of the institution' and that 'principals will be expected to work in a collaborative relationship with their staff' (pp. 10–11), but all the clauses which define what principals are to do emphasize their managerial functions. As board members, principals will be legal employers of staff, involved in appraisal, salary determinations and decisions relating to conditions of employment. They are to be responsible for 'the allocation of duties and detailed objectives amongst staff', and they are to be responsible for 'the development of performance objectives and measures to assess that performance' (p. 11). The thrust of these statements is undoubtedly towards an industrial model of management founded upon a positivist knowledge base. It is a model of management consistent with the economic rationalism that both the Treasury and the State Services Commission had been advocating for some time before their involvement in the education reforms.

The managerialist agenda had first appeared in the 1984 Treasury brief to the incoming Labour government with a description of what the document calls 'the ideal management system' for organizations operating within a competitive market. If applied in the public service, this model, according to the document, would require the following: clear measurable objectives set by the owners of an organization (i.e., the government); a management plan to meet those objectives; regular review of the objectives and the management plan; freedom for managers to choose the best mixture of inputs to get the agreed output, within the overall financial limits set by the government; and, finally, 'appropriate incentives to encourage the management and staff of each organization to perform effectively' (*Economic Management*, 1984, p. 288).

This managerial ideology was to become a central feature of state sector restructuring, including the corporatization of state departments and the establishment of what are now called 'State Owned Enterprises'. A further move to impose it upon the education system came in 1990 when the government appointed a Committee to Review the Education Reform Implementation Process (chaired by N.V. Lough). The Lough Committee was essentially a committee of officials, chaired by an ex-Treasury secretary and comprising the Treasury education manager, a State Services Commission economist, the National Bank strategic planning manager and the chief executive of the Ministry of Education. The review was carried out in eight weeks with only token consultation with schools and no opportunity for submissions from education groups. It was an entirely bureaucratic exercise based upon the tenets of economic rationalism. The report, entitled *Today's Schools*, addresses several aspects of the administrative reforms. Significantly, education is hardly mentioned. The report is all about management, and the recommendations put forward are unmistakably drawn from the industrial management model. Schools are seen to lack clearly defined operational objectives, an overall plan to achieve these objectives, mechanisms to monitor progress, personnel management systems and clear role definitions.

The Lough Report proposes that schools implement administrative systems which incorporate 'objective setting, planning, effective management, internal monitoring and reporting, and external reporting' (p. 19). Educational effectiveness is reduced to role differentiation. Thus, 'for there to be effective administration at the school level, the distinction between operational and policy activities must be clearly defined' (p. 20). Boards govern, principals manage and teachers operate. The quality of education is reduced to 'key performance indicators' which cover education, personnel, property and financial management. Partnership is reduced to constant and extensive reporting. Staff commitment and collaboration are reduced to personnel management, which includes pay flexibility so that incentives can be offered. Educational leadership is provided by 'establishing an educational plan for the school and by communicating it to all staff and students' (p. 23). What this defines is a culture of managerialism in which ends are separated from means and where people are valued only for what they produce. It involves the importation into education of the instrumentalist values of economic rationalism.

Ignoring the Lessons of History

Managerialism produces an organizational culture that is hierarchical, competitive, individualistic and highly task-oriented. It is a culture that is totally alien to the New Zealand experience, and if it is imposed upon schools, it is a culture that tends to be undemocratic and wasteful of human initiative and capacity. Nowhere is this more clearly demonstrated than in Raymond Callahan's classic study, *Education and the Cult of Efficiency* (1962), in which he traces the social forces that shaped the administration of American public schools from 1910 to 1930.

This period preceding the Great Depression was one in which the American economy was in decline. Politicians placed their hope for future prosperity in the hands of leading businessmen and industrialists. Men like Carnegie and Rockefeller became figures of national leadership so that, according to Callahan, '. . . quite naturally their values and beliefs (including the economic philosophy which had made it all possible) were widely admired and accepted' (Callahan, 1962, p. 2). Over time this business view of the world was to have a major influence on education and was to become a powerful force in shaping the organizational culture of schools. As Callahan points out: 'The procedure for bringing about a more business-like organization and operation of the school was fairly well standardized from 1900 to 1925. It consisted of making unfavourable comparisons between the schools and business enterprise, of applying business-industrial criteria (e.g. economy and efficiency) to education, and of suggesting that business and industrial practices be adopted by educators' (Callahan, 1962, p. 6).

One such set of practices was a new system of industrial management known as 'scientific management' devised by Frederick Taylor (1911). 'Taylorism', as it is now called, was a system of management first used to make the north-eastern railroads more efficient so that wages could be increased without increasing costs. It involved breaking down the labour process into its component tasks, carrying out a time and motion study of each task and planning more economical ways of reaching predetermined objectives. By the 1920s it was the dominant form of industrial management and had become the administrative counterpart of the Fordist mode of production. It also had a major influence on the administration of the public schools which at that time were under attack for being wasteful of taxpayer's money and too much under the control of inefficient teachers. Callahan describes what happened as follows: 'The sudden propulsion of scientific management into prominence and the subsequent saturation of American society with the idea of efficiency together with the attacks on education by the popular journals made it certain that public education would be influenced greatly. But the *extent* of this influence was increased by the vulnerability of the leaders in the schools — the superintendents — to public opinion and pressure' (Callahan, 1962, p. 52). Reference here to the 'vulnerability' of educators in the face of alien ideological forces strikes a familiar chord in the current New Zealand context.

Another manifestation of the cult of efficiency described by Callahan, which is worth noting for its contemporary significance, was the fanatical preoccupation with recording and reporting. Efficiency had to be not only done, but it had to be seen to be done. Efficiency was to be continually demonstrated through the incessant production of records and reports. Educational cost accounting became the order of the day. Teachers were required to keep records, accounting for every hour and every day of the week. Administrators were forever occupied in writing reports and policy statements. Needless to say, there was less and less time for teaching, and schools became places of tedium, ritualistic order and bland routine. Ironically, they became less and less 'efficient' in an educational sense.

By the late 1920s these attempts to reform American schools had produced a system that was weighed down by its own inertia and managerial oppression. The cult of efficiency had become a cult of managerialism which eventually proved to be totally unworkable in educational institutions. Liberation would come in the 1930s as the progressive educators, Dewey, Kilpatrick and others, succeeded in defeating managerialism and reconstructing American schooling on a basis of democratic educational values. In his final chapter Callahan writes about what he calls 'an American tragedy in education'. He opens his conclusion with the statement that:

> The study of various aspects of the actions administrators took between 1910 and 1929 in applying business and industrial values and practices to education, together with an attempt to explain *why* they took these actions has formed the substance of this volume. It seems in retrospect that, regardless of the motivation, the consequences for American education and American society were tragic. And when all of the strands in the story are woven together, it is clear that the essence of the tragedy was in adopting values and practices indiscriminately and applying them with little or no consideration of educational values or purposes. (Callahan, 1962, p. 244)

It is often said that those who ignore the lessons of history are destined to repeat them. Educational administrators in New Zealand, therefore, need to ask some hard questions about where the ideologues of economic rationalism and the new cult of efficiency are taking them.

Similar questions should be asked of market liberalism, which is the other major ideological influence behind the move to self-managing schools in New Zealand. One of the most paradoxical elements in this move has been the continued claim of its proponents that problems of efficiency and equity can be overcome by increasing the degrees of choice that exist within the system.

Promoting Consumer Choice

In the 1987 Treasury brief to the incoming government the rhetoric of market liberalism is used with considerable force to defend policies that, if implemented, would substantially reduce the state's role as the principal provider of education. The authors of this Treasury document take the view that state intervention in education is neither equitable nor efficient. Although the evidence they give for this view is both equivocal and inconclusive, they go further to assert that such intervention for equity purposes would probably 'produce effects that reduce rather than further some kinds of equity' (Treasury, 1987, p. 39). This assertion then becomes the major premise from which to advocate policies that would enable education to enter the marketplace and thus lead to increased choice among its consumers.

As the reform agenda unfolded, the promotion of choice was to become one of the central policy objectives — a key that would presumably unlock all that is both desired and desirable in education. The Picot Taskforce, for instance, proclaim 'choice' as the first of their core values and state that this 'will involve providing a wider range of options both for consumers and for learning institutions' (1988, p. 4). Moreover, they 'see the creation of more choice in the system as a way of ensuring greater efficiency and equity' (1988, p. 4). The promotion of choice as a primary social objective, and the reference to parents or learners as 'consumers', clearly locates these statements within a market liberal discourse that connects the New Zealand education reforms with those that have occurred elsewhere (Ball, 1990).

Chester Finn, educational adviser to the Reagan administration and one of the vanguards in the so-called 'excellence movement' in the United States, claims that parental choice is a direct form of accountability. People, in his words, 'will voluntarily exit from bad schools and head for good ones' (Finn, 1989, p. 28). Such a comment undoubtedly has commonsense plausibility, and after pointing out the unquestionabie desirability of engaging parents more deeply in the education of their children, Finn continues: 'Educational choice, moreover, by fostering competition among schools, will itself lead to diversity and individuality. In addition, choice can widen opportunities for disadvantaged and minority youngsters by giving them access to educational options not available in their immediate neighbourhoods' (p. 28). Those who hold to market liberalism do so with a faith that is blind to social reality. The assumption here is that making choice available is exactly the same as enabling all people to choose. Given the choice between a 'good' school and a 'bad' school, any rational parent would always choose the 'good' school for their children. But the so-called 'good' schools are only perceived as such when they can be distinguished from another group of schools that are perceived to be 'bad'. It is not possible, moreover, for all parents to be in comparable social positions from which to choose between 'good' and 'bad' schools. Some will have available to them more financial and cultural resources than others, and their very choice of what they perceive to be a 'good' school becomes a self-fulfilling prophecy. Thus the exercise of choice by some becomes a capacity to determine what is good, and therefore limits for others the opportunity to choose. Ruth Jonathan has argued that this follows from the nature of education as a 'positional' social good, which she defines as 'the sort of good whose worth to those who have it depends to some extent both on its general perceived value and on others having less of it' (Jonathan, 1989, p. 333).

Recent British legislation (Education Reform Act, 1988) has enabled schools to opt out of local authority control if a majority of parents so determine by ballot. Describing the effects of this and other policies extending parental choice, Ruth Jonathan argues that:

> ... it is probable that some schools will get better and others worse, with those parents who are most informed and articulate influencing and obtaining the 'best buy' for their children, thus giving a further twist to the spiral of cumulative advantage which results when the state is rolled back to enable 'free and fair' competition between individuals or groups who have quite different starting points in the social race. (Jonathan, 1989, p. 323)

The conclusion that this points to is that the promotion and enhancement of consumer opportunity and choice in education can be achieved only with a consequential cost in terms of social justice. In a more recent paper Jonathan maintains that:

> ... in the distribution of a 'positional' good such as education, measures to increase individual opportunity bring about a decrease in social justice and lead to a head-on clash between two commonly accepted duties of the state: to maximize individual freedom and to promote justice for the group as a whole — this clash being exacerbated in direct proportion to the resultant increase in social competition. (Jonathan, 1990, p. 16)

Thus policies that promote educational choice, such as the removal of zoning regulations, have the effect not only of extending individual liberties but of ensuring that rational consumers will tend to use them to pursue their self-interest. When parents do this on behalf of their children, their actions have a prima facie moral justification. We expect parents to look after their children's interests. However, this overlooks other social realities relating to the scarcity of educational resources. Jonathan's argument, therefore, shows that policies which increase the discretionary power of educational consumers give priority to individual liberty over social justice. This presents an ethical problem that lies at the heart of the New Zealand education reforms.

The Ethical Base of Market Liberalism

The ethical theory that underlies market liberalism can be recognized as a form of utilitarianism. In terms of this theory, a moral decision is justified

Figure 1.   Ethical Framework for Educational Administration

	Market Liberal Utilitarianism	Social Justice as Fairness
Primary social objective	Choice	Equity
What is distributed?	Education as a preferred good (exchangeable commodity)	Education as a primary social good
Distributive principle	Utility (optimal average benefits for all — even if disparities are wider)	Fairness (inequalities are justified only if they benefit those who are disadvantaged)
Main criterion for resource allocation	Efficiency (invest to maximize aggregate gains)	Need (invest to improve opportunities for least advantaged)
Major educational outcome	Increased educational productivity	Fairer distribution of educational benefits
Major social effect	Disproportionate acquisition of resources by most advantaged (profit by some)	Redistribution of benefits by limiting choice (welfare for all)

if it produces the greatest amount of happiness for the greatest number of people. Thus, in the distribution of a good such as education, utilitarianism would seek to maximize the average distribution even if the disparities were wider as a result. Efficiency, according to a utilitarian ethic, means that as many people as possible get more of what they want even if some end up getting less. This may be achieved by increasing both opportunities for choice and competition among individuals.

Education, in market liberal utilitarian terms, is considered to be a *preferred good*, that is, something we expect some to want and others not to want. It is something we choose or earn, and because it involves the acquisition of marketable skills, it does not differ essentially from other exchangeable commodities. Such preferred goods do not produce positive externalities or benefits to others apart from those who receive them. The distributive principle within a utilitarian framework is that of utility, which means that a preferred good such as education is distributed so as to gain optimal average benefits for all, even if the least advantaged become worse off. This entails an ethical position that differs in a number of essential ways from the social justice ethic that has traditionally informed educational policy-making in New Zealand. The major differences between these two ethical frameworks are summarized in Figure 1.

Social justice as fairness refers to an ethical framework in which equity is given priority over choice as the primary social objective. In its simplest form, equity is taken to mean 'redress', that is, giving more to the less advantaged. Social justice, however, as Rawls (1972) argues, requires a much more subtle concept of equity. In developing his very influential theory of justice, Rawls posits two principles. The first principle is that: 'each person is to have an equal right to the most extensive total system of equal basic liberties compatible with a similar system of liberty for all' (Rawls, 1972, p. 250). The second principle, which he calls 'the difference principle', is stated as follows: 'Social and economic inequalities are to be arranged so that they are both (a) to the greatest benefit of the least advantaged and (b) attached to offices and positions open to all under conditions of fair equality of opportunity' (Rawls, 1972, p. 83). The application of these principles to education would mean that resources were to be allocated 'so as to improve the long-term expectation of the least favoured' (p. 101) rather than simply evening out existing inequalities or improving the economic efficiency of the system. Because education is necessary to the very formation of people's wants, it constitutes what Rawls calls a *primary good* (p. 62). This is a substantially different conception of education from that assumed by market liberal utilitarianism.

Primary social goods are things that all reasonable people would want because without them they cannot even choose the kind of life they would want. For example, reasonable people would want to be able to participate in decisions that affect their welfare, and to be able to develop skills and acquire knowledge necessary to participation in the political and economic institutions of society. Education, in these terms, becomes defined as a basic human right. It is not something we can simply choose to have from a position of not having it. Education is not something we simply acquire: it changes who we are.

Rawls argues that a just society is one in which primary goods are distributed fairly, according to people's needs. This implies that '. . . resources for education are not to be allotted solely or necessarily mainly according to their return as estimated in productive trained abilities, but also according to their worth in enriching the personal and social life of citizens, including here the less favoured' (Rawls, 1972, p. 107). Within this view, educational policies are justified by the extent to which they produce a fairer distribution of educational benefits, rather than in terms of economic efficiency or improved consumer choice. Social justice obligates the state to invest in education, not to maximize the gains for all, nor to allow some to profit at the expense of others, but rather to safeguard conditions of welfare for all and, where necessary, to limit the choice of some in order to redistribute the benefits more fairly.

This view contrasts strongly with the market liberal position in which the state invests in education to improve the overall productive capacity of its citizens. The aim of market liberalism is to achieve a maximum return on investment. Where this involves an unequal distribution of resources, it is based upon the ability of people to profit from these resources, and it is assumed that the resulting increased productivity eventually will provide benefits for all. However, this 'trickle-down' theory of economic and social justice, which is commonly used in defence of market liberal policies, does not bear closer ethical scrutiny. As Ronald Dworkin points out: 'Children denied adequate nutrition or any effective chance of higher education will suffer permanent loss even if the economy follows the most optimistic path of recovery. Some of those who are denied jobs and welfare now, particularly the elderly, will in any case not live long enough to share in that recovery however general it turns out to be' (Dworkin, 1985, p. 209). Dworkin argues that market liberal utilitarianism, which 'attempts to justify irreversible losses to a minority in order to achieve gains for the large majority' is contrary to the principle that people must be treated with equal concern. Thus the utilitarian ethic, which gives priority to the maximization of people's opportunity to have what they happen to want, denies the principle of equity that is central to social justice as fairness.

The point was made earlier that market liberalism has had a major influence on all areas of government policy in New Zealand since the election of the fourth Labour government in 1984. Its influence on education, however, was not apparent until the government set out to reform educational administration. Following the return of the government in the 1987 election, giving an apparent mandate for its market liberal reforms, these ideas began to materialize in the form of specific policy proposals. At the same time, however, some important aspects of the Labour government's education policies were being developed within a more traditional social justice framework. Consequently, the recent education reforms are fraught with serious internal contradictions. These have been exacerbated since 1990 following the return of a National government that has quickly moved to abolish school zoning, to increase financial aid to private schools and to promote even more self-management among state schools.

In rhetorical terms the recent reforms have been concerned with parent participation in education, with providing clear and explicit objectives for all learning institutions, with promoting learner achievement and increasing the productivity of teachers, and with ensuring that learning institutions are responsive and flexible. In reality, however, the same reforms can be seen to be fostering a climate of harmful competition among schools, promoting unfair degrees of parental choice, exacerbating inequalities between communities, and promoting disparities in resources for special needs and teacher support. What we have, it seems, is a discrepancy between the ends that have been proclaimed for these reforms and the means that are being taken for their achievement. What we have, in other words, is a crisis of educational leadership.

When administrative decisions are based upon market liberal assumptions, yet at the very same time are advanced in the name of equity and social justice, the effects will inevitably be contradictory. When education policy is shaped by demands for economic efficiency and managerial control, administrators have very little scope for the pursuit of educational values or purposes. In the final section an alternative conception of educational leadership is outlined. It is a form of leadership that has the potential for a democratic reconstruction of schooling within the context of a new educational order.

The Search for a Moral Vision

In an address to school administrators more than fifty years ago John Dewey argued that democratic principles were essential to the *educational* mission of schools and other learning institutions. For Dewey, this meant that classroom teachers and school communities would have more organic participation in the formation of the educational policies of the school. It would involve a merging and integration of roles rather than the sharp delineations advocated by managerialists. The traditional hierarchical system, in Dewey's view, only leads to educational waste. Moreover, he asks:

> Is not the waste very considerably increased when teachers are not called upon to communicate their successful methods and results in a form in which it could have organic effect upon general school policies? Add to this waste that results when teachers are called upon to give effect in the classroom to courses of study they do not understand the reasons for, and the total loss mounts up so that it is a fair estimate that the absence of democratic methods is the greatest single cause of educational waste. (Dewey, 1958, p. 65)

It is indeed paradoxical that economists and managerialists, in their quest for market efficiency, are capable of producing so much educational waste.

What Dewey argued against so strongly was instrumentalism in all its forms, or what Habermas (1970) was later to call technocratic rationality. This is a form of political rationality in which ends and means are separated. Once the ends or objectives are determined, it is merely a contingent matter to ascertain the most effective or efficient means of reaching those ends. We decide on our destination, and then it is simply a technical matter as to how we reach it. This is the logic of economics. We set our inflation objective, and then we determine the most effective means of reaching it. This logic, Dewey argued, does not work in education. In education, values are intrinsic, not extrinsic — the means are constitutive of the ends. How we reach our objectives will in itself give substance and meaning to those objectives. At best, instrumentalism distorts educational purposes; at worst, it destroys them.

Two examples of instrumentalism in the new education structure spring to mind. One is the separation of policy from operations. The Lough Report asserts this as though it were a self-evident truth. The making of policy must be separated from its implementation at all levels, from the ministry itself to the smallest educational institution. Another example of instrumentalism is to be found in the notion of contestability of services. If teacher support, for example, is reduced to technical know-how, if it is simply a question of alternative means to the same end, then contestability makes sense. If, however, the quality of such support and the effects it has, are actually determined by the shape and form of its delivery, then contestability may well destroy it or force it into a commodified form which fits the economic logic, but in the long term is more wasteful of human resources.

When instrumental effectiveness usurps more important educational aims, we are more likely to have schools in which the needs of society and the economy are given priority over the development of rational autonomy and independent thought. Under these conditions, political forces are better able to ensure that the school remains an instrument for social control committed to the dominant social and political values and the perpetuation of the existing economic order. In these circumstances, schooling loses its capacity for democratic social renewal and the promotion of social justice.

The cult of managerialism and efficiency, with its emphasis on role definition, planning and control, treats teachers as workers rather than professionals and thereby diminishes their commitment to the values and principles which define the field of educational practice (Codd, 1989a). Specification of objectives, performance reviews and other management techniques may encourage teachers to behave in ways that are antithetical to certain fundamental educational values such as intellectual independence and imagination (Codd, 1989b). Conformity to institutional norms may ensure that minimal levels of performance are maintained and managerial competence can improve efficiency, but educational excellence derives from personal initiative and professional autonomy.

Particular managerial skills may be useful, but for the educational administrator, 'a fully professional commitment is always to a set of values and principles for practice rather than to a particular institution in which the individual happens currently to hold an appointment' (Taylor, 1976, p. 44). Professional educators, whether they be involved in policy-making, administration or teaching, are inevitably in the business of judging and deciding what ought to be done. This is a moral enterprise. Education is about values. Whether they are determining ends or means, educators cannot escape a commitment to values such as openmindedness, tolerance and cultural sensitivity. As a practical activity, therefore, educational administration should entail responsible deliberation and decision-making, enabling teachers within the school to have an active role in producing an educated community of individuals who will have the capacity to promote a fair and democratic social order.

If there is to be education *for* democracy, there must be education *in* democracy. This can be achieved only within an institutional environment that is itself democratic. With the move to self-managing schools, New Zealand education has experienced a crisis of confidence — not in the teaching profession or its leaders, but in its politicians and policy-makers. Not only has the pace of reform been frenetic, but the process at times has been a travesty of democracy, and there has been almost no concern to evaluate the effects of change. If New Zealand schools are to become democratic, open and self-reflective communities in which an ethic of social justice can prevail, then the current forces of managerialism and market liberalism must be defeated. Only their defeat can avert the educational tragedy that is looming.

References

BALL, S.J. (1990) *Politics and Policy Making in Education*, London, Routledge and Kegan Paul.

BARRY, N. (1986) *On Classical Liberalism and Libertarianism*, London, Macmillan.

CALLAHAN, R.E. (1962) *Education and the Cult of Efficiency*, Chicago, Ill., University of Chicago Press.

CODD, J.A. (1989a) 'Educational Leadership as Reflective Action', in J. SMYTH (Ed.), *Critical Perspectives on Educational Leadership*, Lewes, Falmer Press, pp. 157–78.

CODD, J.A. (1989b) 'Evaluating Tomorrow's Schools: Accountability or Control?' *Delta*, 41, pp. 3–11.

CODD, J.A. (1990) 'Educational Policy and the Crisis of the New Zealand State', in S. MIDDLETON, J. CODD and A. JONES (Eds), *New Zealand Education Policy Today: Critical Perspectives*, Wellington, Allen and Unwin, pp. 191–205.

CODD, J., GORDON, L. and HARKER, R. (1990) 'Education and the Role of the State: Devolution and Control Post-Picot', in H. LAUDER and C. WYLIE (Eds), *Towards Successful Schooling*, Lewes, Falmer Press, pp. 15–32.

DEWEY, J. (1958) 'Democracy and Educational Administration', in J. DEWEY, *Philosophy of Education (Problems of Men)*, Totowa, N.J. Littlefield, Adams, pp. 57–69.

DWORKIN, R. (1985) *A Matter of Principle*, Cambridge, Mass., Harvard University Press.

EASTON, B. (Ed.) (1989) *The Making of Rogernomics*, Auckland, Auckland University Press.

EDUCATION REFORM ACT (1988) London, HMSO.

FINN, C. (1989) 'Reforming Secondary Education in the United States', in L. KRAMER, *Education: Pathways to Reform*, Policy Issues No. 8, Melbourne, Institute of Public Affairs, pp. 22–8.

GORDON, L. (1992) 'The Bulk Funding of Teachers' Salaries: A Case Study in Education Policy', in H. MANSON (Ed.), *New Zealand Annual Review of Education*, Wellington, Department of Education, Victoria University, pp. 28–58.

GRACE, G. (1990) 'Labour and Education: The Crisis and Settlements of Education Policy', in M. HOLLAND and J. BOSTON (Eds), *The Fourth Labour*

Government: Politics and Policy in New Zealand, 2nd ed., Auckland, Oxford University Press, pp. 165–91.

HABERMAS, J. (1970) *Towards a Rational Society*, trans J.J. SHAPIRO, Boston, Mass., Beacon Press.

HOLLAND, M. and BOSTON, J. (Eds) (1990) *The Fourth Labour Government: Politics and Policy in New Zealand*, 2nd ed., Auckland, Oxford University Press.

JESSON, B. (1988) 'The Libertarian Right', in B. JESSON, A. RYAN and P. SPOONLEY, *Revival of the Right*, Auckland, Heinemann Reed.

JONATHAN, R. (1989) 'Choice and Control in Education: Parental Rights, Individual Liberties and Social Justice', *British Journal of Educational Studies*, 37, 4, pp. 321–38.

JONATHAN, R. (1990) 'State Education Service or Prisoner's Dilemma: The "Hidden Hand" as Source of Education Policy', *Educational Philosophy and Theory*, 22, 1, pp. 16–24.

KING, D.S. (1987) *The New Right: Politics, Markets and Citizenship*, London, Macmillan.

LOUGH, N.V. (Chairperson) (1990) *Today's Schools* (Lough Report), A Review of the Education Reform Implementation Process, Wellington, Government Printer.

MCLEAN, M. (1988) 'The Conservative Education Policy in Comparative Perspective: Return to an English Golden Age or Harbinger of International Policy Change?' *British Journal of Educational Studies*, 34, 3, pp. 200–17.

MINISTER OF EDUCATION (1988) *Tomorrow's Schools*, Wellington, Government Printer.

ORGANIZATION FOR ECONOMIC COOPERATION AND DEVELOPMENT (1983) *Review of National Policies for Education: New Zealand*, Paris, OECD.

RAWLS, J. (1972) *A Theory of Justice*, Oxford, Clarendon Press.

TASKFORCE TO REVIEW EDUCATION ADMINISTRATION (1988) *Administering for Excellence* (Picot Report), Wellington, Government Printer.

TAYLOR, F.W. (1911) *The Principles of Scientific Management*, New York, Harper.

TAYLOR, W. (1976) 'The Head as Manager: Some Criticisms', in R.S. PETERS (Ed.), *The Role of the Head*, London, Routledge and Kegan Paul, pp. 37–49.

TREASURY (1984) *Economic Management*, Brief to the Incoming Government, Wellington, Government Printer.

TREASURY (1987) *Government Management*, Brief to the Incoming Government 1987, Vol. 2, Wellington, Government Printer.

WYLIE, C. (1992) *The Impact of Tomorrow's Schools in Primary Schools and Intermediates 1991 Survey Report*, Wellington, New Zealand Council for Educational Research.

10 Teaching Cultures and School-based Management: Towards a Collaborative Reconstruction

Andrew C. Sparkes and Martin Bloomer

To say that teaching is going through a period of crisis is something of an understatement, and what is likely to emerge in the coming years is likely to differ in significant ways from teaching as it was characterized in the 1960s, a time that, according to Ozga (1988), signalled the 'zenith' of teachers' professional autonomy. One way in which to gain some insights into this current crisis is to consider the manner in which the occupational culture of teaching is being reconstructed by a variety of agencies, including teachers themselves. In adopting this cultural lens, we hope to indicate that what on the surface appears to suggest radical changes in the relationships teachers have with other interest groups associated with the world of education could, in fact, be but another strand in the ongoing deprofessionalization and control of the teaching force.

The chapter begins by briefly considering the concept of culture in relation to schooling before outlining some of the key features of the occupational culture of teaching that act to maintain the status quo. It is emphasized that cultures should not be taken to be unitary, fixed, monolithic, normative or inert, since the creation, maintenance and recreation of the teaching culture and its features is a dialectical process involving forms of production and reproduction that are themselves historically located. How these features operate in relation to the process of educational change is examined in the context of some recent initiatives formulated by the New Right in the United Kingdom. To highlight key issues, a case study of the changing relationship between school governors and a secondary school teacher in different historical periods is presented. This illustrates how changes inside schools are shaped within a framework of differential power resources and competing sets of interests. Our analysis of events provides a challenge and critique of the prevailing rhetoric of school-based management that, for us, fails to problematize the issue of culture and masks the manner in which recent initiatives act to reinforce those aspects of the teaching culture that negate critical reflection, professional development and real change in schools. The case study material is also used to illustrate the dangers outlined by Hargreaves and Dawe (1990) of mistaking conditions of contrived collegiality with those of a collegial culture in relation to school-based management. Having exposed the tensions contained within current notions of school-based management, we then speculate on the prospect of a deconstruction of the occupational culture of teaching and its reconstruction within a collaborative framework grounded in professional accountability.

Adopting a Cultural Lens

In drawing upon the concept of culture in our analysis, we place ourselves on shaky ground. After all, Gibson (1986) claims, 'Culture is one of the most complex and elusive concepts we possess' (p. 66), while Erickson (1987) comments, 'Culture is a term that presents difficulties as well as interesting possibilities when we try to apply it to the school as a whole' (p. 11). Essentially, it is a contested concept. However, despite the wilful lack of precision with which it is a applied to schools and despite the range of definitions available, Feiman-Nemser and Floden (1986) point out that many studies that have focused upon culture have made the assumption that it provides a common base of knowledge, values, and norms for action that people grow into and come to take as the 'natural' way of life. In relation to this Clarke *et al.* (1981) suggest that culture is the distinctive ways in which the material and social organization of social life expresses itself:

> A 'culture' includes the 'maps of meaning' which make things intelligible to its members. These 'maps of meaning' are not simply carried around in the head: they are objectivated in the patterns of social organization and relationships through which individuals become a 'social individual'. . . . Culture is the way the social relations of a group are structured and shaped: but it is also the way those shapes are experienced, understood and interpreted. (pp. 52–3)

This viewpoint is important for our purposes since it emphasizes that the creation and maintenance of culture is a *dialectical process*. As Bates (1986) reminds us, it is not just about the passing on of performed belief systems from one generation to the next, since culture is 'constructed and reconstructed continuously through the efforts of individuals to learn, master and take part in collective life. . . . Learning a culture, living a culture, changing a culture is, therefore, to take part in the process of history. In this process there are both *possibilities* and *constraints*' (p. 10; emphasis added).

As a consequence, cultures should not be taken to be unitary, fixed, monolithic, normative and inert, since they are continually recreated in an ongoing process of production and reproduction. Indeed, as Swindler (1986) comments:

> all real cultures contain diverse, often conflicting symbols, rituals, stories and guides to action. . . . A culture is not a unified system that pushes action in a consistent direction. Rather, it is more like a 'tool kit' or repertoire . . . from which actors select differing pieces for constructing lines of action. Both individuals and groups know how to do different kinds of things in different circumstances. . . . People may have in readiness cultural capacities they rarely employ; and all people know more culture than they use. (p. 277)

The tool kit metaphor is useful because it allows us to consider both similarities and differences in cultures and how they come about via the complex interactions of agency and structure. For example, in reacting to similar sets of structural constraints and dilemmas they experience on a daily basis in their classroom work with children, such as large classes, lack of equipment and other resources, evaluation procedures, the timing of the school day and the length of teaching periods, and the hierarchical organization of the school, teachers will call upon certain tools from their tool kit that, if successful, will favour their use over others in the future. Eventually this constant use of a limited set of tools ensures that their application and operation become routinized and taken for granted, which creates a selective inattention to other possibilities as teachers constantly restructure the world that they are familiar with in order to maintain regularities and routines (see Schon, 1983). Certainly, as Gitlin (1987) argues, these structures do not totally determine how teachers behave, but they do have a powerful influence, and 'teacher behaviour reflects a compromise between teacher values, ideologies, and the press of school structure' (p. 107).

Several analysts have outlined how the norms of the cultures of teaching have evolved as a response to the structure of schooling and the wider cultural values that establish what is the appropriate role of the teacher. For example, Bullough (1987), Fullan and Hargreaves (1992) and Hargreaves (1989) suggest that the sacred norms of teaching encourage teachers to be present-oriented, conservative and individualistic. According to Hargreaves, they tend to 'avoid long-term planning and collaboration with their colleagues, and to resist involvement in whole school decision-making in favour of gaining marginal improvements in time and resources to make their own individual classroom work easier' (p. 54). Essentially, for Hargreaves, teachers are dominated by a classroom-centredness that is itself constantly reinforced by their experience of classroom isolation. In relation to this isolation, McTaggart (1989) draws upon case study material to talk of a commitment by teachers to privatism that apparently includes a 'moral commitment to keep ideas about teaching private, except under very special conditions. Privacy was recognized as a commitment for one-self, and as a virtue and right for others. In this sense, privatism appeared to be an ethic of teaching' (p. 247).

These norms, as selected tools from the tool kit, have developed in response to the daily routines of teaching and have provided a form of protection for teachers from the insecurities and contradictions they experi-ence in their roles as educators. For example, teacher isolation, according to Bullough (1987), has high utility value for teachers since it is linked to autonomy in their minds and this has high cultural value. That is, in the face of a range of stresses and strains that include the changing attitude of society towards teachers, coupled with the ongoing deterioration of their image, coupled with calls for greater public accountability and assessment of performance, the classroom becomes a sanctuary. Once the classroom door is shut, the teacher feels in control. For Bullough, 'It is behind closed classroom doors that they work out tentative solutions to the problems that confront them without fear of being questioned' (p. 92). Teachers tend to feel secure in the privacy of their own classrooms, and their isolation acts to protect them from a range of pressures so that they can cope with the demands of institutional life. However, as Bullough points out, this understandable response is not without its problems, since it allows many aspects of school life such as dependence upon expert opinion, the denigration of personal interests coupled with a growing alienation from work, the ambiguous celebration of isolation masquerading as autonomy, a distrust of other teachers and a narrow concern with the means of education to the neglect of aims, to go unquestioned and un-challenged. Of course, this is not to suggest that all schools operate with such norms. As Feiman-Nemser and Floden (1986) comment: 'The as-sumption of cultural uniformity is, however, untenable. Teachers differ in age, experience, social and cultural background, gender, marital status, subject matter, wisdom and ability. The schools in which they work also differ in many ways, as do the groups of students they teach. All these may lead to differences in teaching culture' (p. 507).

The tool kit metaphor utilized earlier strongly suggests that teachers are skilful users of culture and not just merely cultural dopes who are passive recipients of the views of dominant groups in society (see Sparkes, 1991). This metaphor also fractures the notion of a singular, monolithic, teaching culture, since different tool kits contain different combinations of tools that can be used creatively. Indeed, despite the dominance of isolation, some schools do have norms of collegiality (see Little, 1982). In these schools the cultural norm of joint work (Little, 1990) supports such col-laborative practices as teachers observing each other during team teaching, providing suggestions for improvement, joint planning, openly discussing professional problems, mentoring and engaging in action research. All these are seen to have a positive influence upon the frequency of teacher interaction, the quality of teaching, the promotion of a shared technical culture among teachers and increased pupil achievement.

Contrived Collegiality and Collaborative Cultures

Not surprisingly, in recent years notions of collegiality and collaboration via their association with school/teacher improvement have become something close to buzz words in the educational community as a range of initiatives has attempted to promote more collaborative forms of professional development within and between schools. In relation to these initiatives, Fullan and Hargreaves (1992) note, 'Attractive concepts like collegiality and collaboration are often imbued with a global sense of virtue' (p. 63). However, this sense of virtue has not gone unchallenged. For example, Hargreaves and Dawe (1990), in commenting upon the paradox whereby teachers are being apparently urged to collaborate more, just at a time when there is less for them to collaborate about, suggest that in a socio-political context characterized by centrally generated and bureaucratically driven forms of control in education, the widespread administrative support for collaborative forms of teacher development may not be as altruistic as it seems at first sight:

> collaborative forms of teacher development may in many instances not be empowering teachers towards greater professional independence at all, but incorporating them and their loyalties within processes and structures bureaucratically determined elsewhere. They may be fostering training, not education, instructional closure rather than intellectual openness, dispositional adjustment rather than thoughtful critique. (pp. 228–9)

In relation to this, Hargreaves and Dawe (1990) draw attention to the contrasting conditions of contrived collegiality and collaborative cultures. According to Fullan and Hargreaves (1992):

> Contrived collegiality is characterized by a set of formal, specific, bureaucratic procedures to increase the attention being given to joint teacher planning, consultation and other forms of working together. It can be seen in initiatives such as curriculum coordinators, mentor schemes, joint planning in specifically provided rooms, school-based management, formally scheduled meetings and clear job descriptions and training programmes for those in consultative roles. These sorts of initiatives are administrative contrivances designed to get collegiality going in schools where little has existed before. They are meant to encourage greater

association among teachers and foster more sharing, learning and improvement of skills and expertise. Contrived collegiality is also meant to assist the successful implementation of new approaches and techniques from the outside into a more responsive and supportive school culture. . . . In some of the most questionable forms of contrived collegiality, colleagueship and partnership are administratively imposed, creating a degree of inflexibility that violates those principles of discretionary judgment which make up the core of teacher professionalism. There are many examples of imposed collegiality which deceptively sail under the flag of collaborative culture. (pp. 78–9)

Similarly, Hargreaves and Dawe (1990) argue that, since contrived collegiality consists of administratively contrived interactions among teachers so that they can meet and work to implement the curricula and instructional strategies developed by others, it enhances administrative control. In contrast, Fullan and Hargreaves (1992) draw upon the work of Nias *et al.* (1989) to suggest that what characterizes collaborative cultures are not formal organization, meetings or bureaucratic procedures. Likewise, cultures of collaboration are not seen to be mounted for specific projects and events; 'Rather, they consist of pervasive qualities, attitudes and behaviours that run through staff relationships on a moment-by-moment, day-by-day basis. Help, support, trust and openness are at the heart of these relationships. Beneath that, there is a commitment to valuing people as individuals and valuing the groups to which people belong' (pp. 65–6). They go on to provide some of the key characteristics of collaborative cultures which include acknowledging and giving voice to the teacher's purpose; sharing and discussing failure and uncertainty with a view to gaining help and support; a continuous process that examines values and purposes; the celebration of and making allowances for the teacher as a person; the creation and maintenance of satisfying and productive work environments; and the simultaneous valuing of the individual and the group. Such cultures foster both teacher and curriculum development and are evolutionary in nature. Fullan and Hargreaves comment:

Because collaborative cultures do not evolve quickly, they can be unattractive to heads looking for swift implementation expedients. Collaborative cultures are difficult to pin down in time and space, living as they do mainly in the interstices of school life. Collaborative cultures are also unpredictable in their consequences. The curriculum that will be developed, the learning that will be fostered, the goals that will be formulated — these things cannot always be predicted confidently beforehand. . . . For some administrators, this unpredictability can be disconcerting. What is fostered, formulated and developed by these collaborative cultures may not always correspond with administrators' own preferred purposes or current priorities of the LEA — or the governors, or even the national education system. (1992, p. 77)

This is not to suggest that managerial guidance and intervention have no part to play in fostering and facilitating the development of a collaborative culture. But collegial support and partnership cannot be mandated. Indeed, the very notions of collegiality and partnership are themselves socially constructed and negotiated in the working context of the school day that is permeated by power relationships. One way of illuminating these issues in all their complexity and richness is via detailed case studies of interactions between managers and teachers in different contexts. Hence we now turn our attention to what on the surface might appear to be a case of collaboration between a school governor and a physical education (PE) teacher in England but which, in fact, is one of contrived collegiality. In choosing this case, we also hope to highlight the changing nature of teachers' work in the last thirty years, which is intimately linked to a variety of external changes among which are the increased powers of school governors to influence the work process and school curriculum. We want to suggest the need for extended and informed interactions between teachers and a range of interested groups so that a collaborative culture based on teacher professionalism is nurtured. Finally, in presenting this single case, we would stress that its purpose is illustrative rather than verificatory. Further cases would be necessary for a full analysis of the problem.

School Governorship in the 1960s: A Grammar School Teacher's Perspective

Sally is a PE teacher and is now in her late 40s. In the 1960s the cultural characteristics in England were relative affluence, upward mobility, increased leisure time and options, greater autonomy of lifestyles, and a belief that those who would be affected by decisions should participate in their making. The 1960s was also a time of 'licensed autonomy' that, according to Dale (1979), prevailed when:

an implicit license was granted to the education system, which was renewable on the meeting of certain conditions. Just how those conditions could be met was again subject to certain broad limitations. . . . The educational expansion of the decade from the early sixties to the early seventies stretched the terms of the education system's license to new limits. . . . The major source of teachers' authority was that they could expect to be backed up by their employers and their representatives as long as they stayed within certain implicit boundaries of curriculum, pedagogy, and evaluation. (pp. 100–5)

These conditions shaped the experiences of Sally during the early part of her teaching career. What follows is a brief extract from her reflections on governors during a period in the mid-1960s when she was employed as an assistant teacher of PE in an all-girls grammar school.

> The advent of the thrice yearly School governor's meeting created little more than a ripple of interest in the school itself. The groundsman was instructed to tidy up the already immaculate front garden, while 'pressganged' sixthformers slaved to produce delectable morsels (suitable to tempt the governors' palate) in the cookery room. . . . Governors' meetings were therefore something of a mystery to us lesser mortals. Held behind closed doors no one would dare ask what went on, and I doubt if even the deputy head was privy to any of the proceedings. How they filled the time was therefore only a subject of mere conjecture. For while it was understood that governors had to approve new staff appointments, and changes in the curriculum, we had it on good authority that they always complied with the wishes of our somewhat domineering Headmistress, making this exercise in all probability something of a mere formality, rather than the subject of rigorous debate.
>
> Governors were always referred to by senior members of staff in those hushed tones which are synonymous with deference, and carefully shielded from the exigencies and unpleasantness of reality. Their only direct contact with the staff was at the post Speech Day tea party, and as far as I knew they never actually met the pupils. They were certainly never to be seen around the school, and even when attending the annual concert, carol service, and school opera — inordinate sense of duty again ensured a good turnout — they assembled in the Head's office to be shepherded to their reserved front row places only after everyone else had been seated. They also left immediately afterwards while the 'hoi polloi' waited patiently for them to wend their way again in the direction of the Head's office and a restorative glass of sherry.
>
> It would be difficult to collectively describe this worthy band, for they were indeed a group of very different individuals. However, they did appear to share certain common characteristics. They were all 'well spoken', middle class, middle aged citizens, acutely aware of the honour which membership of a small town grammar school governing body conferred. Many had 'connections' in the town, and although it was not the 'done thing' for school governors to flout political beliefs in the course of duty, there was little doubt that their sympathies lay with the Conservative County Council of the time. Above all they were considered honest, well thought of, and *eminently respectable*. (Sparkes, 1990a, pp. 42–3)[1]

School Governorship in the 1980s: A Comprehensive Teacher's Experience

Things have changed for Sally. From the mid-1970s onwards there was a marked shift in the social climate in which, according to Hoyle (1986):

> Affluence was replaced by economic stringency. Demographic changes resulted in the reduction in the allocation of public funds to education. The numbers of unemployed increased substantially. . . . A new political ideology founded on monetarism emerged, in which the market was held to ensure that all activities were judged according to their contribution to the economy, and 'enterprise' was emphasised as a cultural theme. (p. 40)

The Conservative government's ongoing commitment since its election in 1979 to reconstructing schooling and education within a market economy framework is evidenced clearly in the 1988 Education Reform Act, particularly with regard to financial delegation, variously known as local financial management (LFM) or local management of schools (LMS). Since April 1990, every primary school in England and Wales has been 'formula funded', with each school's budget being allocated according to the numbers of pupils and their ages. This means that schools now compete for students in any given area and the finances they bring with them. As Hargreaves and Reynolds (1989) comment, 'Schools and secondary schools in particular, it seems, will be allowed to flourish or flounder according to the market dictates of parental choice. Schools are being and will increasingly be placed in the position of competitive enterprises seeking parental custom' (p. 5).

Furthermore, it is planned that by April 1993 all primary and secondary schools with 200 pupils or more will receive 'delegated budgets', the responsibility for which lies in the hands of the governing bodies. Within this framework the governing bodies will be responsible for the appointment of staff, staffing levels, implementation of the National Curriculum, the school's budget and disciplinary and grievance procedures. In schools that choose to opt out of local government control the powers of the headteachers and governors are even greater; Broom (1989) comments that, subject to the requirements of the National Curriculum, they will 'be free to determine the school policy on everything from maths teaching to the purchase of toilet paper' (p. 6). Therefore, LMS would appear to have the effect of emphasizing the accountability of the school to parents and strengthening the accountability of the staff to governors.

These pressures are felt by Sally, who now teaches PE at a school which competes with two other schools in the town for clients. There are rumours that one school might be closed or turned into a sixth form college. The morale of the teachers in Sally's school has been lowered by other events, such as the constant undermining of the profession by the media and press, the asides by government about teaching quality and the general devaluing of teachers and teaching. In such a context Sally describes her experiences of governorship in the late 1980s. Her comments focus on a period following an announcement to the staff by the headteacher that each of the school governors had volunteered to take a special interest in each particular department in the school, and would shortly be contacting the relevant head of department.

> Mine, as it soon became apparent, had every intention of taking this responsibility seriously. Determined to be positive about this unexpected turn of events, my hopes were raised. Perhaps my governor might be instrumental in updating our almost mediaeval equipment, and help resolve some of the more pressing departmental problems. This new style of school governorship might even mark the birth of that new partnership envisaged by the Taylor Report (Department of Education and Science [DES], 1977), nearly a decade before. The first inkling that my hopes might not be realized dawned as I became aware that the 'bloke' who kept 'dropping in' for a gossip with one of my junior colleagues in the department was in fact *my governor*. Already on familiar first name terms with everyone in the department except me, I remember feeling vaguely uncomfortable as he disappeared with a male colleague in the direction of the boys' changing room. This was hardly the mode of professional intercourse I had expected!
>
> It was soon evident that my preconceived hopes of a fruitful and supportive relationship were naive and hopelessly optimistic. My governor turned out to be a man with a mission, a man who saw it as his duty to become something of a messiah. Reason and rationality did not feature prominently in a single minded approach to his perception of the situation. His intent, it became clear, was not only to 'sort out the PE department', but to save the school in the process as well. By revolutionising our facilities, and exhorting, supporting and extolling the virtues of the winning school teams he had conceptualized, he was to fulfil cherished ambitions to restore the school's somewhat tarnished public image.
>
> His ambitions, no doubt fuelled by good intentions, were nonetheless supported by an intransigent attitude that permitted neither negotiation nor compromise, let alone consideration of alternative points of view. . . . He heard only what he wanted to hear, and wanted no truck with anything unlikely to improve the school's public image. Matches, matches, and yet more matches were called for — especially against those schools who were enjoying greater

popularity. Anything creative, aesthetic, or which would not attract public attention were dismissed as irrelevant. My comments
such as, 'only fifteen per cent of the school population participate
in competitive sports, don't you think we should offer activities in
which all children can participate?', fell on stony ground. He even
suggested that the trampolining and dance club which were en-
joying considerable popular support should be abandoned in favour
of running more inter-school fixtures.

Since assuming responsibility for my department I have endeavoured
to transform what had previously been an elitist, skills dominated,
and very competitive regime into one more compatible with
contemporary educational thinking. Thus equality of educational
opportunity, and relevant experiences for all were becoming accepted as a justifiable approach to this subject. The added dimensions of personal and social development plus a health focus
not only ensured that pupils received the type of physical education
to which they were *entitled* (DES, 1985), but came near to supporting official curricular views as set out in *The School Curriculum*
(DES, 1981). As one colleague kindly commented, I had moved
the department through 'light years' to a more enlightened and
forward looking position. At one blow a school governor had dismissed all this innovation as not only irrelevant but undesirable. So
much for hopes of a prosperous new partnership! (Sparkes, 1990a,
pp. 43–5)[2]

Locating the Case in a Wider Landscape

Sally's case has been dealt with in more detail elsewhere (Sparkes, 1990a,
1990b, 1992); the point here is that on the surface, to an outsider, the case
might have seemed to be an example of collegiality in action. However,
as Sally's words suggest, it is really a case of contrived collegiality. Of
course, the governor involved probably had the 'good intentions' and the
'interests of the school' at heart. Yet these terms form a 'symbolic canopy'
(Popkewitz and Lind, 1989) that is central to the discourse of management
that masks key issues of power and interests in the contemporary negotiation of relationships between teachers and governors. As a consequence,
we need to see Sally's experiences with a school governor in a wider socio-
historical context in which there has been a shift from 'licensed autonomy'
to 'regulated autonomy'. The latter, according to Dale (1979), involves a
tightening control over the education system, largely through the codifi-
cation and monitoring of processes and practices that were previously left
to teachers' professional judgment. In comparison to the 1960s it would
appear that indirect rule has been replaced by direct rule. In summarizing

the current situation, in which the freedom of teachers to manoeuvre is greatly reduced, Ball (1988) comments, 'Choices have been removed or preempted and certain functions have been withdrawn. In effect the lines of control are now visible rather than invisible, direct rather than indirect, explicit rather than implicit' (p. 291). Part of these visible lines now includes the assertive interventionist stance of school governors armed with increasingly greater powers to shape the school curriculum and the working lives of teachers.

Such conditions do not lend themselves to the development of collaborative cultures in schools but certainly do provide a strong foundation for contrived collegiality. It is more than likely that in the coming years teachers may find themselves delving into their tool kit and choosing, for very good reasons, their well tested tools to assist them to survive. Consequently, the sacred norms of the teaching culture that were described earlier may well be reinforced as teachers attempt to cope with their changing work conditions. Such reinforcement in itself would assist the ongoing process of deprofessionalization that is in operation, since it disempowers teachers from making any collective response to the dilemmas they face as an occupational group.

School-based Management Reconstructed: Some Speculations for a Collaborative Future

Logically, there are two approaches that teachers might take to arrest their own deprofessionalization. The first, via the ballot box, is a rare opportunity and even if there were a change of government, there is nothing to suggest that the opposition parties in Britain have any real intention of dismantling the free market educational economy. The second opportunity to contest current developments demands the close re-examination of teaching and professionalism by teachers themselves as a precursor to the deconstruction and reconstruction of a teaching profession. It is this opportunity, and our own optimism, that we explore in the remainder of this chapter.

The deconstruction of the teaching profession will entail among teachers a critical awareness of the 'new orthodoxies', and a preparedness to contest these on professional grounds. It will require that they challenge the mechanisms of control currently perpetuated in the name of school-based management and accountability in order to lay bare the crude ideology that underpins them. It will be necessary to demonstrate to a general public the qualitative effects of recent changes in educational planning and administration. To do this will require the informed and confident projection of teaching as a specialist activity, a difficult task given that teaching is all too readily regarded as depending upon relatively low level subject knowledge coupled with visible technical skills, or 'gifts', that somehow enable teachers to control unruly classes or make lessons interesting. But, as Carr and Kemmis (1986) note, '[Teaching expertise] consists of spontaneous and flexible direction and re-direction of the learning enterprise, guided by a sensitive reading of the subtle changes and responses of other participants in the enterprise. . . . [It] does not [simply] consist of designing a set of sequenced means or techniques which "drive" learners towards expected leaning outcomes' (p. 37). Somehow, such a view of teaching must be clearly projected to a general public — parents, governors and the community at large — but first it must be recognized by the teachers themselves. Only then can the technical-rationalism which lies behind deprofessionalization be publicly exposed and contested.

A fuller public recognition and acceptance of the values of education, and of the specialist expertise and more subtle qualities of teaching, are prerequisites to any effective reconstruction of teaching simply because it is accountability to others who hold a legitimate interest in education that is the very cornerstone of true professional autonomy and status. We speak here of an open, public, professional accountability (see Sockett, 1982a, 1982b; Simons, 1982) whose criteria are continually validated against educational aims and not, as contemporary accounting mechanisms are, selected for their simplicity. Professional accountability gives minimal attention to crude quantitative 'performance indicators' which, in themselves, stripped of context, provide little useful insight into the quality of education; it more often focuses upon the 'unmeasurable'; it is conducted in qualitative rather than quantitative terms; and it does not readily facilitate comparisons of individuals and institutions given its primary concern to elicit the idiosyncratic qualities of particular cases.

A reconstruction of teaching grounded in professional accountability is entirely consistent with the form of collaborative culture discussed earlier in this chapter. It is a form of accountability and collegiality that is bounded and shaped only by legitimate interests in education. It is neither task driven nor predictable; nor is it constrained by the offices of its participants. The case for collegiality that embraces school and community has already been put by Fullan and Hargreaves (1992).

> Collaborative schools are highly plugged into their environments — the local community, the regional, and even the national contexts. It is possible to become collaborative despite the environment, but it is not possible to stay collaborative without active involvement in and support from the environment. . . . There are at least two reasons why this is the case. First, in the same way that openness is necessary within the school, it must also characterize how the school connects with the outside. As more schools are opting out of Local Authority control, and individual schools compete for pupil numbers and sheer survival, this principle becomes particularly important. New ideas, better practices elsewhere, stimulation, pressure to take into account societal needs,

and dissemination (of what one has to offer to other teachers and schools) are all part of the spiritual vitality of collaborative schools. Nor can schools succeed if they do not establish close working relationships with parents and the community. (p. 70)

Of course, it is easier to speak of openness and collaboration than it is to achieve them, and we do not wish to understate the difficulties of achieving a confident and assertive position in times of widespread demoralization. Nor do we overlook the fact that a collaborative culture requires a significant shift from the occupational culture of teaching referred to earlier. Teachers' tool kits will need to be restocked; some tools may be retained and modified, while other will have to be replaced altogether. Teachers will need to break from the established routines that have arisen more from repetitive practice than from anything else. Specifically, teaching must be made a much more open and visible activity and the old habits of individualism, presentism, conservatism and isolationism abandoned.

It is the occupational culture of teaching and its associated habits, further hardened by recent pressures for contrived collegiality, which has served to cut teachers off, not only from one another, but from the public at large and from parents in particular. It is parents, we would argue, who are crucial to the reconstruction of both the teaching profession and the concept of school-based management. Both teachers and parents have a strong vested interest in the education and welfare of the young, and both are essential to the achievement of that end. Yet the occupational culture of teaching has sustained some indifference among teachers to the real interests of parents, and the practice of teaching has been largely divorced from that of parenting. Such observations informed the Taylor Report (DES, 1977) and *The Parents' Charter* (DES, 1991), both of which sought to extend opportunities for the participation of parents in schooling. However, it is significant that the 1988 Education Reform Act, which sought to achieve similar ends, did so not by encouraging parent entry to the 'secret garden' of education but by inviting parents to become governors with the potential to divert the course of education in accordance with criteria imposed through a market economy framework without any reference to the would-be professional body of teachers, as Sally's case has illustrated.

There is growing evidence of parental concern about recent developments in education, but it appears that parental conceptions of education are fuelled by at least two forms of knowledge: that which they gain through the experiences of their own children in school; and that which they acquire from elsewhere, from their past experiences, the mass media and street gossip. When asked to judge schools and teachers upon the basis of their own experiences as parents, parents present a very favourable account indeed. For example, a recent study by Hughes *et al.* (1992) found that 86 per cent of parents commented, that they were happy with their choice of school, usually because they felt their child was happy, although a few of these expressed some reservations. The reservations took a number of forms, such as a concern about the physical conditions of the school, about discipline, about their child's lack of progress, and about headlice, although it should be made clear these reservations were only expressed by a small number of parents. A similar proportion of parents (83 per cent) thought that on the whole the teachers were doing a good job, with nearly a quarter of them being particularly enthusiastic — 'Very good', 'very impressed' and 'brilliant under the circumstances'. (p. 61)

However, when asked to comment on 'the state of education' on the basis of more generalized experiences, the picture is quite different; schools and teachers are seen to be failing to a much greater degree.

The distinction between specific knowledge and generalized knowledge is most important when it comes to engaging parents in deliberations about education and teacher professionalism. A dialogue between teachers and parents that is based on generalized knowledge can easily be blocked by the rhetoric of 'standards' and dubious generalized images of educational failure (or success), while personal ideological commitments are likely to impede its development if it is grounded only in generalized principles concerning matters such as selection, 'discipline' or pedagogy. However, where dialogue can be based upon specific knowledge concerning the individual welfare of an individual pupil, for example, there is far greater opportunity for discussion to escape disruptive ideological influences and become anchored more securely in empirical evidence and genuine, shared educational concerns.

The relationships between teachers and parents that we envisage here generated their own criteria of accountability. Such criteria are negotiated between those parties immediately concerned with a particular educational case, event or development; they are contextualized, they are elicited from, and are grounded in, teachers' and parents' experience of pupils and their learning. As such, they have meaning for both teachers and parents and assist their open communication, enabling them to get closer to what might be described as the less readily measurable features of teaching and learning. They would, of course, differ quite markedly from the nationally pre-scribed 'performance criteria' which, although giving rise to more readily measurable 'outcomes', contribute little to the achievement of open, honest and useful dialogue between parents and teachers.

The teacher-parent relationship, or partnership, that we have described here provides a marked contrast to the one envisaged under the 1988 Education Reform Act. It is organically grounded, collaborative, even collegial, and not simply contrived by mechanisms of law. The authority of all parties in our preferred teacher-parent partnership rests upon specific knowledge of the educational development of particular young people — knowledge that can and must be continually validated against experience. This is a type of partnership, a type of knowledge and a type of authority that many governors do not have and can never have, and that is noticeably absent from many contemporary examples of school-based management. It is our view that the considerable strengths of a teacher-parent partnership must be fully harnessed in order to stimulate the political will to deconstruct the legacies of entrepreneurial and technicist ignorance and to form the foundations of a professional, accountable and collaborative alternative.

We have already argued that teaching is a complex activity and that teachers need to make the specialist nature of their expertise explicit to a wider audience. The process of making teaching explicit will require the development of a new discourse that will, on the one hand, capture the complexities of teaching, while, on the other hand, assist rather than alienate outsiders' understanding. It will also require that teachers 'return to first principles' of their practice and examine their work very closely, maybe redefining their work and themselves in the process, in order that they will be able to establish firm foundations upon which to build. This will require that all those who engage in such an activity do so with openness and honestly, that they suspend self-interest and proceed only with reference to the educational interests of their pupils who, in turn, should provide the single most important source of validation for all developments. It will not be a straightforward task; it may well prove painful at times but offers, in the long term, the only real opportunity for teachers to reconstruct a sense of worth.

The critical inspection of teaching and of education must not be carried out in isolation. While initially it might centre on small groups of teachers, it must soon involve parents and later all teachers and others with legitimate interests in schooling and the prescribed locality. It must be based upon a genuine partnership between teachers and parents; it must be truly collaborative, not the contrived collegiality so evident in many existing parent-teacher or parent-governor-teacher or parent-manager-teacher relationships.

Such a partnership, we claim, will facilitate a wider recognition of the professional nature of teaching, but this will only become possible if it is accompanied by a requirement for full professional accountability. Professional status offers autonomy within the terms of professional practice but demands accountability in terms of the intrinsic qualities of that practice. The reconstruction of teaching will require a dramatic transformation of the occupational culture of teaching; some of the characteristics of this transformation have already been referred to in this chapter. Most dramatic of all, however, are its implications for management and governance. The function of headteachers and governors will be to mediate between the educational and professional interests of the communities (pupils, parents and teachers) that they *represent* and the social, political and economic worlds beyond. It will not be to provide their political masters with the means of *control* over public education.

In this chapter we have stored great faith in the potential of a teacher-parent partnership to agree and articulate the true values of education. On the basis of information that is now becoming available, we believe this faith to be fully justified. We have claimed that such a partnership, involving others with legitimate interests in education, will stimulate the political will to promote a newly democratic form of educational management, administration and accountability that is solidly based in educational, not political or entrepreneurial interests. Only when this happens will the purveyors of glossy brochures, personalized number plates and the perverse rhetoric of 'performance indicators' be exposed as the charlatans we believe them to be. And only when this happens can new and positive meanings, and more accurate meanings, be given to the terms 'professional educator' and 'school-based management'.

Notes

1 From A. Sparkes (1990) 'The Changing Nature of Teachers' Work: Reflecting on Governor Power in Different Historical Periods', *Physical Education Review*, 13, 1, pp. 39–47. Adapted by permission of Ken Hardman as editor on behalf of the North Western Counties Physical Education Association.
2 *Ibid.*

References

BALL, S. (1988) 'Staff Relations during the Teachers' Industrial Action: Context, Conflict and Proletarianization', *British Journal of Sociology of Education*, 9, 3, pp. 289–306.

BATES, R. (1986) *The Management of Culture and Knowledge*, Geelong, Deakin University Press.

BROOM, D. (1989) 'The Blackboard Revolution', *The London Times*, 28 August, p. 21.

BULLOUGH, R. (1987) 'Accommodation and Tension: Teachers, Teaching Role, and the Culture of Teaching', in J. SMYTH (Ed.), *Educating Teachers: Changing the Nature of Pedagogical Knowledge*, Lewes, Falmer Press, pp. 83–94.

CARR, W. and KEMMIS, S. (1986) *Becoming Critical*, Lewes, Falmer Press.

CLARKE, J., HALL, S., JEFFERSON, T. and ROBERTS, B. (1981) 'Subcultures, Cultures and Class', in T. BENNET *et al.* (Eds), *Culture, Ideology and Social Process*, Batsford, London, pp. 53–79.

DALE, R. (1979) 'The Politicisation of School Deviance: Reactions to William Tyndale', in L. BARTON and R. MEIGHAN (Eds), *Schools, Pupils and Deviance*, Nafferton, Driffield, pp. 95–113.

DEPARTMENT OF EDUCATION AND SCIENCE (1977) *A New Partnership for Our Schools* (The Taylor Report), London, HMSO.

DEPARTMENT OF EDUCATION AND SCIENCE (1981) *The School Curriculum*, London, HMSO.

DEPARTMENT OF EDUCATION AND SCIENCE (1985) *Better Schools*, London, HMSO.

DEPARTMENT OF EDUCATION AND SCIENCE (1991) *The Parents' Charter: You and Your Child's Education*, London, HMSO.

ERICKSON, F. (1987) 'Conceptions of School Culture: An Overview', *Educational Administration Quarterly*, 23, 4, pp. 11–24.

FEIMAN-NEMSER, S. and FLODEN, R. (1986) 'The Cultures of Teaching', in M. WITTROCK (Ed.), *Handbook of Research on Teaching*, 3rd ed., London, Collier Macmillan, pp. 505–26.

FULLAN, M. and HARGREAVES, A. (1992) *What's Worth Fighting for in Your School?*, Buckingham, Open University Press.

GIBSON, R. (1986) *Critical Theory and Education*, London, Hodder and Stoughton.

GITLIN, A. (1987) 'Common School Structures and Teacher Behaviour', in J. SMYTH (Ed.), *Educating Teachers: Changing the Nature of Pedagogical Knowledge*, Lewes, Falmer Press, pp. 107–19.

HARGREAVES, A. (1989) *Curriculum and Assessment Reform*, Milton Keynes, Open University Press.

HARGREAVES, A. and DAWE, R. (1990) 'Paths of Professional Development: Contrived Collegiality, Collaborative Culture, and the Case of Peer Coaching', *Teaching and Teacher Education*, 6, 3, pp. 227–41.

HARGREAVES, A. and REYNOLDS, D. (1989) 'Introduction: Decomprehensivization', in A. HARGREAVES and D. REYNOLDS (Eds), *Education Policies: Controversies and Critiques*, Lewes, Falmer Press, pp. 1–32.

HOYLE, E. (1986) 'Curriculum Development in Physical Education 1966–1985', in *Trends and Developments in Physical Education*, Proceedings of the 8th Commonwealth and International Conference on Sport, Physical Education, Dance, Recreation and Health, London, Spon, pp. 35–45.

HUGHES, M., WIKELEY, F. and NASH, T. (1992) 'Dissatisfied Customers? The View of Real Parents', *Perspectives*, 44, pp. 55–66.

LITTLE, J. (1982) 'Norms of Collegiality and Experimentation: Workplace Conditions of School Success', *American Education Research Journal*, 19, pp. 325–40.

LITTLE, J. (1990) 'The Persistence of Privacy: Autonomy and Initiative in Teachers' Professional Relationships', *Teachers College Record*, 91, 4, pp. 509–36.

MCTAGGART, R. (1989) 'Bureaucratic Rationality and the Self-Educating Profession: The Problem of Teacher Privatism', *Journal of Curriculum Studies*, 21, 4, pp. 345–61.

NIAS, J., SOUTHWORTH, G. and YEOMANS, R. (1989) *Staff Relationships in the Primary School*, London, Cassell.

OZGA, J. (Ed.) (1988) *Schoolwork: An Introduction to the Labour Process of Teaching*, Milton Keynes, Open University Press.

POPKEWITZ, T. and LIND, K. (1989) 'Teacher Incentives and Reforms: Teachers' Work and the Changing Control Mechanism in Education', *Teachers College Record*, 90, 4, pp. 575–94.

SCHON, D. (1983) *The Reflective Practitioner*, London, Temple Smith.

SIMONS, H. (1982) 'Process Evaluation in Schools', in R. MCCORMICK *et al.* (Eds), *Calling Education to Account*, Milton Keynes, Open University Press, pp. 119–32.

SOCKETT, H. (1982a) 'Accountability: Purpose and Meaning', in R. MCCORMICK *et al.* (Eds), *Calling Education to Account*, Milton Keynes, Open University Press, pp. 7–9.

SOCKETT, H. (1982b) 'Towards a Professional Model of Teacher Accountability', in R. McCORMICK *et al.* (Eds), *Calling Education to Account*, Milton Keynes, Open University Press, pp. 17–20.

SPARKES, A. (1990a) 'The Changing Nature of Teachers' Work: Reflecting on Governor Power in Different Historical Periods', *Physical Education Review*, 13, 1, pp. 39–47.

SPARKES, A. (1990b) 'The Emerging Relationship between Physical Education Teachers and School Governors: A Sociological Analysis', *Physical Education Review*, 13, 2, pp. 128–37.

SPARKES, A. (1991) 'The Culture of Teaching, Critical Reflection and Change: Possibilities and Problems', *Educational Management and Administration*, 19, 1, pp. 4–19.

SPARKES, A. (1992) 'The Changing Nature of Teachers' Work: School Governors and Curriculum Control in Physical Education', in N. ARMSTRONG (Ed.), *New Directions in Physical Education: Volume 2*, Champaign, Ill., Human Kinetics Press, pp. 1–31.

SWINDLER, A. (1986) 'Culture in Action: Symbols and Strategies', *American Sociological Review*, 51, pp. 273–86.

11 'And Your Corporate Manager Will Set You Free ...': Devolution in South Australian Education

Brendan Ryan

Introduction

Across the Australian states generally there is now a substantial consolidation of central technocratic controls over key educational policy areas, thereby denying any real possibility for substantial inputs by representatives of teacher, citizen and community groups. Given that the centre would thus be made both more powerful and less representative, any real scope for participation would be limited to the local level and to questions concerning how best to implement central policy. But within the 'rational' model of educational planning and administration that now dominates, the responsibility for 'getting the job done' is viewed, in microtechnocratic terms, as mainly a matter for the local professionals, while school principals are assigned a much stronger managerialist role in order to ensure that overall schooling policy is a functional adaptation of the new sense of central purpose. No real space is allowed at any stage of educational planning and implementation for the democratic discussion of viewpoints and concerns and hence for an active community voice. Nonetheless, the rhetoric of devolution does not merely serve a mystifying ideological function but rather has a much more positive political content; it signals that the burden of 'democratic' accountability falls mainly on teachers. Once this position is accepted, issues concerning the production and nature of policy itself would cease to be a matter of focal public concern and debate.

Yet, as I argue in the first part of this chapter, it is issues concerning basic educational policy commitments that should engage educators and democrats, rather than those that focus, in the name of devolution, on little else than structural matters. I focus in particular upon those studies, notably Pusey (1991), that show that public sector administration generally is subsumed within a 'whole-of-government' approach in the corporate state. As a consequence, it would be fundamentally mistaken to view the current tightening of central educational controls as involving mainly a clawing back of real cultural power by 'old-style' educational bureaucrats. Instead, leading educational technocrats would increasingly be constrained to operate within a megapolicy framework, one that establishes expenditure cuts and the pursuit of economic modernization as the determinants of institutional policy. What this means in terms of the practical relationships of educational government is that a new, distinctly economic rationalist tier of controls is being imposed upon existing bureaucracies, thereby indicating that independent educational considerations, even of a traditionally bureaucratic kind, would no longer be allowed to exercise any major influence at any level of decision-making. Instead, a narrowly economic version of the general interest increasingly directs all major areas of educational policy, effectively ruling out, as a mainstream schooling activity, the pursuit of general educational goals that are not economically relevant and also any substantial curricular autonomies that embody a concern for the distinctive socio-cultural needs of particular communities or groups.

Once it is accepted that economic concerns are the only real business of schooling, parents will increasingly be locked into a preoccupation with the exchange value of their children's schooling — rather than seeing themselves in any sense as collaborators with local professionals in the pursuit of distinctive community needs and interests. Typical parental inputs would thus be limited to little else than pressuring schools and teachers to improve student achievement in the 'key competences'. Parents would become more judgmental in their relationships with teachers, precisely in that narrow accountability sense that is now being assiduously cultivated by increasingly powerful central planners. Given the increased importance of schooling credentials, I argue further, competition would become the major currency of classroom relationships, thereby terminating any residual elements of a common cultural life in the modernized school. In terms of the relationships both between and within key stakeholder groups at the local level, divisiveness rather than solidarity would be the defining political characteristic. This would constitute a fragmentation and dissipation of the power of the periphery and a substantial strengthening of that of the reconstituted centre as a consequence (Davies, 1990, p. 31).

The second part of the chapter provides a critical analysis of the South Australian Education Department's blueprint for devolution (Education Department of South Australia, 1991). This assumed the form of a major statement concerning overall educational policy and organization, and thus provides an especially revealing insight into the meaning of current movements in control along the centralization/decentralization axis. The timing of the Education Department's submission was instructive; all government agencies were required to make recommendations to a Government Agencies Review Group (GARG) concerning the more 'efficient and effective' utilization of resources. The bottom-line rationale of devolution South Australian style was cheaper schooling, and its key element as outlined by the Education Department was to be a single, one-line budget. In this climate of parsimony it was clear that the latter was to be managed according to strict accounting criteria. Given this preoccupation with affordability, local demands would soon be prioritized according to what was seen as both necessary and viable, leading to an inbuilt, structural bias across all schools against real educational alternatives.

The Education Department makes it quite clear that the local managers of the finance would be allowed no real share of decision-making power. There is a continuous emphasis upon the coordination of policy across all functionally-based directorates and an insistence upon the strengthening of managerialist controls within each of these. Underpinning this much more active and intrusive pursuit of a systemic, corporate culture is the redesign of the mainstream curriculum so that it would be made to serve narrowly economic ends, and little else. In the manner of corporate management schemes generally, this narrowly focused educational mission constitutes the determining factor in the departmental redefinition of major positions of responsibility down the hierarchical line, notably those of District Superintendents and school principals. As a consequence, the latter would be allowed no real discretion to act in an educationally independent way but would be required, instead, to ensure that school-based operations are made to conform (without substantial residue) to the 'whole picture' that has been centrally determined.

The Department uses the language of the 'effective schools' movement to indicate that, when it comes to the kinds of discretion that would be allowed to local schools, these would be limited mainly to technical assessments of the 'best methods' based on the findings of the 'rationalizing educational sciences' (Pusey, 1981, pp. 12–13). This particular invocation of 'science' serves a cluster of related ideological purposes. What is thereby indicated, in particular, is that, regardless of the cultural purposes being served, the social context or the resources available, all schools would possess the basic scientific means through which to produce significant improvement in general levels of achievement. The Department would then be enabled to disclaim any major responsibility for the persistence of substantial underachievement and misbehaviour; equally tellingly, school-based interventions to help 'the disadvantaged' would be limited to little else than a more concentrated focus, within a narrowly technical model of teaching, on the core skills of the mainstream curriculum. Not even in the name of social justice, therefore, would the modernized school be prepared to countenance multiculturalism in any substantial form. Rather, a crucial source of 'social democratic' legitimation would be given to the increasingly pressing task of cultural assimilation in the national interest. Such an abstract systems perspective upon the conditions of teaching and learning constitutes an idealism of an extreme and retrogressive kind. My analysis of the departmental blueprint indicates that in its sub-servience to the economic imperative, an acceptance of a more elitist form of schooling is unmistakeably signalled. But the view of teaching as a generalizable, rule-governed activity, in nominating teacher's work as little else than an elite form of labour, also signifies that questions concerning general policy are mainly a political/managerial matter, a very functional ideological consequence. The current modernization of education could thus be pursued, unimpeded by the cultural and social concerns that have become prominent among Australian teachers in recent years.

In the interests of both democracy and equality, I conclude, defenders of state provided schooling must give the most urgent scrutiny to current attempts to restructure the nature and conditions of teaching. They must stress, in particular, that a much more powerful state, if it is to claim any real democratic legitimacy, must be prepared to learn more (Walker, 1991). 'The system', in short, must be required to take seriously the evidence of its teachers concerning the effects of policy innovations, an accountability requirement that necessitates a commitment to the need for an inde-pendently minded and public spirited teaching force. These characteristics would be more than ever necessary if schools are to be enabled to respond, in the sense of the educational realism espoused by this chapter, to the facts of increasing cultural alienation and social disintegration within many school communities. Far from being learners, however, what now char-acterizes central planners is a gritty determination to make their ideas the governing consideration at all levels of educational governance and pro-vision. Given the anti-humanist and anti-social nature of their overall agenda, this is likely to lead to a deterioration of basic socio-cultural re-lationships in many schools, a situation that would be made even worse by the requirement that, in the name of current commitments to devolution, school-based responses would be limited mainly to forms of managerialist containment. The educational system would thus be increasingly stripped of any semblance of basic social intelligence and resourcefulness. As a consequence, 'under the pressure of realities that it cannot grasp' (Pusey, 1991, p. 241), it would cease to act as a universal educational provider in any real sense.

Deregulating the Economy, Reregulating Education

Current moves towards the devolution of financial controls within Aus-tralian schools must be seen against the background of broader processes of economic and administrative restructuring. In response to the twin spectres of a traditional economic crisis and a new economic order, more efficient forms of public administration have been sought so that grow-ing fiscal overload would be alleviated. Overall state policy has also been subsumed within a whole-of-government approach that is directed at the achievement of economic rationalist ends. The current 'reform' agenda targets the administration of education above all else, given that it makes the biggest demand upon the public purse and its role in the production of the new skills required by the innovative economy. This significance ascribed to the school's human capital role has given a momentum and focus to current moves towards a national curriculum. Until recently, the various Australian states had insisted on their constitutional controls over the curriculum. Now, however, under the impact of more powerful extra-legal realities, the quality of schooling has been successfully targeted as a matter of pressing national significance and as being too important to be based on the uncoordinated deliberations of the various states and the independent judgments of teachers.

Within the dominant ideology, since the national interest is viewed essentially in asocial, narrowly economic terms, what is being promoted under the banner of a national curriculum is a narrowly focused emphasis on the core skills and knowledge of the 'economically relevant' disciplines, notably the languages, mathematics, sciences and technologies. While some rhetorical deference is still paid to the need for a liberal education, this is usually defended in terms of the increased vocational significance of general cognitive skills in a rapidly changing economy. There is no real attempt within official policy statements to elaborate upon the need for a liberal education in terms of its contribution to the making of an independently minded citizenry or to a genuine social pluralism. Nor is it reasonable to claim, given the strength of commitment to 'economically relevant' schooling, that the independent cultural priorities of conventional schooling can still be taken for granted. Instead, this absence of a distinctively educational perspective in official discourse signals the likely development of a mainstream national curriculum that is little else than the instrument of economic policy.

The culturally restrictive nature of this development is disguised, however, by the fact that it is the political arm of government, through the much increased powers of expanded ministries of education, that increasingly determines policy. As a consequence it can be claimed that the current strengthening of central educational controls would make schooling more accountable to democratic determinations of the general educational interest (while curbing the oft-lamented tendency to authoritarian rule by unelected mandarins in the process). But it is precisely the capacity of the 'social democracies' to articulate and defend a realistic conception of popular interests that must be increasingly challenged. Throughout the 1980s, as the education bureaucracy at both national and state levels was being made more accountable, the apparently more powerful ministries of education were themselves being denied any real freedom for manoeuvre of a conventional, political kind, given the megapolicy status assigned to so-called economic imperatives. As a consequence, there was a movement away from anything even resembling collective Cabinet decision-making towards executive rule by leading economic rationalist ministers (Weller and Lewis, 1989). What this has meant in terms of the practical relationships of government is that while educational ministers now enjoy much enhanced power with respect to educational administrators (and they, in turn, with respect to teachers and community), these ministries are increasingly little else than instruments of the key economic agencies whose political priorities, in the words of Pusey (1991, p. 179), 'ultimately have their origins in the great financial institutions of the private sector.' The current politicization of education, far from constituting the means by which educational institutions would be made more responsive to a viable conception of the public interest, constitutes instead a de facto privatization of the key elements of policy and practice.

Exit Old-style Bureaucracy: Enter New-style Economic Rationalism

In pursuit of such restrictive controls, leading educational administrators are increasingly chosen on the basis of value-free, managerialist competences rather than distinctive educational understandings and experiences. As Pusey (1991) has admirably demonstrated, promotion to all positions of administrative authority within the national bureaucracy is now dependent mainly upon the possession of high-order, abstract intellectual skills (notably in disciplines such as neo-classical economics and psychology) rather than progression through the ranks in particular departments. On the basis of these narrowly instrumental models of social systems and human behaviour, the new mandarins collectively would be able to rationalize and coordinate the various activities of the state, bringing them all into line with the imperial claims of economic restructuring. No real consideration would be given, even in the educational sector, to the complexity of existing social needs and motivations. Rather, these would be redefined and reshaped by the new breed of 'value-free' managers to accommodate the prevailing, narrowly economic version of the 'national interest' (Considine, 1988). Any real commitment to a substantial measure of difference and diversity, far from being seen as an integral democratic requirement within a society which is increasingly plural in character, is nominated, instead, as a sign of a lack of coordination and integration, as both 'soft' and an irrelevance.

In thus being reconstituted as little else than more efficient problem-solvers on terms strictly determined by the corporate state, the new corporate managers would no longer be either willing or able to provide independent educational advice and feedback concerning the strengths and weaknesses of current policy. An important element of the 'checks and balances' that are conventionally associated with the political process within the 'social democracies' has thus been made anachronistic. In their pursuit of very big and very fast educational changes, Australian governments at both national and state levels have demonstrated that they are not prepared to accept a serious learning role — either in advance of policy construction through the establishment of representative decision-making processes or with respect to the most comprehensive accounting of the effects of policy. Rather, such processes of broadly-based collaboration and accountability are ruled out within the dominant rhetoric of 'modernization', since this nominates educational decision-making as both too complex and too pressing for democratic structures of participation. Within this legitimating framework, no case can be made for the independence of the public service in any traditional sense. Senior executives, instead, are required to act as political accomplices in the forging of a new relationship of dominance between state and civil society. In the current Australian context, in short, the closing of the gap between the polity and educational administration cannot be reasonably seen as a democratic response to the excessive independence and inertia of traditional departmental structures. Rather, this convergence constitutes a creeping totalitarianism in which educational institutions are stripped of their public character and many of their most important functions.

Charged with ensuring the effective transmission of new, instrumental cultural objectives as cheaply as possible, state education departments have become increasingly prescriptive with respect to the most important elements of curricular policy and much more inquisitorial in their evaluation of key educational outcomes. Given the growing impact of these restrictive controls, current proposals for devolution would provide a very narrow focus for democracy at the local level, one that would be limited by and large to questions determining how best to implement more tightly defined curricular frameworks in a variety of different socio-cultural contexts. Nor would there be much room for manoeuvre even with respect to the restricted range of decisions that would remain within the local jurisdiction. Thus within the interconnecting sets of control which characterize modern educational systems, no space can be allowed, at any stage of the administrative process, for the democratic discussion of viewpoints and concerns. If such negotiations were allowed, new interests and demands would be forthcoming within a growing spiral of democratic expectations, thereby leading to a corresponding mobilization in favour of the broader educational and social aims of democratic schooling — and placing at risk the new educational imperatives and controls (Cunningham, 1987). The implementation of policy is also to be streamlined, to be denied any expression in terms of considerations of custom, politics and ethics, and to be made mainly a matter of technical expertise.

This requirement is systematized in the new powers given to school principals, now redefined as line managers in undisputed control of school 'operations'. Teachers would thus be required to accept that their roles and responsibilities are basically to be defined by school management plans, 'mini-mission' statements which constitute a functional interpretation and implementation of the 'whole picture' that has been centrally determined. Now more than ever the official demand is for more innovation and enterprise within the nation's classrooms. But such characteristics would not amount to much more than technical experimentation, since they would not be allowed to threaten the new sense of purpose and teamwork that have been assiduously cultivated at all levels of the new machinery of education. This growing division of powers within schools provides further evidence that, contrary to the official rhetoric, corporate systems of educational administration would be characterized by a pyramidal structure even steeper than that associated with traditional bureaucracies — at least in their more recent, liberal forms.

To close the circle, parents are likely to pressure local teachers to get results according to central specification, thereby signalling that current commitments to increased parental participation serve a conservative ideological function. Given the overall commodification of education, parents in general have been ideologically redefined as 'clients' and 'consumers' with little option other than to act as isolated protagonists and choosers in the marketplace of available schools. But this power of choice, precisely because it takes a socially fragmented and alienated form, is all the more pressing upon the schools. All that parents, acting alone and ideologically interpellated as little else than protectors of the ultimate exchange value of their children's education, can typically be expected to rely upon in their market choices are quantitative measures of key schooling outcomes — and, of course, how these compare with typical results across the state. As a condition of survival, therefore, principals, program coordinators and individual teachers would increasingly be subjected to the tyranny of 'the test'. Moreover, in the name of the passive and manipulated form of participation that now passes for devolution, central administrators are enabled to claim a democratic mandate for the universal imposition of standardized testing — and for the subsequent publication, in the public interest, of comparative achievements, school by school and class by class, in the core subject areas.

Competition as the Sine Qua Non

Within the perspective of schools as marketplaces, it needs to be noted, if test scores as measured against standard results are in the red, then no credence could be given to those accounts that stress the complex origins of measured underachievement — and to the need, therefore, for big and slow processes of collaboration and participation (Sawer, 1989). No matter what the ideological sympathies of the parents concerned, parental choice would increasingly have to embody a short-term time-line — or else run the risk, in an increasingly competitive schooling system where the stakes have never been higher, of fatally damaging the life chances of their children. It follows that pursuit of the in-depth, socio-cultural solutions that characterize the best of progressive education, even if of the 'right' (narrowly focused) kind, would be ruled out by consumer demands for immediate improvements (or else). What would be insisted on by the new breed of principal-manager is the 'quick fix'. This is a telling indication of how parental participation as now conceived, far from embodying a genuine flowering of localism, would lead to a further anti-democratic spiralling of cultural restrictions. The corporate state, armed with the 'hard data' and acting through its local managers, would be empowered to seek clarification and refinement of teaching and learning (Dawkins, 1991, p. 10).

In political terms, current commitments to educational devolution signal much more formalized and judgmental assessments of teachers by both administrators and community. Nor is this tendency towards a mechanical and punitive form of teacher accountability just a question of the ideological reconstitution of participation within the overall corporate plan. Given the expanded functions of newly constituted school councils, notably with respect to budgeting, public relations and general planning, typical parent councillors would increasingly be required to provide highly developed forms of specialist expertise (managerialist, accounting, legal and entrepreneurial) — and to adopt the conservative perspectives of efficiency and control in their deliberations. What this means is that the oft-lamented tendency to exclusiveness in the social composition of parent councillors would be exacerbated within the 'autonomous' units of school governance proposed by various ministries and bureaucracies of education. In terms of the *Realpolitik* of basic council relationships, not only would those members who wanted to bring a broader perspective to bear upon the key issues of planning and the curriculum constitute an increasingly small proportion of typical council membership; they would also be dismissed as inefficient and obstructive in a context where schools, denied sufficient numbers of either outside support or internal administrative staff, have been given the responsibility to maintain basic operations. Typical school councillors would limit their initiatives to market-determined forms of calculation and enterprise. They could thus be expected to join ranks with principal-managers in identifying so-called teacher underperformance as the major accountability issue.

As basic educational relationships at the periphery assume a more commercial, contractual form, there can be no real sense in which learning outcomes are seen as a coproduction of principals, teachers and community. Within a narrowly technical model of teaching, students are treated as the raw material of production, to be processed in a standardized way. They would be increasingly categorized by teachers in merely formal terms on the basis of test results which would be treated, in essence, as an objective measure of the essential qualities of the 'learners' involved. Once it is accepted that, within 'the one best system', persistent failure is the consequence either of fundamental, irreducible characteristics of the learner or of poor teacher performance, then the basis for a new divisiveness at the local level is established. Thus teachers would become increasingly alienated from underachieving students, thereby preventing precisely the kinds of interaction between professional and client that are necessary if a commitment to social justice is to have a determining impact upon mainstream educational practice. This inegalitarian tendency would be strengthened by the requirement that attempts at remediation would have to take the form of even more intense standardization, refinement and clarification of the mainstream curriculum and its processes. In the name of this equity, extra barriers would be raised between the life of the school and the cultural identities and social aspirations of many communities. But the effects of class and culture are much more obdurate and significant than the managerialist model allows. The stage is clearly set, therefore, for a further deterioration in relationships between teachers and students in the 'more troublesome' schools, a consequence which would itself have to be 'managed away' at the local level within more devolved systems of administration.

The current modernization of education is also likely to lead to growing divisions within the student body, thereby adding to the fundamental realignment of basic relationships at the level of the local educational community. In the name of the now dominant definition of relevance, children increasingly are being offered only one viable form of future social participation, one that is based upon competitive careerism. Competition would become the major currency of classroom relationships, therefore, effectively terminating any residual elements of a common cultural life within the classroom. Moreover, within the conservative efficiency perspective that is likely to dominate within 'well managed' schools, differences in measured achievement would be seen as necessitating the introduction of selective devices like streaming, an interpretation that would be given added strength by the importance assigned to the early spotting and fostering of talent in the name of the 'national economic interest'. These conclusions do not merely have a formal logical status, but are given concrete historical expression in the current pressures placed on schools and teachers by middle-class parents (who have an intimate everyday understanding of the growing importance of qualifications and who are much more favourably positioned within new structures of educational participation) to provide, from the earliest years, accelerated learning opportunities for *their* children, i.e., for those who are already relatively advantaged in cultural terms. Within this market-inspired perspective, there would be an increased stratification of real educational inputs along class-cultural lines at all subsequent year levels as the cumulative effects of early selection are allowed substantially free expression. This polarization of basic student experiences signals that the new educational order would be both much less socially just and much less culturally harmonious.

In real terms, therefore, educational politics at the local level is likely to become increasingly fragmentary and conflictual, both in terms of growing divisions between the major stakeholders (notably parents and teachers) and in the polarization of interests within parent and student bodies. It follows that a much more purposeful and organized state would be able to exert more active and undisputed controls over 'the periphery'. In a further political coup, moreover, the corporate state would be enabled to distance itself, in the name of its version of participation, from the many messy and intractable problems associated with the 'operational sphere' — ones which, according to this chapter's analysis, are likely to be accentuated considerably within 'modernized' schooling systems. No matter how much they herald 'the facts' of increased educational participation, governments across the social democracies generally are typically giving very little; they are also taking a lot, however, very silently.

Letting the Managers Manage: The Real South Australian Agenda

If we turn now to the South Australian Education Department's submission on devolution, there is no mistaking its fundamental concern with the strengthening of managerialist controls in the pursuit of economic rationalist ends. The language of coordination and integration is its constitutive theme, indicating that a new significance is being given to a 'whole-of-education' approach to educational governance. As the basis for this new sense of coherence across all forms and levels of education, the Department nominates two basic goals, which must be seen as having fundamental analytic and causal significance: (1) 'the development of the human intellect in all its dimensions — cognitive, social, cultural, moral, emotional and physical'; and (2) 'to prepare our children to lead fulfilling and productive lives in the world of work' (Education Department of South Australia, 1991, p. 6).

The first goal stresses the cultivation of the mind in a classical conservative sense as constituting the whole of the distinctively educational realm. Since the development of the emotions, the social instincts and moral awareness would thus be treated as a subset of the intellectual, the school would not be allowed to treat personal development and political formation as involving independent educational considerations of significance. The basic driving force of the reconstituted Department would thus be a perspective upon the curriculum which divides mind from body, individual from society, fact from value — and which would make the former categories in each case the sole organizing concerns of official educational debate, purpose and practice. Basic curricular decision-making would be restricted to a clearly defined operational framework, one in which those with a developed understanding of the various forms of knowledge and generalized laws of childhood development would be sovereign — and in which there would be a clearly established pecking order of subjects based on perceived economic utility. Within this technocratic universe, considerations of culture, politics and philosophy would be allowed no expression in educational governance or provision at any level — except those which endorse the view that new schooling priorities are both rational and inevitable, a necessary adjustment to the laws of motion of postmodern economies.

In emphasizing nothing but the intellect, the Department cannot be reasonably construed as stressing a concern for the ordering and monitoring functions of the mind in the proper development of individual identity and social purpose. Even if it were accepted that a renewed emphasis on the intellect is necessary as a corrective to the supposedly anti-intellectual excesses of South Australian schooling during its 'social democratic' phase, this would not justify the marginalization in the name of education of much that is noble and energizing about living and relating. The imperial claims being made on behalf of the intellect are especially ominous when squared with the fact that major spokespeople for economic rationalist goals find no independent place for 'society' and 'culture' in their lexicon of important terms. Rather, social and cultural 'effects' are to be managed away through the application of stricter labour market disciplines or more punitive 'law and order' remedies. Within the whole-of-government policies that direct public sector activities within the corporate state, it is not all fanciful to suggest that, with respect to the various dimensions of human development, the intellect has been assigned a parallel custodial function by the new breed of educational planners — an interpretation that is strengthened by the fact that, given the narrowly instrumental focus that characterizes current moves towards a national curriculum, the well schooled mind would assume a substantially reconstituted form. General education in the form being advocated would no longer seriously engage either the reflective powers or the social imaginations of students. With respect to the broader cultural, social and developmental commitments of 'social democratic' schooling, a dual reductionism is being officially proposed: these have been redefined as simply intellectual concerns; moreover, the latter have been redefined in terms of little else than the skills necessary for efficient functioning in the 'innovative economy'.

The second defining mission of the Education Department explicitly affirms the vocational functions of schooling. But in the supposedly knowledge-based economy, such preparation for work is officially represented as having none of the restrictive characteristics associated with 'old-style' forms of vocational education but, rather, as consolidating the intellectual basis of schooling by giving an increased priority within the mainstream curriculum to the most prestigious subjects in both an educational and utilitarian sense (Ryan, 1991). Vocationalism thus defined would lead to a narrowing of that strictly intellectual subset of educational activities that is sanctioned by the first of the departmental priorities. There is no sense, therefore, in which school-based vocational preparation would be allowed to include, as a substantial component, a critical-interpretive understanding of the sciences and their technological applications — and hence a constructive engagement with longstanding cultural beliefs and social aspirations concerning basic economic conditions, relationships and priorities within capitalist societies. What is being promoted, instead, through an initiation into little else than the 'key competences' of the specialist disciplines, is an acceptance by workers-to-be that their future roles in the workplace would be limited to efficient functioning, on the terms and according to the reasons dictated by increasingly powerful elites.

This is an especially sobering conclusion since the Department establishes only one form of social participation as a priority consideration, 'the world of work' (1991, p. 6). Not only is education for citizenship not formally acknowledged in this contest. In a significant further twist the Department specifically nominates work alone as constituting the basis for a public life in the society of the future. Thus it stresses the need for a 'wide range of skills' so that students would be enabled to 'take their place as citizens within the workforce' (p. 6). Given growing competition within the labour market and tighter controls in the typical workplace, so-called citizenship of this kind would assume a socially exclusive and culturally restrictive form. Nor is it reasonable to claim that, as a mature 'social democracy', South Australia can take for granted a commitment to public participation across all the major social institutions. A public sphere that is both independent and powerful has never been a prominent feature of Australian political life — and has only recently begun to take root, albeit in a limited way. It follows that, when viewed in a general historical context, the departmental failure to acknowledge a commitment to a broadly-based citizenship cannot be seen as a politically benign omission.

The Chimera of Participative Decision-making

This silence is distinctly retrogressive in the current political moment, given the powerful hold exerted by economic rationalist philosophy over government at both federal and state levels. The Education Department must thus be seen as giving the seal of educational authority to the reduction of mainstream social participation to little else than economic functioning. Only such a reductionism can explain its juxtaposition, without qualification or addition, of the concepts 'citizens' and 'workforce'. Even social democrats of quite traditional stripe, mindful that normal democratic rights and processes do not characterize the world of work within liberal democracies, would be perplexed by such rhetoric. They would not be too hard-pressed to accept that talk of citizenship in the restrictive sense being espoused must be seen as having, in the words of a leading departmental figure in South Australia, the essential characteristics of a 'decoy discourse' (Boomer, 1989, p. 6). In short, the Department wants to have its cake and eat it too. It wishes to invoke the image of a schooling system that is still strongly animated by the values of independence, collaboration and solidarity, precisely those that would be displaced from the main-stream life of the school as the divisive logic of the marketplace is allowed to suborn schooling priorities and practices.

Nonetheless, defenders of social democratic education should not be consoled by the fact that the Department's attempt to coopt the rhetoric of democracy is, to say the least, without foundation. This response is to ignore the crucial political fact that, in order to bring all public institutions and key elements of society to heel, there is now a concerted attempt by the ideologues of the corporate state to recast traditional norms and com-mitments in ways that render them serviceable for economic rationalist ends. This refashioning of emancipatory discourses means that the rapid adjustment of schools to systemic economic imperatives is represented as both distinctly educational and substantially democratic. In the case of the highly interventionist corporate state there is a political truth inherent in such misrepresentations.

The basic framework and rationale thus established, the Education Department's submission then outlines new administrative structures of control which are intended to ensure that these corporate priorities would form the governing consideration at all levels of educational decision-making. In the classic manner of corporate management schemes, it has recommended the establishment of a new 'Policy and Planning Unit' to 'facilitate system-wide planning, policy advice and co-ordination of key strategic directions across the organization' (Education Department of South Australia, 1991, p. 2). This would constitute a thorough appropriation by the politically dominated centre of the most basic ideological controls and the introduction of a megapolicy perspective that would represent a standardization and coordination of various educational directorates and units far exceeding anything done in the name of old-style bureaucracies. This powerful new executive layer means that the key elements of policy, notably to do with the curriculum, staffing and the general uses of resources, would be framed by very restrictive top-down technocratic controls. In terms of the new politics of education, we should not be beguiled by any claims that the shedding of many middle management positions would lead to flatter hierarchies and hence to processes of policy formation that would be more directly responsive to the gamut of legitimate social and cultural interests in civil society at large and at the periphery in particular. Rather, our attention should be directed upwards at those structural in-novations which serve to redefine curricular directorates as merely a link in the chain of corporate imperatives, and hence as unable to exercise any real education or leadership of any kind, whether directive or democratic.

This swing towards stronger executive controls has been a marked feature of South Australian educational administration in recent years. Many new central positions have been created (notably Director of Personnel, Director of Evaluation and Review and two Associate Directors General — Resources and Schools), indicating the consolidation of a new bureaucratic layer between the Chief Education Officer (Director General) and various directors. At the same time these much more powerful leaders have been chosen on the basis of generic managerialist qualities rather than distinctive educational experiences and understandings, reflecting the whole-of-government approach that now characterizes public sector administration. Moreover, this reconstituted centre has been intent on extirpating any residual tendency to educational independence at any level of administration. As a result of the Cox Report (1987), the Superintendents of Schools, the major links between schools and the regional offices, have been required to perform a monitoring rather than an advisory or facilitative role. They have been redefined in a classical managerialist move as agents of the central executive, ensuring that regional offices would no longer be able to provide any leadership of an educational kind.

In its recent submission, the Department has sought to formalize and extend these restrictive controls over regions and districts through a precise, binding, legal mechanism. The proposed new category of District Principals, the functional equivalent, more or less, of the old Regional Superintendents, is to be subsumed within the Government Management and Employment, rather than Education, Act. These educational overseers would be required, as a fundamental condition of employment, to give unquestioning allegiance to the government of the day (and its administration). This requirement would rule out, especially given the range and reach of current cultural controls, any scope for independent educational initiatives by holders of this new position. It is especially revealing, therefore, that a capacity for 'educational leadership' (Education Department of South Australia, 1991, p. 2) is nominated as necessary for this job — in a context where district principals would have no real capacity to criticize or innovate. This is a clear indication of the radical devaluation of what is seen as education by corporate managers; educational decision-making is to be restricted to narrowly technical calculations and operations. With respect to the schools under their jurisdiction, these 'educational leaders' would perform functions on a par with supervisors across the reconstituted public sector generally. The example of the District Principals provides telling evidence that, in its submission on devolution, the Department seeks the radical toughening of managerialist controls. In short, the process of recentralization that was set in train in the 1980s has substantially gained in momentum. In the name of this devolution, the Department is not signalling anything like a substantial break with the most recent trends in administration, but, rather, a dramatic extension of these.

At the local school level, moreover, as a vital element in the chain of corporate imperatives, principals are required to provide 'strong leadership', rather than being seen as the first among professional equals

(Education Department of South Australia, 1991, p. 8). The Department makes it clear that, in the name of devolution, the principal would be in undisputed control over all other local participants, lay as well as teachers. It insists that since (under the Education Act) 'responsibility for the implementation and management of educational programs at school levels rests with the Director-General', delegation can occur only 'to principals but not to school councils' (1991, p. 15). It follows that, when the Department appeals to the need for 'conviction and agreement between the principals, teachers and parents' (p. 8), the bottom line of this supposed consensus must be the acceptance by all of the principal's interpretation of departmental goals and processes. The Department attempts to soften the force of this anti-democratic conclusion by stressing the need for 'ratification by the school council of the School Development Plan' (p. 15). But given the ideological forces at work and the increased powers of the principal, this procedure is likely to have the characteristics of rubber-stamping; the controllers of the means of production, in education as elsewhere, have always called the shots. This most basic of powers would not be softened by the requirement that the principal has to 'consult' the school council during the planning phase (p. 15). Rather, such consultation must be seen as a functional necessity if the principal is to establish a strong support base within the community.

But though the local community is given no real decision-making power with respect to framing educational issues of the purpose and content of schooling, community characteristics and perspectives are given some weighting by the Department when it comes to the determination of appropriate pedagogical strategies. Thus the Department stresses the need for the 'principals, teachers and other staff', in order to 'determine the kind of assistance a student requires', to be 'informed by a school council representative of the community' (p. 9). However, the giving of information is a very passive form of involvement. Its interpretation, moreover, would be a matter for the local professional elite alone. What is thereby ruled out are the distinctive socio-cultural understandings that illumine and are generated from 'the facts' — and which, if allowed serious institutional expression, might lead to a community-based opposition to current schooling priorities. Since no such licence is allowed to the 'facts of the matter' within the departmental submission, these would merely serve the function of alerting the local commissars to the variety of pitfalls that might entrap even the best of plans — and of providing teachers, time, energy and morale permitting, with some scope for remedial activities, albeit of a narrowly technical kind.

Evidence indicates that such limited attempts at compensation, far from constituting a realistic adjustment to the so-called deficiencies of disadvantaged groups can typically only help those whose out-of-school experiences still equip them substantially (if not maximally) for the rigours of increased competition within more standardized and narrowly focused forms of schooling. Within the 'one best system', no matter how assiduously information about the community is gathered and acted upon, only an already relatively advantaged element of 'the disadvantaged' could be helped in real terms. It is especially interesting, therefore, that in its advocacy of school-based 'flexibility' in the 'delivery of education', the Department stresses the 'maximization' of student learning (p. 8), rather than any commitment to the equalization of student outcomes. In the manner of modern educational policy generally, with its politically directive functions, rhetorical nuances such as these should be read as signalling, if not explicitly, real political commitments and consequences. The principle of maximization (of wealth notably), especially in these hard-nosed times, is generally accepted as being antagonistic to the pursuit of the more equitable distribution of social rewards. The corresponding educational premise is that the overall growth in the total of the nation's cultural stocks would be best served by building on, rather than attempting to moderate, current differences in performance levels. The Department's choice of rhetoric in this context, with its roots in the dominant economic discourse, should thus be read as providing further evidence of a movement away from anything resembling a commitment to more equal schooling outcomes. In the name of enhancing the 'productivity of learning' (Education Department of South Australia, 1991, p. 8), instead, a powerful fillip would be given to the case for elitist organizational devices like streaming. Moreover, conservatives would be enabled to claim the high moral ground in dismissing, as an impediment to overall cultural growth, any interventions of substance to help the disadvantaged.

Pedagogical and Curricular Subservience

If the substantial movement within South Australian education is towards a more culturally restrictive and elitist form of schooling, then the general question of school discipline is likely to become a pressing concern for school management, especially in those communities that are increasingly the victims of 'modernization'. Under the departmental construction of devolution, disciplinary problems would be regarded as the sole responsibility of the periphery and in no sense as containing any implications for central planners. Instead, in its pursuit of an orderly school environment (p. 8), the Department sees student discipline, in a narrowly legalistic way, as a matter of correct student behaviour (and, of course, appropriate teacher technique). Within the 'one best system' no scope can be allowed for the expression of cultural differences and their behavioural manifestations. Even in those 'troublesome' schools where there are large numbers of wayward pupils, no official recognition would be given to the social structural basis of school alienation and hence to the need for 'behaviour management strategies' that are socio-cultural rather than remedial/punitive.

It also follows that the likelihood of a growing class bias in parental representation across the schools of the state would serve an important control as well as 'efficiency' function. Typical parent councillors would increasingly be blind to, or uncaring about, community needs and social aspirations that would no longer be seriously addressed as a consequence of current educational reforms. Should the threat of greater student disaffection eventuate, a managerialist framework has been established which would rule out the likelihood of more collaborative and empathic school responses, those that have characterized some forms of alternative education in recent years.

It follows that, increasingly, teacher-student relationships would not be characterized by any search for common social and cultural ground. Rather, teachers would be pressured to maintain the 'correct' cultural ethos and social relationships. Moreover, the Department gives prominence to research findings which signify that the perennial problems of disadvantage can be resolved through improved teaching techniques. In the name of its version of educational science, the Department asserts that 'of all the factors which have an impact on student learning, the knowledge and skills of the teacher are clearly the most important' (p. 8). A moment's reflection should indicate that this claim, in a context where teachers no longer call any of the major shots, constitutes an idealism of an extreme kind, one that avoids a full and objective canvassing of the complexities. But the Department has armed itself with a powerful stick with which to beat the 'underperforming' teacher. In its recent support for performance-based teacher evaluation, the Department has embraced a view of teachers as little else than skilled operatives. It has also provided a detailed checklist of required teacher behaviours, thus indicating that its assessment of teacher competence would be governed by accountability criteria that were both mainly empiricist and inclusive of the whole range of techniques. We have thus been provided with a much clearer perspective upon the real point of the departmental claim concerning the centrality of the teacher. This cannot be seen as a simple acknowledgment of the pivotal significance of classroom teaching (true enough). What is being asserted, rather, is that in pursuit of the 'one best system', the standardization and intensification of the teacher's work remain the major item of unfinished educational business.

In the concerted pursuit of these crucial subgoals of corporate management, the Education Department is not at all fazed by the obvious tension between a commitment to the school-based standardization of teaching and the general logic of decentralization. Instead, in a triumphalist rejoinder to those who point to the abstract character of standardized pedagogies, the manager of the Department's 'rejuvenating the teaching work-force project' invokes a very strong sense of scientific 'rationalism' in his insistence that 'competence' is not 'environmentally determined' (Olah, 1991, p. 7). In the name of this science, the requirements of effective teaching, even at the level of practice, are transcultural and apolitical, 'scientific truths' in the strictest, positivist sense. The most compelling evidence is thus provided that South Australian schools are being provided only with a spurious autonomy, one that is based upon a denial of the case for any significant educational alternatives. Ominously too for teachers, in insisting on a 'considerable clarification' of the criteria of competence outlined by him, an insistence that has been subsequently met, Olah leaves unanswered the question, 'Is a teacher incompetent if he/she fails to do some or all of these things?' (1991, p. 7). He has unmistakeably identified the potential threat to teachers in the use of inclusive descriptors of competence; 'underperformance' in any particular area could be readily claimed by increasingly assertive managers as a cardinal sin — rough justice indeed for many teachers, especially in those communities whose problems and needs find no place within Olah's managerialist calculus.

For Olah, then, all teachers within a particular subject category or year level would be required to possess the same general corpus of abstract competences, whatever the specific socio-economic context. What is ruled out within his model of teacher accountability, therefore, is the possibility that individual teachers could selectively develop, as a defining professional characteristic, distinctive skills and capacities to meet the sociocultural needs of particular groups. What is also ruled out is the possibility that teachers together, on the basis of a range of highly developed specialist interests, could collaboratively plan a distinctive 'whole-of-school' curriculum, one that would constructively integrate a variety of 'in-depth' cultural insights and perspectives. In short, teachers would not be allowed to choose a preferred model of professional development or be given any real voice, either individually or collectively, in the overall determination of school policies. In insisting on nothing but standardized forms of teacher proficiency, the Department cannot reasonably be seen as imposing 'rational' administrative controls over those teachers whose cultural enthusiasms and political commitments have no real professional or democratic basis. Rather, teachers would be forced to act as little else than functionaries of 'the system' — and hence to play their part in helping to adjust different school settings, whatever the cultural complexities and social problems, to the requirements of 'the plan'.

Conclusion

In its pursuit of such far-reaching and narrowly focused forms of standardization, the Department has a powerful industrial weapon on its side in current award restructuring procedures. There is every indication that, in the absence of strong teacher union resistance, these would make Australian teachers, as a requirement of law, increasingly subject to the same processes of central regulation and technical standardization that are a key feature of microeconomic reforms generally. The South Australian Education

Department is obviously intent on proclaiming its commitment to a more 'cooperative' industrial politics along these lines (1991, p. 31). If such co-operation were to eventuate, teacher unions would be coopted to act as collaborators in the production of a much stricter (and more enforceable) means-end division within education. The work of the local educator would be restricted largely to the methodological, or to specialist understandings of a particular area of the curriculum (or to both). Once it is accepted that questions of teacher productivity can be treated as largely self-contained issues, and hence as resolvable without regard to the nature of the ends being pursued, then the ideological framework has been established for a distinctively managerialist politics of education. The other side of the coin is that many 'old-style' union and educational aspirations, notably those progressive agendas which nominated the pursuit of democratic and egalitarian goals as a central, determining aim of schooling policy, have been dismissed as both restrictive and anachronistic. Compelling further evidence is thus provided that current commitments to devolution, when viewed as one element in an interlocking set of corporate controls, would in no real sense promote a form of schooling that is more 'responsive to local needs' (Education Department of South Australia, 1991, p. 1). Rather, real educational autonomy and diversity at the local level are the target, not the objective.

Nonetheless, it must also be stressed that, even though the current 'modernization' of education enjoys something approaching hegemonic status, the substantial narrowing of cultural and social goals that is thus endorsed is fundamentally unrealistic because of its effective disregard of educational norms and commitments that are both necessary and widely valued. Against the current background of rapid socio-cultural change and increased class division, an independently minded and publicly spirited teaching profession is now more than ever necessary if Australian schools are to retain a viable social and cultural identity (and even, in an increasing number of cases, to function at all). Moreover, if the general public is to be enlightened about what is really being done in the name of 'modernized education', then it requires an accounting of new policy commitments, qualitative yet realistic, which is crucially dependent on the 'hands-on' understandings of a teaching force that is still allowed substantial room for manoeuvre and comment. Yet in its single-minded pursuit of economic rationalist goals, the corporate state is blinded to (or uncaring about) the complexities and seeks to limit discussion about the quality of schooling to a range of performance indicators concerning 'the execution' of policy. In the name of this accountability, increasingly powerful ministries and bureaucracies of education would not be called to account in any substantial sense, a radically anti-democratic consequence indeed. In also follows that democrats and egalitarians must be especially alert to the ideological sig-nificance of the blinding political spotlight currently being focused on the so-called problem of 'teacher underperformance'.

References

BOOMER, G. (1989) 'Slugging It Out Down Under', Paper presented to the American Educational Research Association Conference, San Francisco.

CONSIDINE, M. (1988) 'The Corporate Management Framework as Administrative Science: A Critique', *Australian Journal of Public Administration*, 47, 1, pp. 4–19.

CUNNINGHAM, F. (1987) *Democratic Theory and Socialism*, London, Cambridge University Press.

DAVIES, L. (1990) *Equity and Efficiency? School Management in an International Context*, Lewes, Falmer Press.

DAWKINS, J. (1991) *Australia's Languages*, Canberra, Australian Government Publishing Service.

EDUCATION DEPARTMENT OF SOUTH AUSTRALIA (1991) *Submission to the Government Agencies Review Group*, Adelaide, Government Printer.

OLAH, K. (1991) 'Competency, Professionalism and the Quality of Education', *SAIJ Journal*, 21 August, pp. 7–9.

PUSEY, M. (1981) 'How Will Governments Strive to Control Education in the 1980s?' *Discourse: The Australian Journal of Educational Studies*, 1, 2, pp. 9–17.

PUSEY, M. (1991) *Economic Rationalism in Canberra*, Cambridge, Cambridge University Press.

Review of Superintendents in the Education Department of South Australia (1987) (Cox Report), Adelaide, Government Printer.

RYAN, B.P. (1991) ' "The Speedy Agenda": Whose Interests Are Being Served?' *Discourse*, 12, 1, pp. 44–66.

SAWER, M. (1989) 'Efficiency, Effectiveness . . . and Equity?', in G. DAVIS, P. WELLER and C. LEWIS (Eds), *Corporate Management in Australian Government*, Melbourne, Macmillan, pp. 138–53.

WALKER, J. (1991) 'Legitimacy in Education Policy', in C. FASANO and B. WINTER (Eds), *Education Policy in Australia: Practices and Perceptions*, Wollongong, University of Wollongong Press, pp. 98–107.

WELLER, P. and LEWIS, C. (1989) 'Corporate Management: Background and Dilemmas', in G. DAVIS, P. WELLER and C. LEWIS (Eds), *Corporate Management in Australian Government*, Melbourne, Macmillan, pp. 1–16.

12   Managerialism and Market Forces in Vocational Education: 'Balkanizing' Education in the 'Banana Republic'

Peter Kell

In every Australian town there exist two icons of 'European civilization' which tell us much of the Australian identity. The first is usually a war memorial in the familiar decorative flourishes of the art deco style to commemorate the futile slaughter of the world wars; the second is usually a technical college exhibiting a more functionalist facade, celebrating the work ethic.

In contemporary Australia the role of technical and vocational education, as a focus for social and cultural education, is under challenge in a wave of educational reforms designed to address a national economic crisis. The rhetoric of these reforms has incorporated the language and ideology of the 'self-managing' school, stressing the need for autonomy, the devolution of decision-making, the need for flexibility and the participation of stakeholders from the 'real world' of industry and commerce.

Paradoxically, at a time when national economic imperatives call for unity, the reforms in technical education have produced management strategies in some systems which have created competitive enclaves that have fragmented and demoralized an important social institution essential for economic prosperity and social stability. Owing to technical and vocational education's close relationship with the workplace, the adoption of 'self-managing' principles as a solution to wider educational issues has dire implications for the equitable nature of labour and work. The arrival of these reforms is not conceived in a cultural and political vacuum, independent from the changing terrain of struggles between labour and capital. Fundamental questioning is needed to ask critically who will benefit from the 'self-managing' school in vocational education, and what impact the reforms will have on the workplace of the future.

A study of events in Australia, and more particularly of reforms to New South Wales technical and further education, provides important indicators of the 'toxic' effects and dangers of the new orthodoxy of 'self-management'.

The Changing Culture of Work and Learning

The 'Techs', as they were colloquially termed, originated from the railway or mechanics institutes which were established during the 1880s as symbols of colonial self-improvement and achievement. Prior to 1975, vocational and technical education was a fragmented and archaic system of technical colleges funded and managed by state government departments. In most states technical colleges were the only approved training provider for apprenticeship, trade and posttrade qualifications through a process of rigid legalistic award and licensing demarcations. Technical and vocational education, owing to its predominantly working-class origins, was considered a 'poor cousin' to schools and universities, being referred to as the 'blood and bandages' sector of education.

The election of the Whitlam Labor government, and a wide ranging enquiry into technical education chaired by the late Myer Kangan in 1974, ushered in an era of federal government intervention which overhauled the archaic nineteenth century style of vocational training. The subsequent landmark report, *TAFE in Australia* (ACOTAFE, 1974), emphasized the notion of lifelong learning and placed the focus of activity on meeting a wider range of individualized and community needs. The report also developed the acronym 'TAFE', which stood for Technical and Further Education. The terms 'further' and 'adult' education called for TAFE to develop a more flexible notion of vocational training, outside the narrow range of masculinized trade-based courses, with significant priority towards the provision of access courses and the pursuit of social equity. The Kangan Report urged the participation of more women, ethnic, migrant groups, Aborigines and the disabled, whose access to TAFE had been marginal, and recognized the need for general education (McIntyre, 1991).

Administration in TAFE was also typified by a legalistic centralized bureaucracy which implemented its charter as primarily a trainer for trades occupations in an autocratic and paternalistic manner. Mackie colourfully described the unique qualities of educational management practices in TAFE of the mid-1970s: 'Certainly the educational milieu in TAFE seems to derive from a bizarre combination of Adolf Hitler and Dale Carnegie! Rigid unquestioning obedience to a vastly extended bureaucratic hierarchy ensures minimal deviation from the party line. None dare question TAFE directors' (Mackie, 1980, p. 59). The strict hierarchical order was characterized by extraordinary levels of control over teachers and students and their activities. Some of these were plainly absurd examples of moral policing. Full-time day secretraries in NSW during the late 1970s were confined to their buildings unless they received permission to leave. This bizarre caveat even extended to mature-aged married women (Mackie, 1979).

Pedagogically teachers and students were isolated from the focus of a centrally established and assessed curriculum, with changes to courses generally requiring what has been euphemisically termed a 'fast track' period of two years through a bureaucratic maze. The dominating and rigid internal structure of TAFE, according to critics like Mackie, constituted a replication of the social arrangements in the workplace and reinforced the stratified and segmented relationships in industry. Technical education is not a neutral detached monastic site of education, but has been a continuing site of struggle for workers, unions and the interests of commerce and industry to secure advantage. Miller (1982), Bessant (1988), Blackmore (1990) and Watkins (1988) have all documented how the relationships between work education and industry struggle and contestation have been evolving and subject to redefinition in response to changing economic conditions.

While TAFE exhibited many faults as a state funded social institution, it claimed a valuable role in mediating the demands of the competing interests and acted as a vehicle for compensatory programs in areas of high regional unemployment. Its primary strength came from close contact and interaction between workers and managers in small businesses and industries, who were TAFE's traditional stakeholders. In many respects TAFE represented a cultural site with an expectation that it would provide the necessary credentialling for intergenerational social mobility for the working classes. In the euphoria of the post-Kangan era TAFE would market itself as a place for everyone!

Unfortunately, in contradiction to this, TAFE also perpetuated an exclusive masculinized ethos of valued and valid work emphasizing male-based trades, technology and the 'practical' as opposed to the 'philosophical' and 'abstract'. In many ways technical education was symbolic of the ethos of the Australian identity centred on the great myth of white masculine self-sufficiency and practicality. Conforming to this pattern, TAFE exhibited a high degree of gender segmentation, with almost 99 per cent of apprenticeships being male, with the remainder being female hairdressing students (Davis, 1988). In spite of changes in participation and growth of non-vocational and access programs in the era of the Kangan reforms, a paternalistic male ethos remained a dominating corporate culture.

Into the context of this delicate balance between competing interests and meanings surrounding TAFE, the generic calls of the New Right for reform in education emerged as a distinct threat to the consensus surrounding vocational education. The dominance of economic fundamentalism at the threshold of economic catastrophe in the late 1980s saw the educational lexicon changed from notions of 'access', 'equity' and 'social justice' to the technical language of 'productivity', 'efficiency' and 'effectiveness' (Kenway, 1990).

Peter Kell

A New Focus for TAFE in a Banana Republic

In a moment of great vigour and candour during a commercial radio interview in 1986 Paul Keating, the Treasurer of the Australian government, declared boldly that the external trade position of Australia was so disastrous that the country was in danger of becoming a 'banana republic'. The self-styled 'Placido Domingo' of Australian politics suggested, in his unique style, that the continued reliance on declining international primary produce markets would drive Australia to being a 'basket case' economy, with, presumably, the influence and status of countries like Honduras and Haiti. This announcement struck a raw nerve that triggered panic on the stock market, an immediate dramatic drop in the Australian dollar and a frenetic level of introspection and self-flagellation about what was happening to the 'lucky country'.

The answer to this crisis, according to the Hawke federal Labor government, was the development of efficient and modern 'value adding' technological industries capable of competing aggressively in external markets and turning around the balance of payments. In the context of this, the schooling system, including TAFE, was viewed as an important micro-economic tool in facilitating change in the workplace (Cerny, 1990). Unlike the UK, the impetus for change came from the industry training lobby, an uneasy alignment of big union and business interests and not the cultural restorationists within the education industry; but like the UK, much of the agenda for change was fuelled by the press (see Ball, 1990).

The TAFE system, as with all public education, rapidly achieved the status of a pariah, seen as the catalyst for economic decline. Some hysterical newspaper commentators such as P.P. McGuinness, using the logic of the UK 'Black Papers', argued knowingly that: 'Everyone knows it [TAFE] is not producing results . . . the system has been allowed to fall into disrepute as more and more of its products have entered the workforce unable to do what employers expect of them' (McGuinness, 1992, p. 2). Uncritically, adopting much of the logic of the familiar rhetoric of the right, the Hawke government signalled a new role for vocational education aimed at achieving national economic goals and announced in the 1987 budget that: 'In the light of the urgent need to raise the level of national skills development, the government has decided to sharpen the focus of its financial assistance for TAFE to ensure that funds are spent in accordance with national objectives and priorities' (Dawkins and Holding, 1987, p. 30).

Significant federal government criticism was directed at TAFE, with the suggestion that it lacked clear program goals and targets, was overly concerned with 'inputs', lacked evaluation and failed to develop inducements toward greater private and public sector cooperation. While these criticisms appear vague in a policy context, they indicated the fundamental direction of things to come. The new policy agenda called for TAFE to redress a demonstrated 'lack of a direct relationship to wider economic, industry development or labour market objectives' (Dawkins and Holding, 1987, p. 33).

Managerialism in TAFE: Devolution or Fragmentation?

The proposed resolution of TAFE's problems was the implementation of what Angus (1991) terms 'a seemingly unproblematic notion of basic straightforward and no nonsense management' which offered certainty and an appearance of activity (Angus, 1991, p. 12). This perspective advanced the idea of schooling in the context of a market structure, run and managed using business principles to evaluate success. Education using these criteria became synonymous with a discourse associated with managerial concepts, and educational administrators were encouraged to mimic the behaviour and values of the corporate sector. The new market-based image of schooling urged a corporate image of logos, marketing strategies, corporate plans and portfolio management (see Beare, 1988).

The idea that everything was principally a management problem requiring the right fix took on the status of a universal truth among what Yeatman terms an 'administrative elite more comfortable with techniques than telos' (Yeatman, 1987b, p. 12). The adoption and implementation of the managerialist approach was to exacerbate and expose contradictions between policies advocating a unified national focus, on one hand, and a devolved and market-oriented training system, on the other.

The restructuring of state education systems in Australia along the lines of the corporate sector was a regular feature of the 1980s. In New South Wales (NSW) the largest TAFE system in Australia was substantially restructured, with disastrous results, following a management review designed to achieve the most effective and efficient management practices. Consistent with the technically-oriented managerial focus, educational gaols were subordinated in favour of administrative reforms. The assumption was that they would complement each other and that the administrative changes would support educational goals. The review, conducted and coordinated by private management consultants on behalf of the conservative state government, recommended that the Department of TAFE should become a 'training enterprise', obtaining half of its $800m budget from industry sources (Scott, 1989, p. 16). It was proposed that the new enterprise would not be subject to the legislative controls of the parliament and would need to conduct its charter as a corporation. In terms more familiar with McDonald's franchises, colleges were celebrated as 'points of sale' and educational administrators were encouraged to adopt managerial models of behaviour using 'business plans' (Scott, 1989, p. 27).

The management review attributed the 'root cause' of TAFE's deficiencies to the demotivated effects of inertia in the centralized and rigid bureaucracy. The review argued for several devolved networks focusing on the college level. In this simplified and decentralized administrative structure, senior staff were assigned roles which reflected the status of TAFE as a training enterprise (Scott, 1989). The impression created was that principals would have increased autonomy and discretion and be free to pursue their entrepreneurial schemes. The radical surgery was legitimated on the assumption that 'flat management' structures would facilitate better interaction and participation with teaching staff and allow greater flexibility to cater to industry needs. The theoretical assumptions of the restructure comprised a curious blend of technicist management and the participatory processes described by Caldwell and Spinks (1988) in *The Self-Managing School.*

To some of the practical men of TAFE the emergence of these values came as a relief as the language of management was identical to the technical terminology most of them were familiar with in trades or technology, and the corporate style had a seductive potential to remedy TAFE's 'poor cousin' status. In reaction to the previously rigid centralized systems, the promise of greater managerial autonomy in the networked corporate models appealed to TAFE staff frustrated at the inflexibility of an archaic and legalistic system.

Following a spill of management positions, a private recruitment firm hired a 'new breed' of manager for the reformed entrepreneurial organization. In the identification of characteristics for the new managerial elite, emphasis was placed on generic technical management skills rather than educational competence. One interviewee confessed that there were no questions relating to education other than how it could be sold. A former director general of TAFE, Allan Pattison, commented on the changing role of administrators. 'I was concerned because senior quality talent of the organisation has been decimated. . . . It seems to me that the talents which are sought to run this organisation are no different to the talents which are sought to run a toilet paper manufacturing outfit or sausage factory' (*Daily Telegraph*, 24 July 1990). Claims that enhanced salary packages constructed along private sector lines would attract dynamic executives from the private sector proved to be unfounded, with almost all appointments being allocated internally. In the initial recruitment of managers for network and senior executive service staff, of forty-two only three were external appointees, and only ten of all SES appointments were women (NSW Department of TAFE, 1990a). This type of 'spill', as Yeatman suggests, acts as a purge, vetting people for political and ideological compliance (Yeatman, 1987b).

Senior figures in the state government lamented that 'the old boy network' and 'mateship' had frustrated the development of a more dynamic bureaucracy. Senior sources were forced to admit that, even in the rare instance that private sector appointments had been made, problems existed. A senior official in the government said: 'There is very real problem in that people from the private sector cannot understand that if the Minister has made a political decision, then the public servant must ensure the decision becomes policy. They are not here to argue those political decisions' (Garcia, 1990, p. 11). The experience in NSW offers a classic textbook case study of the deficiencies inherent in applying simplistic instrumental models of management to complex cultural and political settings.

The promise of enhanced autonomy in the devolved system was illusory. Rather than the 'downside-up' focus promised in the management review, greater 'top-down' management control eventuated. Principals found class sizes, enrolment policy, course pricing policy and funding formulas to be non-negotiable impositions. Decision-making was characterized by an increasing level of intervention and control, framed within a context of ultimatum. Participation and consultation were subordinated in favour of managerial prerogatives constructed within exclusive managerial 'think tanks' and 'weekend lock-ups'. The worst aspects of the autocratic culture of management described by Mackie clearly adapted quickly to the new regime's terminology and behaviour, imposing their own agenda. These trends were confirmed by internal TAFE documents: 'There are too many examples of regional structures either "taking over" and becoming "mini-head offices" under a strong regional manager or for the regional office to act as a "post box" between delivery point and the central administration' (NSW Department of TAFE, 1991, p. 15).

Alienated from the focus of decision-making and bewildered at the rapidity of management restructuring, teachers spoke of the collapse of structures to support quality and collegiality. Rather than promote better communication, teachers complained that the new structures isolated them from decision-making, with options for creative educational practice diminishing as financial constraints were imposed by cost-conscious managers meeting 'productivity' targets. Others spoke of a complete 'corporate amnesia' from the endless managerial musical chairs that typified the restructure. Contradictory themes of chaos, control and fear emerged from discussions with participants. TAFE understated the dimensions of a massive morale problem in justifying a second restructure to remedy the problems of the first: 'Teachers feel somewhat alienated from the Training Divisions and consequently a lack of support for their classroom activities' (NSW Department of TAFE, 1991, p. 28).

Publicized as a value-free, neutral, technical operation, the adoption of corporate managerialism operated to alter substantially the balance of power in the workplace at the expense of teachers' professional autonomy. Rather than enhancing the autonomy of teachers, the restructure imposed new technologies of control and surveillance, which enhanced management's ability more directly to impose the priorities of the managerial elite. The promise of devolutionary empowerment has not evolved but precipitated heightened levels of alienation and fragmentation, stratifying and dividing the workplace. Ironically, rather than initiate change, the dysfunctional aspect of reform has entrenched the old paternalistic and autocratic management, a trend which forced the authors of the management review to disown the restructure, saying the 'old guard was too strong' and had become 'authoritarian supervisors' (*The Sydney Morning Herald*, 28 September 1991, p. 1).

Marginalizing Access and Equity

The character of TAFE's educational provision did not emerge from the process unscathed. In arguing for a corporate approach, the management review criticized TAFE's commitment to access and equity programs as attempting to be 'all things to all people' and having overemphasized the importance of individual skill requirements at the expense of workplace relevance by pursuing an 'open access policy'. It was argued that the 'quasi welfare' role had taken precedence over the education and training needs of industry (Scott, 1989, pp. 12–13).

While there was a token recognition of the value of 'second chance' and further education, the management review was conditional in its support, suggesting that funding levels should be reviewed to ensure that the quality and scope of TAFE's activities were consistent with identified needs. In the newly restructured and economically rational organization it was assumed that the industry and social justice roles of TAFE would co-exist as an equal partnership. In spite of this optimism, the ideological themes of economic rationalism and entrepreneurialism signalled a subordinated role for many educationally impoverished and disadvantaged groups who had traditionally participated in, and benefitted from, the post-Kangan initiatives in TAFE. The review facilitated the emergence of an organizational bias towards the revenue-generating potential of commerce and industry and away from the programs for disadvantaged groups who were unlikely to generate funds.

Paradoxically, at a time when community leaders were calling for a greater level of vocational education, invoking the rhetoric of the 'clever country' and 'skills formation', NSW TAFE's enrolment actually dropped 23 per cent in the period of devolution from 1987 to 1990. The exodus was most chronic among groups who traditionally experienced difficulty accessing TAFE, with Aboriginal, disabled, migrant and rural students being jettisoned with the introduction of a 'user pays' course fee policy. Women, whose participation rose in response to the previous Kangan reforms, fell most dramatically (NSW Department of TAFE, 1988, 1990b). In 1988 the Women's Co-Ordination Unit, which was responsible for the provision of special courses to encourage the entry of women into TAFE, was disbanded and assigned a role in individual colleges. Justified in the context of 'mainstreaming' special needs, the experience of women's access courses illustrates well the dangers of leaving equity issues vulnerable to market forces in a devolved system. A teacher narrates the collapse of these specialist programs:

In June 1988. . . . It took the Women's Co-Ordination Unit's staff and the College, with the help of the Counselling Unit, most of the week to interview, advise and/or place the women who attended. Given the hours, we could have filled four courses and probably more. (Bee, 1989, p. 14)

She writes in different terms of the immediate post-restructuring period: 'At the commencement of this year one course is operating and it isn't full to capacity' (Bee, 1989, p. 14). The erosion of access and equity courses illustrates how market theory is used selectively. The organizationally contrived collapse is in an area which featured strong demand and market growth. TAFE's growth in the 1980s came from shorter non-accredited courses and compensated for the decline in apprenticeships in manufacturing industries. High growth in many non-technical service industries such as tourism and welfare industries was recorded (Fricker, 1986; O'Connor, 1991). In this way the growth in access courses, general education and short vocational courses outstripped many of TAFE's traditional time-serving trades courses. The reasons for these distortions in the application in market theory during the restructure are evident in the theoretical biases which characterize the foundations of the technical/managerialist perspectives.

The purposive rational approach of corporate managerialism has facilitated a subordination of values which do not conform to a task-oriented view of public administration. Rather than being a neutral application of technology, the corporate model assigns biases which influence and legitimate knowledge, values and behaviour. Yeatman argues that reliance on technical and financial skills nurtured an 'illiterate in the knowledge and skills required to make judgements about the substantive purposes of public services' (Yeatman, 1987a, p. 342).

Resolutions of issues outside narrow reductionist technical or financial solutions are seen as 'soft options' described as 'philosophical' and 'impractical'. In the context of this thinking, courses outside the mainstream of a technical and scientific focus are viewed as 'mickey mouse' and are considered inferior, being seen as unable to address the 'hard-nosed' national economic goals (see Yeatman, 1987b). As Yeatman also suggests, equity becomes a residual 'add-on' notion considered after the main agenda, that reinforces paternalistic and tokenistic values within an organization (Yeatman, 1990, p. 18).

The further education and non-vocational roles of TAFE are interpreted as mutually exclusive with the needs of industry in this conceptual model. This truism has achieved popularity among senior policy-makers, with the chair of the most influential training board in Australia feeling secure in announcing that 'fine arts people are nice people and dinner company, but not much use in a steelworks' (*The Sydney Morning Herald*, 30 July 1991, p. 15).

As evident in the summary of the restructure in NSW, a mobilization of bias sympathetic to the needs of industry has resulted in an erosion of services to other stakeholders and a legitimation of specific notions of knowledge and pedagogy (see Bates, 1983). Notions of collective and participatory knowledge are subordinated in favour of commodified notions of knowledge featuring measurement and assessment in a scientific and technical focus. Attempts to develop national goals through the education system embracing the corporate managerialist perspective have several flaws. In the first instance, as shown in this study, it reinforces racial and gender segmentation and stratification by excluding participation and marginalizing the dispossessed and powerless. Second, it validates a limited range of strategies, skills and knowledge defined in the context of the sectional needs of corporate industry and business. National recovery requires a more universal and inclusive approach than the confined and distorted views contained in market-based views of education. It is a theme which Ruth Jonathan articulates in forecasting the implications for democratic structures.

> The introduction of market mechanisms into the education systems has damaging consequences in the general society it serves and not only for the least fortunate members. It therefore needs to be shown, not simply that some will be unable to exercise new found freedoms effectively, but that even those who are apparently well placed to do so, in fact are constrained by circumstance to act within parameters which are thus beyond debate and modification. (Jonathan, 1990, p. 21)

Balkanizing the Context of Education and Work

The broad social concerns expressed here have special importance as the new models of management have facilitated, through the rhetoric of devolution and the appeal of less government intervention, a fragmentation of social institutions and structures which, considering TAFE's relationships with the workplace, has a critical impact on the social fabric.

Successive restructures, implementing a corporate model, have reconstructed the notion of a public education system as an unrelated collection of separate and independent colleges. In a commodified context of education the free market orthodoxy sees the notion of a system as being replaced by a loose collection of branch offices or separate institutions striving for market share and serving specific enclaves. This view broadly conforms with the New Right notion that society exists only as a collection of markets, but more importantly fragments unified systems into cantons resembling the loose and troubled federation of the Balkan states.

The restructures in NSW and Victoria have partitioned institutes into territorial allotments. They are viewed as separate and competing 'businesses'. The notion of a unified system is eroded as colleges compete against each other to meet the vague and often contradictory needs of industry. The demands of marketing and the entrepreneurial activities in some colleges act as a distraction from the educational focus, diverting resources from the process of teaching and learning. Inequalities of provision also exist in economically depressed areas and those closer to a vibrant infrastructure willing to enter into partnerships with TAFE. In rural communities, where the agricultural sector is declining and little industry exists, entrepreneurial opportunities are thin on the ground. Inequalities also exist between standard courses offered to the community and custom-built fee-paying courses whose catchy marketing slogans such as 'TAFE Plus' create the image of inequality as a virtue (Bates, 1991).

The managerial model has segmented and dispersed the educational assets and resources into competing enclaves. This fragmentation represents a 'Balkanizing' of public education and has important implications for Australia's social, political and economic development, facilitating a polarized, divided and fragile social structure.

Ewer *et al.* (1991) argue that while the industry restructuring and skills formation debate has taken on an apolitical status being backed by both the major political parties, it has distorted the policy agenda towards the interests of business and industry. They argue that the approach to skills formation adopted by big business and the Canberra bureaucracy aims at an enterprise focus along the lines of the Japanese training model and neglects the system and industry-wide German approach. Training in this context is presented as a narrow operational skill confining relevance to a particular enterprise and offering skills which lack portability. Notions of multiskilling and workplace flexibility in relation to enterprise level training, according to Ewer, are more likely to represent attempts by management to eliminate functions which have proved sites for militancy than to provide learning experiences.

The skills formation debate is also premised on a deficit model which attributes economic decline to deficiencies in the workforce skill level, a theory which tends to blame the powerless victims of economic collapse for their own dispossession. This perpetuates a simplistic view of economic forces and locates the issue as a 'supply problem' where workers do not have the requisite skills for a growth economy. Questions of ownership, imprudent investment decisions and the poor performance of business are not associated with decline at all, remaining obscured in the clamour for training, retraining and more training. By exclusively identifying supply-side problems, industry has been able to attain disproportionate advantage and secure leverage in dictating the character and terms under which the labour market is determined. In short, the skills formation agenda has favoured a buyer's labour market, allowing business to demand often contradictory and unrealistic expectations of higher skill levels from both the vocational education system and workers themselves (Kell, 1992).

Ewer's concern with skills formation is that the conceptual framework presented by business interests 'takes on a more overt political flavour which is undoubtedly motivating employers' (Ewer *et al.*, 1991, p. 130). It means that TAFE does not exist in the cultural and political vacuum implicit in managerialist solutions and that the vocational education system is vulnerable to exploitation in achieving wider more universal political agendas.

The 'Balkanization' of the state vocational education system facilitates the alignment of the public sector education system with the interests of business. It also integrates TAFE with employer demands for collective bargaining, which argues for the abolition of centralized wage-fixing procedures and their replacement with individual enterprise agreements, where wages and conditions are no longer determined through state and federal awards but through a myriad negotiations with workers and owners at the enterprise level. Attacks on the centralized wage system remain one of the central rallying points for New Right market theorists and act as a demarcation point between conservative and labour political alignments. The fragmented nature of the devolved system, operating on the ethos of competition with other colleges, is particularly vulnerable to 'take over' by conservative forces seeking advantage in the struggle with labour. Eagerness to please the customer makes TAFE create an environment where the interests of learners are of secondary importance to securing a 'deal' or meeting the corporatist jargon of 'strategic objectives'. While this might be seen as a conspiracy theory, one TAFE principal confided that in an interview for a promotion they were asked by the recruiting agent what their view was on the 1905 court decision that established the centralized wage system and how they might attempt to establish enterprise bargaining in the college!

With the emergence of corporate managerialism and the corporatist objectives as the organizational rationale within TAFE its role is likely to be closely identified with, and resemble, the agenda of big multinational business and industry, and in the process fragment the industrial relations system. This de facto privatization of TAFE represents a marginalization of the interests of other stakeholders, including smaller business, and a corruption of the more universal and democratic goals associated with education.

Conclusion

There was no golden era of TAFE management in the long distant past. The vocational education system has a history of despotic, autocratic and paternalistic management which has facilitated the development of a compliant and unquestioning workforce that is artificially stratified on the basis of class, race and gender (not very successfully either). While reforms associated with devolution and turning the system 'downside-up' promised much in the way of autonomy and flexibility to make necessary reforms, the rhetoric failed to match the reality. Managerialist strategies introducing new technologies of control acted to confine and restrict the resolution of problematic issues to a managerial elite distant from the focus of the teaching and learning activities of TAFE. Notions of empowerment and autonomy dissolved as the expediencies of managerial imperatives excluded the participation of teachers, students, parents and workers. In totally underestimating the despotic managerial culture in TAFE, architects of the reform process in NSW acted to reinforce the worst aspects of the old monolithic rigidities of the much reviled public system rather than eradicate them. In applying these instrumental strategies, teachers and learners, the people required for national revival, are excluded, demoralized and embittered by increasing levels of control.

From the evidence of the case study of NSW, the market-oriented corporate view of TAFE is not a neutral, value-free administrative reform but an allocation of values and biases which favours a privatized, commodified and instrumental notion of TAFE's role. Reforms utilizing distorted notions of markets redefined the notion of legitimate knowledge and interpreted the rights to participation within a utilitarian and instrumental framework, within the context of national economic goals. Paradoxically, the implementation of market theory has assigned the notion of choice a subordinated status. The reforms and the creation of an exclusive political and bureaucratic elite are a vehicle for a political and economic realignment of the public system to facilitate economic goals more to do with controlling the workplace and less to do with education. In meeting sectional goals, the relative unity and balance achieved within a state system become fragmented and exploited, meeting the sectional needs of the private sector, which has historically lacked a commitment to a training ethos. It is a trend which will accelerate the idea that the TAFE and industry nexus is the only valid expression of vocational education.

The reforms, invoking the rhetoric of empowerment, participation and devolution, in reality represent simultaneous attempts at control and surveillance aimed at the ultimate redistribution and concentration of resources into the hands of multinational corporations (David and Wheelwright, 1990). As suggested by Dale (1989) in the context of wider political struggles, reforms of education are 'writ small' in the modern capitalist state, creating the necessary conditions for the continued accumulation of capital. The reform agenda is blatantly politicized to favour conservative interests, and educationalists need to identify the 'hidden hand' behind the rhetoric of managerial jargon now so popular in the public culture.

While these forces of darkness appear like an unstoppable juggernaut, there are signs that the wheels might fall off. Periodically tensions erupt in the political arena which disturb the balance of power threatening to destabilize the established order. These disruptions resemble Habermas's (1976) legitimation crisis, where the anarchistic tendencies of the market threaten the ambitions and aspirations of the 'life-world' for material and mental security (Habermas, 1987). For example, the state government in NSW, a government which believed in 'letting the managers manage', received an electoral backlash recently, a phenomenon which was not predicted by the political gurus or polling 'superstar soothsayers', leaving the government at the mercy of non-aligned independents. The anger in the electorate at the government's education policy was identified as a major factor in the electoral erosion, with people expressing ballot-box dissent at having local services withdrawn in an impoverished and 'Balkanized' state system. Whether political change will ever alter the hegemonic control of corporate interests is another matter, but there are signs that teachers and educationalists, as active participants in the political process, can capitalize on the discontent generated by the overall destruction of symbolic public institutions and the destruction of the 'life-world'. As the New Right attempts to roll back the welfare state, it is perhaps a matter of arguing for a preferred future.

A participant at a public meeting protesting the cuts to government programs expressed well the frustration that teachers, academics, students and workers might be able to mobilize:

> The actions that this community faces in the forms of cutbacks, transfers, etc. ultimately affect us as people and what they do is tear at a sense of community, because in all of the cutbacks we have grey men operating cashbooks and journals but they forget what they are dealing with is playing with people and their futures, and what we are leaving is a terrible lesson to our children. What we are saying is people don't matter. It doesn't matter the way we care for each other. There is no sense of community. Treat one another the way you like. That's why as a community the overarching reason that we have to say, enough is enough, is that this vital sense of community which makes this town worth living in is being attacked and violated. (public meeting, Bathurst, 22 May 1992)

To fail to answer this stirring rallying call is to condemn the cultural icon of the technical college and democratic notions of education to the same status of that other famous Australian icon, the war memorial, a sombre reminder of other tragic mistakes.

References

ANGUS, L.B. (1991) 'Conservative Educational Reform and Australia's National Interest', Paper presented at the Annual Curriculum Conference of the Australian Curriculum Studies Association, Adelaide, July.

AUSTRALIAN COMMITTEE ON TECHNICAL AND FURTHER EDUCATION (ACOTAFE) (1974) *TAFE in Australia: Report on the Needs in Technical and Further Education*, Vols 1–2, Canberra, April.

BALL, S. (1990) *Politics and Policy Making in Education: Explorations in Policy Sociology*, London, Routledge.

BATES, R. (1983) *Educational Administration and the Management of Knowledge*, Geelong, Deakin University.

BATES, R. (1991) 'Who Owns the Curriculum?' Paper presented to Curriculum Conference New Zealand Post Primary Teachers Association, Christchurch, May.

BEARE, H. (1988) 'School and System Management, in Post Industrial Conditions: The Rationale behind Corporate Managemet', *Unicorn*, 14, 4, pp. 248–5.

BEE, B. (1989) 'Keep Your Mouth Shut', *Education*, April, p. 14.

BESSANT, J. (1988) 'Public Rhetoric and Education: Recurring Phemonena', *The Australian Administrator*, August, pp. 1–5.

BLACKMORE, J. (1989) 'Working the System: Corporate Management, Social Justice and Feminism', *Education Links*, 35, pp. 13–25.

BLACKMORE, J. (1990) 'The Text and Context of Vocationalism: Issues in Post Compulsory Curriculum In Australia since 1970', *Journal of Curriculum Studies*, 22, 2, pp. 137– 48.

CALDWELL, B. and SPINKS, J. (1988) *The Self-Managing School*, Lewes, Falmer Press.

CERNY, P. (1990) *The Changing Architecture of Politics: Structure, Agency and the Future of the State*, London, Sage.

DALE, R. (1989) *The State and Education Policy*, Milton Keynes, Open University Press.

DAVID, A. and WHEELWRIGHT, T. (1990) *The Third Wave: Australia and Asian Capitalism*, Sydney, New Left Books.

DAVIS, D. (1988) *School to Work: The EHW Factor*, Sydney, Nelson.

DAWKINS, J. and HOLDING, C. (1987) *Skills Formation in Australia, 1987–88*, Canberra, Australian Government Publishing Service.

EWER, P., HAMPSON, I., LLOYD, C., RAINFORD, J., RIX, S. and SMITH, M. (1991) *Politics and The Accord*, Sydney, Pluto Press.

FRICKER, L. (1986) 'The Changing Context of TAFE and Its Consequences for the Role of TAFE', *Australian Journal of TAFE Research and Development*, 1, 2, pp. 13–31.

GARCIA, L. (1990) 'Reform Is Far from the Reality', *The Sydney Morning Herald*, 20 December, p. 11.

HABERMAS, J. (1976) *Legitimation Crisis*, Boston, Mass., Polity Press.

HABERMAS, J. (1987) *The Theory of Communicative Action: Vol. 2. The Lifeworld and the System: A Critique of Functionalist Reason*, Boston, Mass, Polity Press.

JONATHAN, R. (1990) 'State Education Service or Prisoner's Dilemma: The "Hidden" Hand as Source of Education Policy', *Education Philosophy and Theory*, 22, 1, pp. 16–24.

KELL, P. (1992) 'Skills Formation and TAFE: An Alternative View for Research', Paper presented to Training and Research in Higher Education, NCVER/ UTS Conference, Sydney.

KENWAY, J. (1990) *Gender and Education Policy: A Call for New Directions*, Geelong, Deakin University.

McGUINNESS, P.P. (1992) 'We Must Make Sure Our Vocational Training Measures Up', *The Weekend Australian*, 14–15 March, p. 2.

MCINTYRE, J. (1991) 'Technical and Further Education (TAFE) and Adult Education in Australia', in M. TENNANT, *Adult and Continuing Education in Australia: Issues and Practices*, London, Routledge.

MACKIE, R. (1980) 'The Unholy Alliance between TAFE and Industry', in D. MCKENZIE and C. WILKINS, *The TAFE Papers*, Melbourne, Macmillan, pp. 65-7.

MILLER, P. (1982) 'Technical Education and the Capitalist Divisions of Labour', *The ANZHES Journal*, 1, pp. 1-15.

NSW DEPARTMENT OF TECHNICAL AND FURTHER EDUCATION (1988) *Statistics Newsletter: Trends in Enrolments 1984-1988*, Sydney.

NSW DEPARTMENT OF TECHNICAL AND FURTHER EDUCATION (1990a) *Restructuring Newsletter*, 1, January.

NSW TECHNICAL AND FURTHER EDUCATION COMMISSION (1990b) *Statistics Newsletter: Trends in Enrolments 1989-90*, Sydney.

NSW TECHNICAL AND FURTHER EDUCATION COMMISSION (1991) *TAFE in New South Wales: Directions for the Future*, Sydney.

O'CONNOR, R. (1991) 'Vocational Education: Issues: The Hare and The Tortoise', Paper presented to AARE Conference, Gold Coast, November.

SCOTT, B. (1989) *TAFE Restructured: Building a Dynamic Vocational Education and Training Enterprise for the 1990's*, Management Review, Sydney, NSW Education Portfolio.

WATKINS, P. (1988) 'Satisfying the Need of Industry: Vocationalism, Corporate Culture and Education', *Unicorn*, 14, 2, pp. 69-76.

YEATMAN, A. (1987a) 'The Concept of Management in the Australian State in the 1980s', *Australian Journal of Public Administration*, 47, 4, pp. 339-56.

YEATMAN, A. (1987b) 'Iron Cage Administrative Reform or Reform and Management Improvement', *Flinders Studies in Policy and Administration*, March, pp. 1-15.

YEATMAN, A. (1990) 'Reconstructing Public Bureaucracies: The Residualisation of Equity and Access', *Australian Journal of Public Administration*, 49, 1, pp. 17-20.

13 Self-Managing Schools, Choice and Equity

Geoffrey Walford

Introduction

Over the last decade England and Wales have experienced a variety of changes in education policy which have gradually given greater autonomy to individual schools and increased the involvement of parents in their management.[1] These changes include the introduction of the right to have parent representatives on school governing bodies given in the 1980 Education Act; the reconstitution of the powers and composition of governing bodies (which included greater parent representation) in the 1986 Act; and, in particular, the 1988 Education Reform Act's restructuring of the education system through grant maintained schools, local management of schools and open enrolment. It might be argued that state-maintained schools in England and Wales have gradually moved towards the model of 'the self-managed school'. However, in this chapter I shall argue that this concept, as originally envisaged by Caldwell and Spinks,[2] has played only a minor part in justifying the range of changes, and that the reorientation of the school system is better understood in terms of the government's desire to increase competition between schools and to create a hierarchy of unequally funded schools which will help perpetuate class, gender and ethnic divisions.

A History of Inequality

Recent changes in education in England and Wales need to be seen against a backcloth where inequality in the schooling available to children from different social groups has consistently dominated the structure of provision. During the nineteenth century the state-maintained sector of schooling gradually developed to fill the gaps in private provision. The class divided nature of schooling was emphasized and clarified through the Newcastle, Clarendon and Taunton Commissions of the 1860s, which examined education for the poor, the upper class and the growing middle classes of the time. These commissions led to a greater separation of schooling for the various social classes, and to the introduction of local school boards to build and control schools for the working class alongside existing church schools (Walford, 1990, Ch. 2).

Local education authorities (LEAs) were established in 1902, and became the channel through which state funding to all elementary schools, whether owned by the state or by the churches, was provided. Secondary education was available only to some — either those with money to pay substantial fees or those passing a special scholarship examination.

The 1944 Education Act, which has still not been repealed but merely amended and added to, embodied the somewhat more egalitarian views of the time, and established free secondary education within the state sector as a distinct stage for all children. In the years following the Second World War secondary schools were provided to 'accommodate all children according to age, ability, and aptitude' which, at the time, was generally interpreted in terms of meritocracy and beliefs from psychology about the necessity for separate provision for three types of pupil. In most LEAs separate grammar, secondary modern and technical schools were proposed to enable children to develop their talents and to fit them for their future place in the occupational structure.

The technical schools within the tripartite system did not last long, so that selection for secondary schools at 11+ became a contest where those who 'passed' went to grammar schools, but where the majority who 'failed' ended up in the secondary moderns. The rhetoric of these schools being 'different but of equal status' rapidly disappeared as it became evident that the two different types of school were offering highly unequal educational experiences. Moreover, during the 1950s and 1960s evidence showed that there was considerable class bias in the intakes to the two types of school. The selective system was reinforcing class differences rather than offering wider opportunities to all (Floud *et al.*, 1957).

Class bias in intake was far from being the only problem with the selective system. Many parents, for example, were more concerned with failings in the 11+ examinations themselves, and in the possibility that selection was being made when their children were too young. But the 1960s did bring a popular demand for comprehensive education in terms of equality of opportunity. There was also a rather smaller number of educationists and intellectuals on the political left who were pressing for greater equity at the societal level. They saw comprehensive schools as a way of reducing class differences in society, and argued that putting all children from an area in the same school, where they would have equal access to high quality teachers and facilities, would bring greater equity within the schools and lead to greater equity outside in the world of work. It was hoped that mixing children from various social backgrounds in school would bring about a lowering of social class barriers and lead to a reduction in class antagonism and class differences.

As a result of these diverse demands for comprehensive education, LEAs gradually reorganized secondary provision to provide common education for all. In 1971 36 per cent of secondary children in state schools in the United Kingdom were in comprehensives, and by 1986 this figure had risen to 93 per cent. Although the Conservatives were fundamentally against comprehensive education and the egalitarian ideas which it incorporated, the changes continued unabated throughout their short period of government from 1970 to 1974 when, ironically, Margaret Thatcher was Secretary of State for Education and Science.

By 1979, although the private sector still educated a small but significant number of children, within the state sector selection of children for separate and unequally provided schools had decreased markedly and schooling was more comprehensive than it had ever been before. There remained some inequalities between schools, of course, and the use of catchment areas as a basis for allocating children to schools meant that there were still considerable class and ethnic differences between the intakes of schools, but these differences were decreasing and the aim was to try to ensure greater equality in the educational experiences being offered.

The 1979 general election brought a decisive change in government, and a prime minister dedicated to an ideology of individualistic competitiveness and a denial of the very existence of such an entity as 'society'. The concept of the 'self-managing' school was one which could be adapted by the New Right to suit its own ends, and used to re-establish separate education for different social groups.

The Path towards 'Self-Management'

In their book of that name, Caldwell and Spinks define a self-managing school as one where there has been significant and consistent decentralization to the school level of authority to make decisions relating to the allocation of resources. These resources include knowledge, technology, power, materials, people, time and finance, yet they somewhat naively see this decentralization as 'administrative rather than political, with decisions at the school level being made within a framework of local, state or national policies and guidelines' (Caldwell and Spinks, 1988, p. 5). Their focus is on raising the quality of learning and teaching — which they believe can be done through securing appropriate involvement of staff, students and the local community in policy-making through a cycle of collaborative school management. The cycle involves goal-setting, need identification, policy-making, planning, budgeting, implementation and evaluation and, ideally, involves staff, students and the local community in the process through a formal structure such as a school council or board of governors. The model of decentralization put forward by Caldwell and Spinks is not simply that schools should be autonomous, but one which envisages individual schools responding to local democratically voiced needs within a wider local and national framework of policies and guidelines to ensure that education meets public as well as private needs. Their model is essentially about improving efficiency and effectiveness, and draws upon a wealth of research showing that schools are more likely to be efficient and effective if those directly concerned with the school are given responsibility for local policy-making and implementation.[3]

There are considerable problems in defining what is efficient and effective within education, and in determining the extent to which the findings of good industrial and commercial practice can be applied to education. There are also questions to be raised about the assumption that self-management can be seen as an administrative rather than political activity. However, these issues will not be discussed here, for, within the context of implementation in England and Wales, there are further important issues. Crucially, various New Right groups in England and Wales have drawn somewhat selectively on the elements of the ideas originally put forward by Caldwell and Spinks, and incorporated these elements within wider ideologies of inegalitarianism. Under such circumstances, ideas which were intended to improve the quality of education available in schools to all children have become part of policies with very different purposes.

In England and Wales the moves towards 'self-management' were initially concerned predominantly with finance. The delegation of part of the LEA education budget to individual schools is far from new for, from 1944 onwards, most LEAs have given heads the freedom to spend a proportion of the budget as they felt fit. However, until recently, the amount of money involved was small and only related to a limited range of spending. In particular, such autonomy rarely included staff salaries, which are the major expenditure item of any school (although the Inner London Education Authority had such a scheme in 1973: see Downes, 1988). During the 1980s there were several experimental schemes where a greater proportion of LEA funding was delegated to schools, but the benefits envisaged by this change were sometimes far from those advocated by Caldwell and Spinks.

A much quoted example of school financial autonomy is that of the metropolitan Borough of Solihull in the English West Midlands, where a scheme was introduced in 1981 which included expenditure on teaching and non-teaching staff as well as on buildings and maintenance. Even though staff were still employed by the LEA, heads were free to spend their budget largely according to their own priorities. But Solihull's experiment was introduced explicitly as a cost-cutting exercise and was not designed to improve schools or make them more responsive to local needs (Humphrey and Thomas, 1986, pp. 513–14). A new chair of the Conservative controlled Local Education Committee had the belief that, if the same sort of procedures were used to run schools as he used in running a small business, savings would be made. Indeed, to ensure that such savings were made, for the first year of operation a bottom line deduction of 2 per cent was imposed on the secondary schools involved. The Director of Education argued that 'standard of service was about to become second fiddle to cost effectiveness' (Humphrey, 1988). As Caldwell and Spinks recognize, this scheme was not introduced to improve schools and did not draw upon the school effectiveness literature — its aim was simply to save money (Caldwell, 1987a). Yet Caldwell and Spinks appear to see this as an aberration, rather than as a potent force behind similar changes.

Self-Management and Choice in the 1980s

Caldwell and Spinks developed their ideas about self-management largely through a study of Rosebery District High School in Tasmania, where Spinks was principal. They state:

> The township of Rosebery is located on the west coast of Tasmania. The town has developed in conjunction with the mining industry. The school of some 600 students serves not only Rosebery but also the neighbouring Hydro-Electric Commission village of Tullah and the mining village of Zeehan. The school is referred to as a K-10 school as students are enroled at the age of four years in kindergarten and continue through until the fourth year of high school, year 10. Approximately one-half of students are of primary age, the other half of high school age. (Caldwell and Spinks, 1988, p. 71)

What is evident here is that the school is isolated and that there was no competition between this school and any others. There were no other public schools nearby! Yet in England and Wales the idea of the self-managed school has become intertwined with ideas of choice of school, competition between schools and funding based directly upon the number of pupils which competing schools can attract. Caldwell and Spinks's original book had little to say about competition or choice, yet in England and Wales this process of linking self-management with choice and competition gradually occurred throughout the 1980s and culminated in the changes in the 1988 Education Reform Act.

In England and Wales the number of 10-year-olds reached its peak in 1975, and there was a decline of some 30 per cent in the years until 1987. It is this dramatic demographic change that does most to explain the increased popular interest in parental choice of school in Britain in the late 1970s and into the 1980s. From the mid-1970s it became obvious that many schools had spare capacity, and the then Labour government was faced with a growing demand from parents to have the right to choose a particular school for their children. An Education Bill was produced in 1977, but a general election was called in 1979 before the Labour Education Bill became law.

Mrs Thatcher's newly elected Conservative government rapidly moved to implement its own version of parental choice through the 1980 Education Act. Much of the Act was similar to the Bill proposed by Labour, simply because it aimed to solve the same problems, but the ideological emphasis was shifted towards moving schools into the market-place and generating more competition between schools. From 1982 parents were given the right to 'express a preference' for a school of their choice, and the LEA was obliged to take this preference into account. However, the Act still gave LEAs considerable powers so that they could manage falling school rolls and plan the overall provision of school places in their areas. It allowed the benefits of the community as a whole to override the benefits to individual parents by giving LEAs the right to refuse parents' preferences if this would lead to some less popular schools having unviable numbers.

Stillman (1986) and Stillman and Maychell (1988) have shown that the effect of this legislation throughout England and Wales was extremely variable, as some LEAs tried to encourage parental choice, while others endeavoured to restrict it. Those offering minimal choice justified their behaviour in terms of catchment area schools fostering better links with the local community. They also argued that catchment areas ensured that the LEA could engage in long-term planning and hence benefit from the most efficient and effective use of resources. During a time of economic depression the government was not keen to be seen to encourage inefficiency and waste, and at this time it also appeared to retain some faith in the LEAs' planning functions.

The next major legislative change came with the 1986 Education Act which greatly increased the powers of school governing bodies (Deem, 1990). The governing bodies established in the 1944 Education Act had previously played a trivial role in the everyday management of schools. Many schools shared their governing body with other nearby schools, and in a few LEAs all schools were served by a single committee. The 1986 Education Act revitalized governing bodies, by ensuring that each school had its own committee and by giving it real powers and responsibilities over appointments, the curriculum and the management of the school. The Act also reconstituted the membership of governing bodies such that democratically elected local politicians and their nominees were no longer in the majority. The aim was that they were to be largely replaced by members of the local community (in particular, people in business and commerce, who were to be nominated rather than democratically elected) and parents of children in the school. The changes were justified in terms of increasing local accountability and fostering stronger links between schools and the world of work, but they can also be seen as encouraging differentiation and generating competition between schools. 'Responding to local needs' has rather different implications for a school in a working-class inner-city area than it has for one in a middle-class suburb.

At the 1986 Conservative Party Annual Conference which preceded the 1987 general election, a dramatic new form of self-managing school was announced under the guise of giving greater parental choice. The Secretary of State for Education and Science announced the creation of a pilot network of twenty City Technology Colleges (CTCs) to cater for 11- to 18-year-olds in selected inner-city areas. These were to be private schools, run by educational trusts with close links with industry and commerce. The governing bodies of these schools were to include many representatives from industry and commerce but to exclude both parent and teacher governors. The CTCs would charge no fees, and sponsors would be expected to cover the extra costs involved in providing a highly technological curriculum and would make substantial contributions to both capital and current expenditure. In order to dampen criticism that the colleges were equivalent to reintroducing grammar schools, they were to admit pupils spanning the full range of ability drawn from a defined urban catchment area. However, selection was still a major feature of the plan, not according to ability alone, but based upon general aptitude, readiness to take advantage of the type of education offered, and the parents' and child's commitment to the college and to full-time education or training up to the age of 18. The desire to increase technological education was a major feature of the plan, but many public political speeches at the time showed that CTCs were also designed to encourage inequality of educational provision, reintroduce selection, weaken the comprehensive system and reduce the powers of the LEAs.

A preliminary study of the first CTC has now been conducted by Walford and Miller (see Walford and Miller, 1991; Walford, 1991a; Gewirtz *et al.*, 1991). Of particular importance is the way in which children are selected for the CTC from those who apply. All of the CTCs are required to 'provide education for children of different abilities . . . who are wholly or mainly drawn from the area in which the school is situated.'[4] The CTC, Kingshurst selects children from a tightly defined catchment area which includes eight LEA secondary schools, and is thus in direct competition with these other schools for pupils. Parents are required to apply for admission to the CTC on behalf of their child. The child takes a simple non-verbal reasoning test which is used to ensure that children are selected with a range of abilities broadly representative of those who apply; they are also interviewed with a parent. The study by Walford and Miller showed that the college took great care to ensure that it was taking children with a wide ability range, but the whole entry procedure means that selection is based on the degree of motivation of parents and children. Children and families where there is a low level of interest in education simply do not apply.

In interviews, heads and teachers in the nearby LEA schools claimed that the CTC was selecting those very parents who have the most interest in their children's education, and those children who are most keen and enthusiastic. They argued that the CTC was selecting children who, while they might not be always particularly academically able, had special skills and interests in sport, art, drama or other activities. These children were seen as invigorating the atmosphere of any school, providing models for other children, and being rewarding for teachers to teach. Heads and teachers in nearby schools thus saw their schools as having been impoverished by the CTC's selection of these well motivated pupils.

Self-Management, Choice and the 1988 Education Reform Act

The New Right in England and Wales saw the potential of the concept of the 'self-managing school' during 1986 and 1987. Stuart Sexton, who was advisor to several Secretaries of State for Education in the early 1980s, had an important role in several New Right groups, including the Institute of Economic Affairs Education Unit.[5] In 1987 that body published Sexton's edited version of a conference on the funding and management of education which included a paper by Brian Caldwell. Caldwell's paper was moderate in tone and explicitly denied the calls for privatization of state maintained schools (Caldwell, 1987b), but the same volume included a précis of Sexton's own vision for a 'system truly based upon the supremacy of parental choice, the supremacy of purchasing power' (Sexton, 1987, p. 11). Sexton's aim is for a highly differentiated and privatized school system which selects according to academic and other abilities, parent and child motivation and parental ability to pay. He proposes that an educational credit for a minimum amount would be usable at any state or private school, both of which would be allowed to charge additional fees. Schools would be fully autonomous, being able to pay teachers whatever they liked. Against such powerful ideas, Caldwell's claim that 'there is no reason to fear that quality and equity will be sacrificed' looks distinctly naive (Caldwell, 1987b, p. 53).

Selection of children was an important part of the autonomy for schools proposed in several other New Right documents preceding the 1988 Act. Various grand-sounding groups were involved in campaigning for greater selection in education and unequal provision; they included the Campaign for Real Education, Parental Alliance for Choice in Education, Social Affairs Unit, Centre for Policy Studies and the Adam Smith Institute. The Hillgate Group (1986) echoed these demands by calling for schools to be owned by individual trusts rather than LEAs and given control over their own admissions.

The 1988 Education Reform Act for England and Wales introduced a wide range of ideas designed to hasten market processes within eduction.[6] Through the introduction of grant maintained schools (where schools opt out of LEA control and are funded directly by central government instead) and in the interlinked ideas of local management of schools and open enrolment for the remaining LEA schools, the major thrust of the Act was designed to increase competition among schools and to encourage parents to make choices among schools.

Of crucial importance here is that funding to individual schools is now largely related directly to age-related pupil numbers. Popular schools gain extra funding as they attract more pupils, while less popular schools lose funding as their numbers decline. The funding formulas which are used to allocate block funding to individual schools have been designed specifically to make sure that LEAs have lost practically all of their power to give extra support in areas of special need, or temporarily to adjust funding to particular schools to ensure that future needs are met. At a time of falling school rolls this means that the choice of which schools will close is left largely to the summation of the decisions of existing parents. The needs of future parents, or the society as a whole, are forgotten.

In many American versions of self-management and choice there is at least the recognition that it might be desirable to allocate more resources to low-income/low-achieving schools to ensure equity (for example, O'Connell, 1991), but in England and Wales LEAs have had to fight central government to retain even minimal powers to adjust the per pupil funding. What is happening in England and Wales is in direct contrast with the ideas expressed by Caldwell, who states that the 'crucial prerequisite for success in self-management is that the lump-sum allocation of resources to schools should take account of factors which distinguish pupils' needs and interests (1987b, p. 27). He continues, 'A single formula allocation on a per pupil basis will be as inequitable as the most centralised decision-making process.'

The Act was also designed to reduce the powers of LEAs in other ways. LEAs are currently allowed to retain a small proportion of their educational funding for services which are best provide centrally rather than at the school level. Thus LEAs provide help for those with special learning difficulties, pay for local school inspectors, curriculum advisors, planners and administrators, develop curriculum innovations, support multicultural and anti-sexist work, operate field centres, media centres and a host of other activities. One of the main reasons why schools have wished to become grant maintained is that the schools receive 'their share' of these central costs. They are then able to buy whichever of these services they wish from any supplier. The LEA thus loses power to encourage curriculum developments which it feels to be particularly relevant to the children in the region. If a grant maintained school becomes oversubscribed, it can begin to select the children that it wishes to accept. The ability of parents and children to choose a school quickly leads to schools being able to choose the pupils they want.

Reasons for Choice and Who Makes the Choice

The greater choice of school that followed the 1980 Education Act for England and Wales has encouraged research on the criteria that parents use in making their choice. Janet Hunter, for example, who conducted an interview survey of parents with children in eighteen inner-London secondary schools, found the four most commonly cited reasons for choice were good discipline, good exam results, single sex intake, and proximity to home (Hunter, 1991). The third of these is somewhat special to London where there is a high proportion of single sex schools and a high ethnic minority population. Anne West and Andreas Varlaam questioned parents before their final choice of school had been made. Their sample was small and drawn only from six inner-London primary schools, but the results are very important to the debate on choice and standards (West and Varlaam, 1991). Under these conditions a fairly similar list of reasons for choice was elicited from parents, but with some important additions. They found that three-quarters of the parents had particular schools that they did *not* wish the child to attend, mainly because of the school's 'bad reputation'. They also found that the positive factor mentioned most frequently (when not prompted) was that the child himself or herself wanted to go to a particular school. Thus, at the time the choice is made, parents appear to give high status to the choices of their 10-year-old sons and daughters. After the event, parents may rationalize their decision in terms of the criteria they believe the researcher might want to hear, but before the event they are prepared to admit that their child's happiness in attending a particular schools is an extremely important factor.

West and Varlaam also asked their sample of parents why they thought their child wanted to go to a particular school. The most important reason was simply that the child wished to go to the same school as his or her friends or relations. Other reasons given were good sports facilities, the school's convenient location or because it was single sex. None mentioned academic reasons.

This is in agreement with Edwards, Fitz and Whitty's study of the Assisted Places Scheme, where they found the most striking difference between parents of able children at LEA comprehensive schools and those of children in private schools was the extent to which they considered their child's desire to keep with friends (1989, p. 191). Those who chose the private sector for their children were more likely to ignore their children's wishes. A comparison between two small-scale studies of parental choice in socially different areas, reported by West (1992), also suggests that middle-class parents and parents of more academically able children are likely to take less notice of their child's view.

While children appear to play a large part in the process of choosing, until recently they have rarely been questioned about their reasons for wishing to attend one school rather than another. One small-scale study was part of the wider study of the City Technology College, Kingshurst discussed earlier (Walford, 1991b). The majority of children at the school completed questionnaires, and a representative sample was individually interviewed. It was found that nearly half of those interviewed believed that it had been they who had made the final choice to apply to the CTC and not their parents. A further 40 per cent stated that the decision had been a joint one with their parents. Significantly, in a specific question asking whether the fact that it was a *technology* college had been important, less than half agreed that it had. In this case the most common reason given was simply that they saw the CTC as offering them a 'good' or 'better' education, but this was often seen in terms of newer or better facilities and a better physical environment.

For comparison, interviews were held with sixty-one pupils in their first year at three nearby LEA schools which were within the CTC catchment area.[7] Fifty-five per cent of these children stated that the choice of school had been their own decision, with a further 30 per cent saying that it had been a joint decision with their parents. Reasons given for choice were varied, with differing patterns among the three schools. In all three schools, however, the fact that friends and relations were either already attending the school or were due to do so was important. The most common response in the interviews was that the pupil simply thought it was a 'good school' or that they just 'liked it'. Negative comments about other possible schools were also common.

What is of great importance here is the high proportion of children from this largely working-class area who stated that the choice about secondary school had been made by them rather than their parents. While it must be recognized that parents may use various subtle techniques to influence their children's choice, this was not the impression gained from these interviews. Most of the children who stated that it had been their choice were adamant that they had made this decision — sometimes against the wishes of their parents.

This degree of delegation of responsibility has also been found in a small-scale study of children in two urban junior schools in northern England conducted by Thomas and Dennison (1991). In that study of seventy-two children 60 per cent claimed that they made their own choice of secondary school. A further 30 per cent said it was a joint decision with their parents. Interviews with a sample of parents confirmed that most gave their children the 'biggest say' in the choice, and that their main concern was their children's happiness. Again, decisions were made on the basis of a mixture of factors, with friendship being a major factor for children. Of those children who chose a secondary school which was not their nearest, existing patterns of friendship represented the single most important factor in accepting the longer journey.

The results from another study of slightly older children in an outer-London borough indicate a small, but still significant, proportion of children making the choice of school themselves (West *et al.*, 1991). Eighteen per cent of the children from twelve middle schools reported that they had made the choice of high school themselves, with a further 66 per cent reporting that it had been a joint decision with their parents or guardians. These different proportions could be related to the social class composition of the outer-London sample. This study also discusses ethnic group differences; while the numbers involved are small, the differences are significant. Compared with white European children, a higher proportion of African/Afro-Caribbean children stated that they had made the choice themselves, while a far lower proportion of Asian pupils made this statement.

Conclusion

In their most recent book Caldwell and Spinks (1992) emphasize their view that self-management of schools is an important part of increasing equity in schooling available to all children. They point out that historic funding has often led to inequalities between schools and argue that a funding formula which allocates funding according to need, and based on the Need Weighted Pupil Unit, will lead to greater equity. They state that they 'no longer believe that the equity issue is any longer a valid argument against self-management, although all with an interest in the issue must remain vigilant' (Caldwell and Spinks, 1992, pp. 195–6).

It is a sad reflection of their depoliticized view of educational administration that, even by 1992, they have not recognized the underlying purpose of the 1988 Education Reform Act in England and Wales. They seem to assume that all government will 'naturally' wish to promote equity, and that it is only administrative difficulties which stand in the way of such ends. But the British government has no interest in equity in educational provision. It is using the competitive market version of self-managing schools to return to a more inegalitarian past where children are schooled in ways deemed 'appropriate' to their social class and ethnic group. During the early 1980s there were several attempts to reintroduce selective education within Conservative controlled LEAs, but these were all unsuccessful due to popular revolt (Walford and Jones, 1986). The self-managed school concept has allowed the New Right to introduce differentiated schooling and selection covertly instead.

Within England and Wales many of the more positive aspects of the cycle of collaborative school management envisaged by Caldwell and Spinks have been forgotten; and they have been replaced by an emphasis on choice and competition. Sadly, in more recent work, while still voicing concerns about the need for social factors to be taken into consideration in the allocation of block grants, Caldwell and Spinks see increased competition as a positive aspect of self-management (see, for example, Hill *et al.*, 1990).

One of the main justifications now used for greater self-management and choice of school is that it is anticipated that efficient and effective schools will thrive while the inefficient and ineffective ones close. Little thought is given to those children who will remain in these schools over the years of decline, but it must also be noted that such closures can only occur at a time of falling school rolls. Once less popular schools have closed in line with the falling pupil population, those remaining will be full. Without overcapacity in schools, parents will quickly find that their choices are severely curtailed, and that it is the schools who choose which children to accept rather than the parents and children choosing a school. Control will have passed to individual schools and their governing bodies. At the City Technology College, Kingshurst, for example, there were over 1000 applicants for 180 places on offer for September 1991. Far more parents were denied their choice than granted it, and the CTC was able to select the children it thought most suitable.

The idea that greater choice leads to higher standards is based on the assumption that choice of school will be made by parents, and that these parents will be well informed. It is supposedly the 'bad' schools that close and the 'good' ones that expand. However, it has been shown that parents make choices on a broad range of criteria and that academic issues appear to feature quite low on their list or priorities. There is little evidence for equating 'popular' with 'good' in terms of parental choice.[8] Moreover, recent evidence has shown that the child's wishes are of great importance to many parents, and that a large number of parents appear to delegate the decision entirely to their child. This concern with the wishes of the child may mean that she or he has a happier time at secondary school (which is not insignificant!), but there is even less evidence that the choices of 10-year-old children are likely to be informed choices and primarily related to the academic effectiveness of the schools. More fundamentally, it is highly unlikely that the sum of many such choices will automatically lead to higher educational standards for all.

It does seem likely, however, that choice will lead to better quality schooling for *some* children, for some parents and children will be more concerned and better informed about the effectiveness of various schools than others. Some parents are more able to pay for the transport of their children to school, and some parents are more likely to impose their decision about schooling on their children. It is not coincidental that these differences among parents in their relationship to schooling are likely to be class and ethnic group biased. In practice, the government's embrace of self-management and choice has little to do with any desire to increase educational standards and even less with equity, but conceals and mystifies a desire to construct a hierarchy of schools with unequal provision, into which children can be fitted to equip them for their preordained roles in society. As choices are made and pupils selected, the schools will become more differentiated. Some will be able to draw on parental financial support for new buildings and equipment or to pay for additional teachers and helpers. Other schools will not be so lucky.

Eventually this continuum of schools will offer different educational and social experiences to pupils, and various children will be fitted into these schools through a process of mutual selection. However, the final decisions will be made by the schools and their governing bodies. Control of education will be in the hands of a series of small, largely unelected groups. The evidence that we already have about choice suggests that this process of mutual selection will probably be closely linked to social class and ethnicity, and discriminate in particular against working-class children and children of Afro-Caribbean descent. There is also likely to be greater social segregation among social and ethnic groups and less mutual understanding. The pre-existing social order of wealth and privilege is likely to be confirmed. In summary, the main purpose of the recent moves towards greater choice is not to build a more democratic and fair educational system but to put an end to egalitarianism, and to rebuild a differentiated educational system which will more closely aid social reproduction. The ideology of choice and self-management acts partially to mask this process; and while it may allow a few individuals to benefit, the majority have much to lose.

Notes

1 Some of the ideas in this chapter are drawn from my article, 'Educational Choice and Equity in Great Britain', *Educational Policy*, Spring 1992.
2 As put forward by Brian J. Caldwell and Jim M. Spinks (1986) *Policy-Making and Planning for School Effectiveness*, Hobart, Tasmania, Education Department; (1988) *The Self-Managing School*, Lewes, Falmer Press; and Brian J. Caldwell (1987) *The Promise of Self-Management for Schools: An International Perspective*, London, Institute for Economic Affairs.
3 The school effectiveness literature is well reviewed in Hedley Beare, Brian J. Caldwell and Ross H. Millikan (1989) *Creating an Excellent School*, London, Routledge, Ch. 1.
4 1988 Education Reform Act, para. 105.
5 See Clive Griggs (1989) 'The New Right and English Secondary Education', in Roy Lowe (ed.), *The Changing Secondary School*, Lewes, Falmer Press for a discussion of New Right groups.

6 This area is dealt with in more detail in Geoffrey Walford (1990) 'The 1988 Education Reform Act for England Wales: Paths to Privatisation,' *Educational Policy*, 4, 2, pp. 127–44; Geoffrey Walford (1991) 'Educational Reform in Great Britain,' in Peter W. Cookson, Alan R. Sadovnik and Susan F. Senmel (Eds), *Handbook of International Educational Reform*, New York, Greenwood Press. A good guide to the Act is Martin Leonard (1988) *The 1988 Education Act*, Oxford, Blackwell.

7 These interviews with LEA children were conducted by Sharon Gewirtz, Henry Miller and the author as part of an ESRC funded research project on City Technology Colleges directed by Tony Edwards and Geoff Whitty (research grant no. C00232462).

8 The major study by D. Smith and S. Tomlinson (1989) argued that it was clear that parents in their study could not identify the schools that were doing well in terms of pupil progress.

References

CALDWELL, BRIAN J. (1987a) *The Promise of Self-Management for Schools: An International Perspective*, London, Institute of Economic Affairs Education Unit.

CALDWELL, BRIAN J. (1987b) 'New Roles and Responsibilities for Resource Allocation in Education: An International Perspective', in STUART SEXTON (Ed.), *The Funding and Management of Education*, London, Institute of Economic Affairs.

CALDWELL, BRIAN J. and SPINKS, JIM M. (1988) *The Self-Managing School*, Lewes, Falmer Press.

CALDWELL, BRIAN J. and SPINKS, JIM M. (1992) *Leading the Self-Managing School*, Lewes, Falmer Press.

DEEM, R. (1990) 'The Reform of School Governing Bodies: The Power of the Consumer over the Producer?' in MICHAEL FLUDE and MERRIL HAMMER (Eds), *The Education Reform Act 1988*, Lewes, Falmer Press.

DOWNES, P. (Ed.) (1988) *Local Financial Management in Schools*, Oxford, Blackwell.

EDWARDS, T., FITZ, J. and WHITTY, G. (1989) *The State and Private Education: An Evaluation of the Assisted Places Scheme*, Lewes, Falmer Press.

FLOUD, J.E., HALSEY, A.H. and MARTIN, F.M. (1957) *Social Class and Educational Opportunity*, London, Heinemann.

GEWIRTZ, S., MILLER, H. and WALFORD, G. (1991) 'Parents' Individualist and Collectivist Strategies at the City Technology College, Kingshurst,' *International Studies in Sociology of Education*, 1, pp. 171–89.

HILL, D., SMITH, B.O. and SPINKS, J. (1990) *Local Management of Schools*, London, Paul Chapman.

HILLGATE GROUP (1986) [Caroline Cox, Jessica Douglas-Home, John Marks, Lawrence Norcross, Roger Scruton] *Whose Schools? A Radical Manifesto*, London, Hillgate Group.

HUMPHREY, C. (1988) *Financial Autonomy in Solihull*, London, Institute of Economic Affairs.

HUMPHREY, C. and THOMAS, H. (1986) 'Delegation to Schools', *Education*, 12.

HUNTER, JANET B. (1991) 'Which School? A Study of Parents' Choice of Secondary School,' *Educational Research*, 33, 1, pp. 31–41.

Geoffrey Walford

O'CONNELL, M. (1991) 'The Genesis of Reform', Equity and Choice, 8, 1, pp. 7–13.

SEXTON, S. (1987) Our Schools: A Radical Policy, London, Institute of Economic Affairs.

SMITH, D. and TOMLINSON, S. (1989) The School Effect: A Study of Multi-Racial Comprehensives, London, Policy Studies Institute.

STILLMAN, A. (Ed.) (1986) The Balancing Act of 1980: Parents, Politics and Education, Windsor, NFER/Nelson.

STILLMAN, A. and MAYCHELL, K. (1988) Choosing Schools: Parents, LEAs and the 1980 Education Act, Windsor, NFER/Nelson.

THOMAS, A. and DENNISON, B. (1991) 'Parental or Pupil Choice: Who Really Decides in Urban Schools?' Educational Management and Administration, 19, 3, pp. 243–9.

WALFORD, G. (1990) Privatization and Privilege in Education, London, Routledge.

WALFORD, G. (1991a) 'City Technology Colleges: A Private Magnetism?' in GEOFFREY WALFORD (Ed.), Private Schooling: Tradition, Change and Diversity, London, Paul Chapman.

WALFORD, G. (1991b) 'Choice of School at the First City Technology College,' Educational Studies, 17, 1, pp. 65–75.

WALFORD, G. and JONES, S. (1986) 'The Solihull Adventure: An Attempt to Reintroduce Selective Schooling', Journal of Education Policy, 1, 3, pp. 239–53.

WALFORD, G. and MILLER, H. (1991) City Technology College, Milton Keynes, Open University Press.

WEST, A. (1992) 'Choosing Schools: Are Different Factors Important for Different Parents?' Paper given at the British Education Management and Administration Society Research Conference, April.

WEST, A. and VARLAAM, A. (1991) 'Choosing a Secondary School: Parents of Junior School Children,' Educational Research, 33, 1, pp. 22–30.

WEST, A., VARLAAM, A. and SCOTT, G. (1991) 'Choice of High School: Pupils' Perceptions,' Educational Research, 33, 3, pp. 207–15.

Notes on Contributors

Gary Anderson is a member of faculty in the College of Education, University of New Mexico. His interests include the paradigms that underlie research in educational administration and critical ethnography in education.

Alexandra Dixon is principal of New Futures School, an alternative school for pregnant and parenting teens in Albuquarque, New Mexico.

Lawrence Angus is Senior Lecturer in Education at Monash University. Among his most recent works is *Continuity and Change in Catholic Schooling* (Falmer Press). His current interests and research are in technical/managerial and participative/professional perspectives in educational organizations.

Stephen Ball is Professor in the Centre for Educational Studies, University of London. Some of his more recent publications include: (editor) *Foucault and Education: Disciplines and Knowledge* (Routledge); and *Politics and Policy Making in Education* (Routledge). His research interests focus on various aspects of educational reform and policy-making.

Marie Brennan is lecturer in Social and Administrative Studies of Education at Deakin University. Her research interests are on aspects of school improvement, particularly participative approaches.

John Codd is Associate Professor of Education at Massey University of New Zealand. He has published extensively in books and international journals of educational policy. He has taken a particular interest in 'flagging' the lessons to be learned from the activities of the New Right in his country.

Jack Demaine is a faculty member at Loughborough University. His particular interests are in the manner in which New Right thinking has come to underpin educational reforms, particularly in Britain, and in the 'market orientation' being taken by universities.

David Hartley is in the Centre for Continuing Education, University of Dundee, Scotland. Over several years he has had an interest in how aspects of surveillance and social control have an impact on teachers. He is currently preparing an anthology on that topic.

Peter Kell is a classroom teacher who takes up a position shortly at James Cook University of North Queensland. His particular interests are in educational reform as they affect technical and further education institutions.

Susan Robertson is Director of the International Institute for Policy and Administrative Studies, Edith Cowan University, Western Australia. Her interests are in various aspects of teachers' work and how the politics of the wider aspects of work (such as post-Fordism) influence and shape what goes on in school.

Brendan Ryan is Senior Lecturer, University of South Australia. He has published widely in national and international journals and his interests are in technocratic rationality in education, and whose interests are served by educational reform.

John Smyth is Professor of Teacher Education at Flinders University of South Australia, prior to which he was at Deakin University. Among his recent books are *Teachers as Collaborative Learners* (Open University Press); (with Gitlin) *Teacher Evaluation: Educative Alternatives* (Falmer Press); (editor) *Critical Perspectives on Educational Leadership* (Falmer Press); and *Educating Teachers: Changing the Nature of Pedagogical Knowledge* (Falmer Press). His current research interests are in teachers' work and the changing labour process of teaching.

Andrew Sparkes and Martin Bloomer are from Exeter University. Their interests focus on the cultural context in which schooling occurs and how this shapes the occupational culture and practices of teaching and how critical reflection can be a part of this.

Geoffrey Walford is in the Aston Business School, Aston University, Birmingham. Among his more recent works are: (with Henry Miller) *City Technology College* (Open University Press); and *Private Schooling: Tradition, Change and Diversity* (Chapman). His particular interests are in the way in which so-called 'choice' shapes and distorts equity and social justice in schooling.

Peter Watkins is Senior Lecturer in Social and Administrative Studies of Education at Deakin University. He has interests in the relationship between school, work, workplace democracy and the critical analysis of organizations.

Index

Accord, 120, 133n6
accountability, 3, 15–16, 17, 18, 24,
    29, 50, 66, 96, 117, 124, 126,
    132, 139, 143, 144, 154, 156,
    162, 179, 182, 183, 185, 187,
    191, 192, 194, 197, 199, 208,
    209, 210, 234
Adam Smith Institute, 37, 236
    Omega Report, 37
administration
    and 'whole-of-government'
    approach, 191–2
adult education, 214
AEC
    see Australian Education Council
Anderson, G.L. and Dixon, A., 4,
    49–61
Angus, L., 4, 11–33, 217
Angus, M., 117, 125, 131
Apple, M., 18, 21
Ashenden, D., 141
Assisted Places Scheme, 238
Assisted Places Scheme [Scotland],
    109, 110, 112n5
Australia
    see also New South Wales; Queens-
    land; South Australia; Victoria;
    Western Australia
    as 'banana republic', 216–17
    curriculum in, 142–3
    educational reform in, 3, 5–6, 8–9,
    12–13, 15, 30, 83–98, 117–33,
    192–3, 201–10, 213–26
    Fordism in, 121
    social formation in, 121
    social relations in, 118
    vocational education in, 213–28
    war memorials in, 213, 226
Australian Education Council (AEC),
    142–3
Australian Teachers' Federation, 126,
    127

'back to basics' movement, 51
Ball, S.J., 7, 18, 29, 63–82, 122, 130,
    182
Bates, R., 172
Beazley, K., 134n9
    see also Beazley Report
Beazley Report, 123, 134n9, 134n10
Bell, D., 99–100, 105
Bennis, W. and Nanus, B., 26
Bentham, J., 101
Berger, P. and Luckmann, T., 106
Bessant, J., 215
Better Schools in Western Australia,
    124–5, 128, 131, 130
BHP, 143
'Black Papers', 216
Blackmore, J., 215
Bloomer, M.
    see Sparkes and Bloomer
Boston Compacts program, 104,
    105
Bourne, Cardinal, Archbishop of
    Westminster, 37

Bowles, G.
  see Fidler and Bowles
Brennan, M., 3, 83–98
British Telecom, 141
Broom, D., 179
Brown vs Board of Education, 51
Budgetary Reform, 122
budgets
  school, 16, 17–18, 20, 21, 23–5, 30,
    35–6, 40, 46, 60n5, 67–9, 73, 76,
    77, 80n5, 86, 102, 110, 125, 179,
    193, 199, 232–3, 237
Bullough, R., 173, 174
bureaucracy, 12–14, 58–9, 196–8
  see also managerialism
  'responsive', 12–14
bureaucratic rationality, 24
Burke administration, 119, 134n9
Burrell, G. and Morgan, G., 53–4,
    60n2
Business Council of Australia, 139,
    140, 143–4
Business Round Table [New
    Zealand], 157

Caldwell, B.J., 86, 236, 237
Caldwell, B.J. and Spinks, J., 4–5,
    11, 19–29, 36, 39–40, 68, 69, 71,
    79, 87–9, 91, 92–3, 94, 96, 97,
    218, 229, 231–2, 233, 240, 241
  see also Self-Managing School, The
Callahan, R., 159–61
Cambridgeshire Local Education
    Authority, 80n5
Campaign for Real Education, 236
capitalism, 2, 6, 99–100, 105–6, 100,
    120–1, 137–50
  and crisis of accumulation, 99,
    120–1, 147
  and crisis of legitimation, 99, 100,
    149
  and crisis of motivation, 99, 100
Carnegie, D., 160
Carr, W. and Kemmis, S., 183
Catley, B., 120
Centre for Policy Studies, 236
choice
  in education, *see* parental choice
Chresiomathia, 101

Chubb, J.E. and Moe, T.M., 111
Circular 7/88 [DES, UK], 65
City Technology College,
    Kingshurst, 235, 239, 241
City Technology Colleges (CTCs),
    235–6
  aims of, 235
  selection for, 235–6
Clarendon Commission, 229–30
Clark, J., 141
Clarke, J., *et al*, 172
Clarke, K., 43
classroom practice, 64, 67
Codd, J., 4, 153–70
collaborative cultures, 175–7, 183–6
collaborative school management
    cycle, 24–5, 39–40, 68, 87–8,
    92–3, 94, 231, 241
collegiality, 118, 124, 132, 172,
    175–82, 183–4, 186
colonization of the life-world, 138,
    146, 147–50, 226
  see also Habermas
Committee to Review the Education
    Reform Implementation Process
    [New Zealand], 159
Committee of Review of Post-
    Compulsory Education, 143
*Common and Agreed National Goals for
    Schooling in Australia*, 142–3
Commonwealth Schools
    Commission, 133n1
community participation
  see participation
compacts
  education-business, *see* Compacts
    Initiative program
Compacts Initiative program, 100,
    103–7, 108–9, 111
  aims of, 104
  and egalitarianism, 103
  and evaluative state, 103
  and outcomes, 105–6
competition, 3, 200
comprehensive schooling, 44, 230–1
  and 'giantism', 44
Conservative government
  see also Conservative Party; New
    Right

and comprehensive education, 231
and educational reform, 36, 41–3,
    46, 63, 76–7, 179, 234
Conservative MPs, 'No Turning
    Back Group' of, 39
Conservative Party, 20–1, 36, 41–3,
    46, 53
    see also Conservative government
    compared with New Right, 36,
    41–3, 46
    Conference (1983), 43
    Conference (1986), 235
    Election Manifesto (1987), 20–1
    and self-managing schools, 41–3
    and voucher systems, 43
Considine, M., 7, 142
'consumer' politics, 65
contestability, 168
contractualism, 153
corporate federalism, 143
corporate management, 14, 16–17,
    29, 118–19, 122–3, 142, 193,
    196–7, 204, 205, 208, 217–22,
    224–5
    see also managerialism
    in Technical and Further Education,
    217–22, 224–5
Cox Report, 205
Crough, G. and Wheelwright, T.,
    120
CTCs
    see City Technology Colleges
Cuban, L., 64
cultural assimilation, 193
cultural engineering, 68–9
culture
    definitions of, 172–3
    and schooling, 172–5
Cumming, J., 90–1
curriculum, 4, 15, 29, 64, 103, 142–3,
    193, 199, 200, 201, 209
    see also national curriculum; unit
    curriculum
    as 'whole-of-school', 209
Curriculum Corporation [proposed],
    142

Dale, R., 7, 177, 181, 225
Davies, D., 78–9

Dawe, R.
    see Hargreaves and Dawe
Deal, T. and Kennedy, A., 26
decentralization
    and conflict management, 56–7
    in education, *see* education, and
    decentralization
    and efficient site management, 14–16
    and legitimation, 56–7
deindustrialization, 120
Demaine, J., 5, 35–48
denationalization, 120
Dennison, B.
    see Thomas and Dennison
Department of Education [New
    South Wales]
    sale of headquarters of, 14
Department of Education [Victoria],
    86
Department of Management and
    Budget (DMB) [Victoria], 86
deregulation, 120, 194–5
desegregation
    in schools, 51
devolution, 1–2, 4–5, 8, 12–13,
    17–18, 35, 53, 58–9, 60n4, 77,
    80n5, 110, 117–33, 154–7,
    101–211, 217–22, 128–31,
    192–3, 201–10, 222–5
devolved management of resources
    (DMR), 110
Dewey, J., 167
dezoning
    of schools, 17, 166
Dimmock, C., 141
discipline
    in schools, 207–8
District Principals [South Australia],
    205
District Superintendent [South
    Australia], 193
Dixon, A.
    see Anderson and Dixon
DMB
    see Department of Management and
    Budget
DMR
    see devolved management of
    resources, 110

Downes, P., 80n5
Dunleavy, P., 148
Dworkin, R., 166

Economic Management, 155
economic rationalism, 118, 120, 133,
    138, 143, 146–8, 149–50, 153,
    155, 157, 159, 161, 192, 194–8,
    201–2, 203–4, 210, 220
economic restructuring
    global, 120–1
education
    see also educational reform; school
        self-management
    aims of, 28, 30, 201–3, 210
    'Balkanization' of, 222–4
    and business, 138–40, *see also*
        Compacts Initiative; education
        and industry
    and centralization, 2–8, 39, 42, 46,
        137, 143–4, 147–8, 154, 191–2,
        204
    choice in, *see* parental choice
    'commercialization' of, *see*
        education, and market orientation
    and competition, 17
    and consumer choice, *see* parental
        choice
    context of, 11–33, 50–1, 118–23,
        154–7, 192, 194–5, 210, 213,
        222–4, 229–30
    control in, 77–8
    critical reflection on, 30–1
    and culture, 27, 172–5, 278
    decentralization in, 2–8, 12–16,
        144, 153, 192, 208, 231–2
    democracy and, 18, 202, 203–4
    and devolution, *see* devolution
    and disadvantaged, 206–7
    and divisiveness, 198–201
    and economy, 6–7, 16–17, 51–2,
        194–6, 203, 216; *see also*
        economic rationalism
    and equity, 20–1, 229–31,
        240–2
    and ethnicity, 8
    funding of, 110, 111, 149, 156–7,
        229–30, 237, 240; *see also*
        budgets, school

as human right, 165
and industry, 7, 23–5, 68–9,
    130–1, 143, 160–1, 216,
    232–3
instrumentalism in, 167–8
managerialism and, *see*
    managerialism
and market orientation, 4, 11, 15,
    17, 18, 29, 30, 37–8, 39, 43–5,
    64–6, 70, 74–5, 77, 110, 111,
    130–1, 137–50, 161–3, 179,
    198–9, 200, 201–2, 203–4,
    217, 222–3, 224–5, 234, 237
modernization of, 198–201, 207,
    210
motivation crisis in, 100
and outcomes, 207
and participation, *see* participation
policy implementation in, 24–5,
    93–4, 168
politicization of, 196
as primary good, 165
privatization of, 37–8, 43, 196
and producer capture, 37, 69
and provider capture, 16
and social class, 8
social justice in, *see* social justice
and the state, 3–6, 65, 77–8,
    99–112, 118–19, 123, 131–3,
    140–1, 147, 155–7, 196–7; *see*
    also economic rationalism
values in, 167–9
vocational functions of, 202–3; *see*
    also Technical and Further
    Education
and voucher systems, *see* vouchers
Education Act [South Australia], 205,
    206
Education Act (1944) [UK], 42, 230,
    234
Education Act (1980) [UK], 229, 234,
    238
Education Act (1986) [UK], 234
Education Bill (1977) [UK], 233–4
education credits, 37
Education and the Cult of Efficiency,
    159–60
Education Department [South
    Australia], 192–3, 201–10

Education Department [Western
  Australia], 124
Education Policy, 37
Education Reform Act (1988) [UK],
  15, 42, 60n4, 66, 71–2, 113n6,
  153, 163, 179, 184, 185–6, 229,
  233, 236–8, 240
Education Review Office [New
  Zealand], 156
Education (Scotland) Act (1981), 109
Education: A Framework for Choice, 37
educational administration
  critical theory and, 53, 54, 55, 60n3
  and objectivist paradigm, 53–4, 59
  phenomenology and, 53, 54
  positivism and, 53–4
  and subjectivist paradigm, 53–5
  theories of, 53–5
Educational Institute of Scotland
  (EIS), 107–8
educational reform
  see also school self-management
  conservatism in, 16–19, 41–3, 64,
    117–33, 142–50, 225
  and corporate managerialism, *see*
    corporate management
  and management, *see* management
  models for, 50
  New Right and, *see* New Right
  in Australia, 3, 5–6, 8–9, 12–13,
    15, 30, 83–98, 117–33, 192–3,
    201–10, 213–26
  in New Zealand, 4, 14, 153–70
  in South Australia, 191–211
  in Technical and Further Education,
    213–26
  in United Kingdom, 14, 18, 20–1,
    35–48, 60n4, 63–82, 171,
    177–87, 229–44
Edwards, T., *et al*, 238
Effective Local Management of
  Schools, 69
effectiveness, 2, 14–16, 17, 23–4, 25,
  29, 49, 143, 192–3, 215, 232,
  233, 234, 241
efficiency, 2, 11, 14–16, 17, 23, 50,
  84, 100, 143, 160–1, 162, 164,
  165, 166, 168, 192–3, 199, 200,
  203, 208, 215, 232, 234, 241

11+ examinations, 230
Employment Department [UK], 104
England
  see also United Kingdom
  choice of schools in, 238–40
  educational reform in, 233–42
  educational system in, 229–3
  parental choice in, 233–40
  pupil enrolments in, 233
  school self-management in, 8,
    63–82, 109, 232–42
  social class and education in,
    229–31
enterprise bargaining, 224
entrepreneurialism, 7, 220
equity
  see social justice
Erickson, F., 172
evaluation
  participatory, 90–3, 96, 97n2
  principles for, 91
evaluative state, 100–15
Ewer, P., *et al*, 223–4
excellence movement, 162

Feiman-Nemser, S. and Floden, R.,
  172, 174
Ferguson, K., 58–9
Fidler, B. and Bowles, G., 69
'50 Schools Faced Classroom Chaos',
  125
'Fightback' policy [Australia], 145
Financial Administration and Audit
  Act (1986) [Western Australia],
  123
Finn, C., 143, 162
  see also Finn report
Finn report, 133n3, 133n8
Fligstein, N., 143
Floden, R.
  see Feiman-Nemser and Floden
Ford, H., 134n7
Fordism, 66, 121, 138, 160
  see also post-Fordism
  definition of, 121
Foucault, M., 66–7, 78
'free marketeering', 2
Freire, P., 112
Fritzell, C., 103

Fullan, M. and Hargreaves, A., 173, 175–7, 183–4
functionalism, 23–5, 26–7, 28
further education, 214
    see also Technical and Further Education
Further Education Unit (FEU) [UK], 105

gender
    in Technical and Further Education, 215, 220–1
General Teaching Council for Scotland (GTC), 107–8
Germany
    training model in, 223
Gibson, R., 172
Gilbreth, 146
Gintis, H., 29
Gitlin, A., 173
Goodchild, S., 68
Gordon, D., 122
governing bodies
    see school governing bodies
Government Agencies Review Group (GARG) [South Australia], 192–3
Government Management and Employment Act [South Australia], 205
Grace, G., 153–4
grant-maintained status (GMS), 38, 40, 42, 46, 109, 110, 229, 237
Gude, Mr, 144–5

Habermas, J., 138, 146, 147–8, 149, 150, 167, 226
Halsey, A.H., 36, 40–1, 46
Hargreaves, A., 173
    see also Fullan and Hargreaves
Hargreaves, A. and Dawe, R., 172, 175, 176
Hargreaves, A. and Reynolds, D., 179
Hargreaves, D.H. and Hopkins, D., 67, 69
Harmann, E., 119
Hartley, D., 6, 99–115, 143
Hawke government, 216
Hayek, F.A., 37

headteacher, 25–6, 39, 75, 79, 110, 179, 186–7
    see also leadership; principal
Hill, D., *et al*, 36
Hillgate Group, 39, 236
Hobson vs Hansen, 51
Hopkins, D.
    see Hargreaves and Hopkins
How to Become a Self-Governing School, 109
Hoyle, E., 179
Hughes, M., *et al*, 184–5
Hunter, J., 238

IBM, 130, 143
IEA
    see Institute of Economic Affairs
In Search of Excellence, 23–4, 25
Independent Schools Salaries Officers Association [Western Australia], 126
individualism, 102, 144–6
industrial management model, 7
industrial relations
    post-Fordist, 118–23, 138–40
Industrial Relations Commission (IRC) [Australia], 126
industry
    and education, *see* education, and industry
Inner London Education Authority, 60n4, 232
Innovations and Priority Schools Programs, 117
Institute of Economic Affairs (IEA), 37, 38
    Education Unit, 236
instrumentalism, 167
Into Work, 104
IRC
    see Industrial Relations Commission

Japan
    post-Fordism in, 140
    scientific management in, 146
    training model in, 223
Jesson, B., 155
Jonathan, R., 162–3, 222
Joseph, Sir Keith, 43

Journal of Economic Affairs, 38
justice
   see also social justice
   theory of, 164–5

Kangan, M., 214
   see also Kangan Report
Kangan Report, 214, 215, 220
Keating, P., 216
Kell, P., 5–6, 213–28
Kemmis, S.
   see Carr and Kemmis
Kennedy, A.
   see Deal and Kennedy
Kent County Council, 43
Kickert, W., 65–6, 71

Labor government [Australia], 214, 216
Labor government [Victoria]
   and bureaucratic reform, 86
   and educational reform, 12, 84–7
Labor Party [Australia], 53, 148
Labor Party [Victoria], 84
Labour government [New Zealand],
   155, 166
Labour government [UK], 35
Labour Party [UK], 36, 41, 46
Lange-Douglas government, 155
Laver, 143
leadership, 25–8, 166–9, 205–6
   see also headteacher; principal
Leading the Self-Managing School, 25
'learner-centred', 102
learning
   constructivist theory of, 103
   lifelong, 214
   student-centred, 102–3
LEAs
   see local education authorities
LFM
   see local financial management
Liberal Party [Australia], 148
Lingard, R., 143
Littler, C., 140
LMS
   see local management of schools
local education authorities (LEAs), 17,
   20, 40–1, 42, 65, 163, 230, 231,
   232, 234, 236, 237–8

local financial management (LFM),
   179
local management of schools (LMS),
   14, 17, 24, 29, 40, 42, 46, 65, 67,
   76, 80n5, 109, 110, 112–13n6,
   179, 229, 237
Local Management of Schools, 36
London Street primary school
   [Edinburgh], 109
Loton, B., 137, 139
Lough, N.V., 159
   see also Lough Report
Lough Report, 159, 167–8
Luckmann, T.
   see Berger and Luckmann

McGuinness, P.P., 216
Mackie, R., 214, 215, 219
McTaggart, R., 173–4
Main Committee, 107
Malen, B. and Ogawa, R., 57
management, 27, 65–71, 101,
   217–20
   see also managerialism; performance
      management
   entrepreneurial, 68–9
   as financial, 67–8, 69
   and human relations, 101
   as professional, 67, 69
   and self-monitoring, 101
   and worker discretion, 101
managerialism, 4, 118, 124, 146–50,
   157–9, 160–1, 168, 193, 201, 205,
   209, 210
   in Technical and Further Education,
      217–20
Managing Change in the Public Sector,
   122–3
market liberalism, 154–7, 161–3
   see also economic rationalism
   aims of, 165–6
   ethical base of, 163–7
Maychell, K.
   see Stillman and Maychell
Mayer report, 133n3
Maymen, J., 119
mechanics institutes, 214
   see also Technical and Further
      Education

Mexico
decentralization of education in,
60n4
microeconomic reform, 121, 209
Miller, H.
see Walford and Miller
Miller, P., 215
Ministerial Papers [Victoria], 12–13,
84–5, 86–7, 94
Ministry of Education [New
Zealand], 156
Ministry of Education [Victoria], 21
Ministry of Education [Western
Australia], 124–5, 126–8
modernization, 197
Moe, T.M.
see Chubb and Moe
Morgan, G.
see Burrell and Morgan
multiculturalism, 193

Nanus, B.
see Bennis and Nanus
National Board of Employment and
Training, 143
National Committee for the In-
Service Training of Teachers
(NCITT) [Scotland], 107
National Companies and Securities
Commission, 120
national curriculum, 4, 20, 56, 59, 63,
66, 70, 130, 131, 143–4, 195,
202
see also National Curriculum [UK]
National Curriculum [UK], 71, 75,
79n1, 179
NCITT
see National Committee for the
In-Service Training of Teachers
Neave, G., 102
New Right, 2, 4, 5, 11–12, 15, 18,
20–1, 30, 35–48, 64, 120, 171,
215–26, 222, 224, 226, 231, 232,
236–8, 240
definition of, 36–7
New South Wales
decentralization of education in,
14–16
deregulation of school zones in, 15

Technical and Further Education in,
5–6, 213, 217–22, 223, 225, 226
New Zealand
consumer choice in, 161–3
economic rationalism in, 153–7
educational reform in, 4, 14,
153–70
managerialism in, 157–9
market liberalism in, 153–7
school self-management in, 153–70
social justice in, 153, 155, 157, 163,
164–7, 169
Treasury in, 155–6, 157, 158, 159,
161–2
Newcastle Commission, 229–30
Newsom Report, 100
Nias, J., *et al*, 176
'No Turning Back Group', 39
Norman, M., 139–40

OECD [Organisation for Economic
Cooperation and Development],
153
Ogawa, R.
see Malen and Ogawa
Olah, K., 209
Orrock, N., 104, 105
Our Schools: A Radical Policy, 38
output financing, 102
Oyakata system, 140
Ozga, J., 171

Paine, T., 37
Panopticon, 101
Parental Alliance for Choice in
Education, 236
parental choice, 3, 17, 18, 20, 29, 36,
44, 45, 53, 64, 65, 77, 111, 154,
161–3, 162, 198–9, 233–4,
236–42, 243n8, 233–6, 237,
238–42
parents
see also parental choice
and knowledge of education,
184–6
and participation, *see* participation
and school management, 28–9
and teachers, 185–6, 187, 192, 198,
201

Parents' Charter, The, 184
Parents' Charter in Scotland, 108, 109, 110, 112n5
Parents in Partnership, 41
participation, 12, 13, 20, 27–9, 30–1, 40, 41, 46, 52, 57–8, 59, 84, 85–6, 91–6, 124, 154, 157, 158, 166, 184, 203–7, 218, 229, 234–5
Partido Revolucionario Institutucional, 53
partnerships
  education-business, *see* Compacts Initiative
Pattison, A., 218
pedagogy
  learner-centred, 101, 102–3, 105, 106
  reflective, 100–1, 106
performance indicators, 110, 159, 183, 187, 210
performance management, 122
  see also management
Peters, T. and Waterman, R., 23–4
Piagetian psychology, 102
Picot Report [New Zealand], 156, 158, 162
policy group
  in school management, 24–5
Policy and Planning Unit [proposed, South Australia], 204
post-Fordism, 118, 121–2, 128–32, 137–50
  see also Fordism
  definition of, 121
principal, 18, 25–7, 49, 144, 158, 193, 197–8, 199, 205–6
  see also headteacher; leadership
program budgeting, 21–2, 23, 84, 86–7, 92–3, 97n1
  see also budgets, school
programme team
  in school management, 24–5
'pupil entitlements', 37
pupils
  and Compacts Initiative program, 104
  and competitive careerism, 200
  consent of, 100
  and motivation, 102, 104–5

and outcomes, 199–200
and school choice, 238–40, 241
and self-management, 102–6, 111
Pusey, M., 191, 196

Qualifications Authority [New Zealand], 156
Queensland
  teachers' pay in, 127

railway institutes, 214
  see also Technical and Further Education
Rawls, J., 164–5
Reagan administration, 51, 155
Reforming the Australian Public Service, 122
Regional Boards of Education [Victoria], 84
remedial activities, 200, 206
Reynolds, D., 23
  see also Hargreaves and Reynolds
Riddle of the Voucher, The, 38
Rights of Man, The, 37
Robertson, S.L., 3, 117–36
Rockefeller, 160
Rosebery District High School [Tasmania], 233
Rothwells Bank, 119
Rousseau, J-J., 102
Rowland, S., 103
Rustin, M., 121
Ryan, B., 5, 191–211

Salt Lake City, Utah
  site-based management in, 57
Save Our Schools, 39
Schon, D., 106
school-based management
  see school self-management
school boards, 109
School Boards Act (1988) [Scotland], 109
school councils, 13, 15, 93–4, 199, 206
School Curriculum, The, 181
school development plans, 94, 125, 206
school governing bodies, 229, 234

school governor, 177–82, 186–7
  case study of collaboration with
    teacher, 177–81
School Improvement Plan (SIP)
    [Victoria], 83–6, 90–3, 96–7
  aims of, 85, 96
  development of, 84–5
  end of, 96–7
  and evaluation, 90–3, 96
  and participation, 85–6, 95
  and school networking, 85, 86
School Level Program Budgeting
    (SLPB) [Victoria], 83–4, 86–7,
    96
  aims of, 96
  context of, 86–7
  development of, 86
  and management, 94
  and planning, 87–90
school management cycle
  see collaborative school
    management cycle
School Management: The Way Ahead,
    101, 109–10
school management plan (SMP),
    72–3, 67
school self-management, 1–9, 4, 5–6,
    19–20, 35–48, 64–71, 101,
    109–11, 124, 132–3, 139, 187,
    229, 231–42
  see also education; schools
  and autonomy, 74–7
  and business management, *see*
    education, and industry
  and choice, 233–4
  and competition, 240–2
  context of, 11–33, 40, 117–18, 233
  and control, 78–9, 86
  and corporate management, *see*
    corporate management
  and cost-efficiency, 23–5
  definition of, 39, 231
  and devolution, *see* devolution
  and economic rationalism, *see*
    economic rationalism
  and empowerment, 49–61
  and ethnicity, 240, 242
  evaluation in, 90–3
  and flexibility, 74–7

ideological role of, 77–8
and individualism, 145
model for, *see* Self-Managing School,
    The
'model articles' (1945) for, 35
New Right and, *see* New Right
in New Zealand, 153–70
and organizational culture, 71–4,
    77–8
planning in, 87–90
and polarization of labour, 141
and post-Fordism, 118, 121–2,
    128–32, 137–50
pupils and, 102–6
reform in UK of, 35–48
resistance to, 149–50
and resocialization, 77–8
and school choice, 236–42
and social class, 240, 242
and social reproduction, 242
theoretical perspectives on, 53–5
teachers and, 2, 3, 126–32, 182–7
and teaching cultures, 171–89
and technical and further education,
    213–26
school organization, 64
*School Teachers' Professional
    Development into the 1990s*, 107
schooling
  see education
schools
  see also education; school self-
    management
  and business, *see* education, and
    industry
  and change, 83–98
  and communities, 8; *see also*
    participation
  and 'culture of profit and
    production', 70
  and 'culture of welfare', 70
  desegregation in, 51
  dezoning of, 17, 166
  discipline in, 207–8
  divisions within, 131
  and financial management, 35,
    232–3; *see also* budgets, school
  gap between managers and teachers
    in, 71–4, 112, 141, 158, 159, 198

and grant maintained status, 38, 40,
    42, 46, 109, 110, 229, 237
as islands, 96, 97
and local education authorities, *see*
    local education authorities
and marketplace, *see* education, and
    market orientation
and networking, 96
organizational culture, of, 27, 71–4
as post-Fordist workplace, 132; *see*
    also post-Fordism
quality control of, 11
reasons for choice of, 238–40
and selection, 44, 230, 235–6, 240
and self-evaluation, 91–3
and self-management, *see* school
    self-management
Schools' Commission, 117
Schools Council, 141
Schools Renewal, 14
Schutz, A., 106
scientific management, 16–17, 101,
    138, 143, 144, 145–6, 150, 160
Scotland
    see also United Kingdom
    school self-management in, 6, 100,
        101, 109–11
    16+ National Certificate in, 103
    teacher appraisal in, 107–9
Scott, A., 137, 138
Scottish Action Plan, 100
Scottish Education Department
    (SED), 107–8
Scottish Office Education Department
    (SOED), 101, 109–11
secondary education
    provision of, 230
Secondary Education Authority, 127
Secretary of State for Scotland, 107
SED
    see Scottish Education Department
Seldon, A., 37, 38, 43, 46
selection
    in education system, 44, 230,
        235–6, 240
self-determination, 118, 124, 132
Self-Governing Schools etc.
    (Scotland) Act (1989), 107, 109
self-governing status (SGS), 109, 110

self-managing school
    see school self-management
Self-Managing School, The, 9, 11,
    19–29, 36, 39–40, 218
Sergiovanni T., 26
Sexton, S., 42, 46, 236
SGS
    see self-governing status
Shadow Education Minister [Western
    Australia], 126
Shadow Minister for Industrial
    Relations [Victoria], 144–5
SIP
    see School Improvement Plan
site-based management, 1, 49–61
    see also school self-management
    and control, 58–9
    and individual efficiency, 54–5
    and individual empowerment, 54–5
    and participation, 57–8
    and social context, 55–7
    and social empowerment, 54–61
    and social efficiency, 54–5
'Skill Olympics', 146
skills formation, 223–4
SLPB
    see School Level Program
    Budgeting
SMP
    see school management plan
Smyth, J., 1–9, 120, 133n2
Social Affairs Unit, 236
social equity
    see social justice
social justice, 20–1, 153, 155, 157,
    163, 164–7, 168, 169, 193, 200,
    214, 215, 220
social phenomenology, 102
SOED
    see Scottish Office Education
    Department
Solihull
    school funding in, 232–3
Soucek, V., 120
South Australia
    devolution in education in,
        191–211
    educational reform in, 192–3,
        201–10

'whole-of-education' approach in, 201–2

South East Asia, 6

Sparkes, A.C. and Bloomer, M., 7, 171–89

Spinks, J., 86, 233
see also Caldwell and Spinks

Sputnik, 51

SSTUWA
see State Schools Teachers' Union of Western Australia

Starratt, T., 26

state
see also education, and the state
as evaluative, 101–2

State Board of Education [Victoria], 84

State Schools Teacher's Union of Western Australia (SSTUWA), 125, 126–7
Annual Conference (1989), 127

State Services Commission [New Zealand], 157, 158, 159

'steering at a distance', 65–6, 71, 72, 77

Stillman, A., 234

Stillman, A. and Maychell, K., 234

Strathclyde Region
devolved resource management in, 110

streaming, 200, 207

Suchman, L.A., 88–9, 90

symbolic interactionism, 102

TAFE
see Technical and Further Education, 214

TAFE in Australia, 214

Tailby, S. and Whitson, C., 140, 141

Taskforce to Review Education Administration, 156, 162

Taunton Commission, 229–30

Taylor, F.W., 101, 134n7, 143, 145–6, 160
see also scientific management

Taylor Report, 35, 36, 40, 41, 180, 184

Taylorism
see Taylor, F.W.

teachers
see also school self-management; schools
and accountability, see accountability
appraisal of, 107–8, 208
and autonomy, 3, 70, 177, 181, 209, 219
case study of school governor/ teacher collaboration, 177–81
and classroom isolation, 173–4, 184
and collaboration, 174–81, 183–4, 186
and collegiality, see collegiality
and competence, 208–9
and compliance, 100
and control, 7, 65–6
and curriculum reform, 124, 142
and deprofessionalization, 171, 182, 183
and educational performance, 45
and empowerment, 3
and incentives, 145
and 'licensed autonomy', 177, 181
and management, 65–71, 72–4, 168
and morale, 128, 179–80
and motivation, 100
occupational culture of, 171, 173, 186
and output, 108
and parents, 185–6, 187, 192, 198, 201
and productivity, 210
and professional development, 107
as 'professional educators', 187
and professionalism, 5, 177, 182–7
and pupils, 199–200, 208
as reflective practitioners, 106
and 'regulated autonomy', 181
role of, 93–4, 95
as rule-governed, 194
salaries of, 38–9, 107, 108–9, 126–8, 141–2, 144–6, 157
and school governors, 177–82
and school self-management, 2, 3, 126–32, 182–7
and self-management, 100, 106–9, 131–3
as skilled operatives, 208

and strike action, 126–8
in Technical and Further Education, 219, 225
and uncertainty, 130–1
and unit curriculum, 129–30, 132
working conditions of, 38–9, 44, 80n4, 107, 126–8, 131–2, 144–6, 157, 182, 208
Teachers' Credit Society [Western Australia], 119
Technical and Further Education (TAFE), 5–6, 214–26
access to, 214, 215, 220–2, 225
administration of, 214–20
'Balkanization' of, 222–4
context of, 215, 222–4
corporate managerialism in, 217–22, 224–5
criticisms of, 216–17
decentralization in, 218
and disadvantaged, 220–3
and economy, 216
enrolment in, 220–1
and entrepreneurism, 218, 220
and gender segmentation, 215, 220–2
and industry, 215, 220–4, 225
management review of, 217–20
managerialism in, 217–22, 224–5
and market orientation, 216–18, 222–3, 224–5
masculinized ethos in, 215
and multinational corporations, 224, 225
New Right and, 215–26
paternalistic ethos in, 215, 221
pedagogy in, 215
restructuring of, 217–24, 225
and social equity, 214, 220–2
teachers and, 219, 225
and unions, *see* trade unions
Women's Co-ordination Unit of, 220–1
technical colleges, 213, 214
see also Technical and Further Education
technocratic rationality, 138, 167
see also economic rationalism
Tertiary Entrance Exam, 127

testing, 4, 15–16, 29, 71, 79n1, 131, 198, 199–200
Thatcher, M., 6, 20–1, 43, 231, 234
see also Thatcher government; Thatcherism
Thatcher government, 155
Thatcherism, 65, 102, 110, 140
see also Thatcher, M.
Thomas, A. and Dennison, B., 239–40
Thomas, H., 42
Times Educational Index, 6, 112
Today's Schools, 159
Tomorrow's Schools, 156, 158
Tories
see Conservative Party
'tracking', 51
trade unions, 125–8, 138–9, 141, 144, 145, 209–10
Trades and Labour Council [Western Australia], 126
Training Agency, 100, 103, 105, 112n3
TVEI [Technical and Educational Education Initiative, 100, 104

unit curriculum, 123–4, 125, 126, 128–30, 132, 134n9
see also curriculum
assessment in, 129–30
United Kingdom
see also England; Scotland; Wales
Compacts program in, 103
educational reform in, 14, 18, 20–1, 35–48, 60n4, 63–82, 171, 177–87, 229–44
United States of America
commissioned reports on education in, 51, 52, 60n1
education and business in, 103, 160
education and economy in, 51
educational reform in, 49, 50–3, 56, 59, 160–1
educational standards in, 51–2
equity and education in, 51, 59
first wave of educational reform in, 51–2
Fordism in, 121
parental choice in, 53

participation and education in, 52, 59
partnership-in-education movement in, 103
second wave of educational reform in, 52
school desegregation in, 51
site-based management in, 49, 52–61
testing in, 59
United States Supreme Court, 51
utilitarianism, 163–7

Varlaam, A.
see West and Varlaam
Viall, P., 26
Victoria
bureaucratic managerialism in, 14
educational reform in, 3, 8–9, 12–13, 15, 30, 83–98
equity in educational system in, 12–13
evaluation and school change in, 90–3
Liberal/National Coalition policy in, 15
participation in, 12–14, 15, 84
School Improvement Plan in, *see* School Improvement Plan
School Level Program Budgeting in, *see* School Level Program Budgeting
vocational education, 202–3, 213–26
see also Technical and Further Education
vocationalism, 102, 202–3
'voucher economy', 42
see also vouchers
vouchers, 18, 35–6, 37–8, 40, 42, 43, 44, 46, 111
and top-up fees, 44, 46

WA Inc., 119
wage systems, 224
Wales
see also United Kingdom
educational reform in, 229–44, 233–42
educational system in, 229–31
parental choice in, 233–40

pupil enrolments in, 233
school self-management in, 8, 63–82, 109, 232–42
social class and education in, 229–31
Walford, G., 8, 229–44
Walford, G. and Miller, H., 235
Waterman, R.
see Peters and Waterman
Watkins, P., 6–7, 8, 96, 137–52, 215
Watts, A., 68
Weber, M., 109
Weick, K., 26
Weiler, H., 7–8, 56–7
West, A., 238–9
West, A. and Varlaam, A., 238
Western Australia
business and politics in, 119–20
curriculum in, 123–4, 125, 126, 128–30, 132, 134n9
devolution in, 128–32
educational reform in, 3, 117–33
fiscal crisis in, 119–20, 126–7
industrial action in, 117, 125–8
post-Fordism in, 118–33
public sector reform in, 118–23
state and corporate sector in, 119–20
teacher unions in, 125–8
teachers' pay in, 126–8
youth unemployment in, 123
Western Australian Chamber of Commerce, 119–20
Westminster system, 119
Wheelwright, T.
see Crough and Wheelwright
White Paper (1986) [Western Australia], 122–3
White Paper (1992) [UK], 41–2, 43
Whitlam government, 214
Whitson, C.
see Tailby and Whitson
whole school planning, 94
Witzel, M.L., 108
Wolferen, K., 140
Wood, S., 122
workplace organization, 121–2, 145–6

Yeatman, A., 217, 218, 221